W9-BKU-927

BETH MAJ.
COLLEGE

WITHDRAWN

Religious Origins
of Modern Science

BUCHANAN
LIBRARY
COLLEGE

Religious Origins of Modern Science

Belief in Creation in Seventeenth-Century Thought

BL
245
K52

by

Eugene M. Klaaren

REGIS
BIBL. M.
COLLEGE

WITHDRAWN

33189

William B. Eerdmans Publishing Company

Dedicated to Mom and Dad

Copyright © 1977 by Wm. B. Eerdmans Publ. Co.
255 Jefferson Ave. S.E., Grand Rapids, Mich. 49503
All rights reserved
Printed in the United States of America

Library of Congress Cataloging in Publication Data

Klaaren, Eugene M   1937-
  Religious origins of modern science.

  Includes bibliographical references and index.
    1. Religion and science—History of controversy.
  2. Creation.   I. Title.
  BL245.K52   509   76-53838
  ISBN 0-8028-1683-5

Preface

This study in intellectual history has a dual purpose. As an inquiry into the history of theology it aims to show the profound cultural significance of Christian belief in divine creation. At the same time, as an inquiry into the history of science as it is broadly conceived, this study advances an explanation of the beginnings of modern natural science. Conflict and reformation in Western theologies of creation made the rise of many natural sciences from older natural philosophy a distinct and lively possibility; belief in divine creation was presupposed in the rise of modern natural science.

A thesis of such scope cannot be advanced without making some assumptions, which in this case are related to a secondary purpose. My chief assumption is that a viable explanation of the epochal rise of modern science can be advanced by focusing on mid-seventeenth-century English intellectual history. The secondary purpose here is to advance a unified interpretation of the highly representative and diverse works of Robert Boyle.

Before this project was undertaken, I studied the classical Christian views of creation (from Genesis and Augustine to Thomas, Calvin, and Jonathan Edwards) and found that Christianity bespeaks a mysterious drama in three acts. The first act of divine creation is prior to sin and redemption. Despite Schleiermacher's claim in the name of religious experience that creation turns upon sin and redemption, and despite Barth's formally similar proclamation in the name of divine revelation that creation turns upon redemption and sin, creation is primary — in all senses of the term. Apart from this truth, the moving yet jagged drama intrinsic to Christianity is doomed at best to historical finality, a necessarily tragic form of existence.

At worst, apart from creation, Christianity oscillates between sin and redemption.

Partly due to this studied conviction, as well as a growing interest in history of science, I came to see that there have been at least three major theologies of creation in classical Christian thought. Besides traditional views oriented to divine Being, frequently neglected visions of the Creator as Spirit and still other perspectives on creation ordered to the Will of the Creator have played influential roles in our past.

Such theological presuppositions of creation have governed many quite different Western stories and accounts of the process of creation, not excluding those discernible in Genesis. To demonstrate this would require a separate volume. Yet, despite the fact that this book concentrates on the structures of various basic theologies of creation according to the Being, Spirit, and Will of the Creator, at the expense of showing how these theologies were worked out in the detail of such inherited contents as, say, the six "days" of creation and the Sabbath, one should not underestimate the immense significance of belief in divine creation for the course of classic Western Christendom. Prior to the eighteenth century, Western culture was so deeply attuned to divine creation that it could hardly sustain an alternative basic presupposition about the origin of the world.

Another source of this essay was an intense interest in methodology that accompanied my late graduate studies in the history of science. Upon studying seventeenth-century chemistry I was most interested in the nature and validity of claims made about the advent of this science. This, in turn, led me to consider the general validity of Collingwood's method of combining history and philosophy, a venture partly moved by soundings in the history of natural sciences, and one which he termed the "search for absolute presuppositions." In that peculiar purity of spirit of one who loved methodology, at one time I set out to write an all-purpose methodological prolegomenon for explanations of the origin of modern science. Traces of that grandiose project surface here in running critical debates with Merton, Zilsel, and others. The issues deserve a full and separate treatment. (Such a treatment would provide a further test for my methodological proposals in the third section of the first chapter, which, incidentally, might also be profitably read after the material argument of the remaining chapters.)

Those arguments explaining the new science which turned on religion proved to be particularly fascinating, for they were often simultaneously philosophical, theological, sociological, historical, and so forth. There is something about the peculiar power and elusiveness of religion, particularly in its connections to other things, that calls forth a variety and richness of methodological concerns. Witness the long and lively aftermath of the Weber thesis, a discussion which shows no sign of subsiding.

Searching into the worth of such arguments I decided that I could do just as well — or better, that I could strengthen what was left so often in the mode of suggestion in Whitehead, Collingwood, Merton, Foster, Torrance, and others. Such an effort is central to this study. This involves methodological care throughout, particularly in joining historical and systematic inquiry. Collingwood's broad approach to the riches of intellectual history has been my general guide. The task also requires attention to what is significantly novel in the new science, and not least, critical discernment of the plethora of religious styles and beliefs so deeply held in early modern times. This includes a fresh study of both well-known and neglected figures such as Calvin and Helmont.

One rare book-length study in this area, R. J. Hooykaas' *Religion and the Rise of Modern Science*, has also been helpful for my work, although my argument was formed independently. Although I have sought to steer away from Hooykaas' tendency to over-emphasize distinctively Protestant influences upon modern science, the historical sensitivity to both science and religion in his impressive work remains instructive. However, more sociological footwork is clearly necessary to determine the alleged bases of the new science in definite Reformation and Puritan communities. This is work for another day, and no doubt will also require further methodological consideration.

I hope that this venture checks the split character of much early modern, seventeenth-century study. The field of the history of philosophy has its own canon of continental rationalists and British empiricists, and does not sufficiently engage Newton, Boyle, and Galileo. Studies in the history of science stress the latter figures often at the expense of Leibnitz, Spinoza,

Hobbes, and the Cambridge Platonists. There are also separate and largely neglected canons of divines. Indeed, not only are Perkins, Ames, and Edwards overlooked by most historians of philosophy and of science, they are also slighted in the history of theology. The typical jump, particularly in Protestant schools, is from the heroic Reformers to much later Enlightenment philosophers.

I resist the perpetuation of these separate canons. However, I would not have attempted to understand and relate the thinkers they include had I not discovered the fascinating work of Johan Baptist van Helmont. This mystical natural philosopher put it all together: the Holy Spirit, Air, gas and medicine. One long summer I was baffled by his conflation of philosophy, theology, and science in a surprising mixture of speculation, prayer, vision, and experimentation. This forced me to come to terms with the extraordinary intellectual range and its significance in many other seventeenth-century thinkers frequently locked into recent historical specialties.

My research for this volume was largely completed during the academic year 1973-74. Although some recent relevant studies and debates, particularly among early modern historians, have not been taken into account, it is time for this study to see the light of day.

After the initial chapter on method, Chapters 2 and 3 are relatively more historical than Chapters 4 through 7, which develop the central argument. Quotations from primary materials have not been altered for spelling and punctuation. Notes with multiple page references normally follow the order of quoted material in the text. See the Appendix for the dates of publication and writing of Boyle's works. I have used the five-volume, 1744 edition of *Boyle's Works*, edited by Thomas Birch. In the notes, a particular work of Boyle is specified, followed by the volume number of the 1744 edition (not the section number of the particular work cited), and the page reference (for example: Boyle, *Notion of Nature*, IV, 400). All page references to volume I are to the second pagination series of that volume, except for Birch's biography of Boyle, which is independently paginated at the beginning of the volume. References to primary works of Bacon, Calvin, Helmont and others are fully cited when their works are initially discussed; lengthy titles in the notes are shortened after initial citation.

The notes for this volume are extensive. Although most refer to primary materials, many refer to and discuss the various secondary literatures which have grown up around the historical and systematic problems of interpreting religion and the rise of modern science. Some of the notes amplify important terms of analysis such as differentiation, basic presuppositions, etc. Other notes indicate the grounds of novel interpretations. To facilitate use of these notes, which are collected at the rear, the Analytical Index of Principal Subjects refers to the notes as well as the text.

For encouragement and criticism I am indebted to a number of scholars in the history of science, theology, and philosophy, who read earlier versions of this study in its entirety. Everett Mendelsohn, J. E. McGuire, Arnold Thackray, John Dillenberger, James Preus, Arthur McGill, Louis Mink, and Eugene Golob, as well as my colleagues in the Wesleyan University Department of Religion, have been central to this study in more ways than they know. Of course, they are not responsible for the line I have pursued. I am also grateful for the editorial skills of the late Wayland Schmitt and for the typing skills of Diane Brennan. And my wife, Mary, but that is another story.

Middletown, Connecticut

Contents

CHAPTER ONE:

Introduction

The chief purpose of this essay is to show that religion was conducive to the advent of modern science, specifically that belief in divine creation was a major presupposition in the emergence of natural science in seventeenth-century England. Any attempt to advance this argument must take account of the historical explanations of modern science, especially those which have stressed the religious roots of the new science. But R. G. Collingwood's methodology for intellectual history, which will be adopted here, has a wider scope than this specific argument. Even so, the materials of natural philosophy, science, and theology in sixteenth- and seventeenth-century Western culture have a tendency to expand with increasing inquiry.

A truly adequate explanation of the rise of modern natural science would require a complete historical philosophy of early modern Western culture in relation to prior and subsequent epochs. Such an explanation would also deal with a wide range of comparisons between Western and non-Western culture.[1] It would involve not only the history of science per se, but also histories of philosophy, technology, religion, politics, economics, and so on. And not only the integrity of these disciplines, but also their capacities of synthesis would have to be analyzed. Furthermore, histories alone, no matter how comprehensive, would not suffice. Something like an historically informed philosophy of culture, guided by careful methodology, would be necessary to advance so massive a project.

No explanation of this scope exists. Indeed, it is striking that the phenomenal rise of modern science has received relatively little attention, at least in comparison to phenomena of similar immensity, such as the advents of modern capitalism and democracy. Despite the hyperbolic talk of the "scientific revolution," no account of modern science is so arresting as Marx's account of modern capitalism. None remains so intriguing as Weber's of modern rationalization. Benjamin Nelson has described the present situation well:

> The early modern revolution in science and philosophy has been arduously studied and discussed for at least two centuries now. Contemporary scholars and publicists are everywhere continuing, with undiminished vigor, to explore archives, plumb sources, and to dispute one another's interpretations. Nonetheless, few would claim that the roots and outcomes of the seventeenth century 'break through' had been reliably established. Indeed, many of the central issues are hardly more clear to us than are the circumstances and ideas which explain the breathless 'takeoff' of our own century.[2]

Taken in isolation from much of the work that has been done, this judgment may be too severe. Nevertheless, it does highlight the lack of a truly compelling and complete explanation of the rise of science in early modern culture.

The achievement of Marx and Weber is, first of all, marked by an impressive synthesis of disciplines. Marx fused history, politics, economics, and philosophy — to say nothing of his critique of religion and psychology — into an account of immense scope. Weber's lifelong effort to explain modern rationalization, beginning with *The Protestant Ethic and the Spirit of Capitalism*, was equally comprehensive.[3] Indeed, so many disciplines are carefully and suggestively integrated by these efforts to understand modern times that it is insulting to simply label Marx and Weber as sociologists. Despite the achievements of an earlier generation of intellectual historians — Cassirer, Koyré, and Burtt — no explanation of the rise of modern science possesses so vast and impressive a synthesis of disciplines.

Furthermore, a critical mass of experience is built into the work of Marx and Weber. Marx was both irrevocably alienated from and deeply respectful of the capitalist achievement, just as Weber was both fascinated and appalled by modern rationalization and the weight of bureaucracy. Their historical explanations of modern capitalism and politics are ruled by passions rooted in the vicissitudes of modern history. But such deeply troubled experience in the West has not yet been manifest in a major explanation of the rise of modern science. Notwithstanding the periodic, or even regular, protests of romantics, the sciences have long been received as blessings in our history. It is peculiarly ironic that in our own times — characterized by pervasive technology — there are so many signs of deep unease with the scientific achievement and its supports in the West.[4] Accordingly, the necessity for a complete explanation of the rise of science in early modern culture manifests an urgent and widely felt demand for critical analysis.

I hope to make a modest contribution to a fuller explanation of the new science by showing its roots in religious presuppositions. However, my fondest hope for this essay is that it might facilitate a more complete criticism of science, primarily by highlighting the gulf between early modern culture and our own. An awareness of the reliance of early modern science upon theological presuppositions enlarges the sense of sixteenth- and seventeenth-century culture as an epochal unity. Taken with Weber's pioneering demonstration that early capitalism presupposed a highly rational socio-religious orientation shaped by Protestantism, and with the subsequent work of Walzer and Little on the religious ideologies at the root of modern politics,[5] this fresh glimpse of the immense differences between our times and the early modern era suggests a far broader topic for study. If early modern science presupposed theologically articulate religion, and if subsequent modern religious developments were delimited by theoretically articulate sciences, our time bears witness to a displacement of both religion and science by technology. A radically new cultural unity, with its own continuities and discontinuities with the modern past, now calls for critical understanding. In our times, theology is hardly an engine of religion, much less of other spheres of culture. Today, the relation of science to technological society may be as pressing an issue as that of religious currents locked into ideological conflict at the expense of critical theological vision.

Of course, most historians of science offer less ambitious explanations. In general, their narrative accounts range from records of more or less steady scientific progress to dramatic stories of the scientific revolution. Thus the development of modern science is related with more or less continuity to Renaissance, medieval, and ancient thought. Most of these narratives also focus upon a relatively outstanding natural science, such as astronomy, mechanics, or mathematics, in order to show the whole phenomenon of the advent of modern natural science.[6] However, this tendency is usually qualified, sometimes decisively, by stressing the significance of far-reaching novel concepts, laws, and experiments. Indeed, it is frequently argued that some ensemble of these novelties — i.e., the hypothetico-deductive method, variously understood — plays the decisive role in the rise of modern science.

My historical argument is deeply indebted to such accounts of the new science. Yet they are not at the center of the inquiry, for a phenomenon as immense as that of the rise of modern natural science refuses to remain confined to narrative possibilities solely internal to the course of the natural sciences. The striking novelty, the new beginning in the rise of modern science, exceeds prior boundaries. The immensity and novelty in such densely rich subject matter must be seen in multiple perspectives.[7] Furthermore, the very drive for explanation refuses to stop short of unity.

Fortunately, developments in both history of science and historical study of religion encourage this approach. Indeed, there is a small group of philosophers, theologians, historians of science, and sociologists who have launched the project of explaining the rise of modern science in relation to religious currents. The bold adventures into congruent Western ideas of nature and God by Whitehead and Collingwood are fairly well known. Robert Merton's sociological efforts, partly indebted to Weber's work, on relating the new science to Puritanism are perhaps even more familiar. Charles Raven, an Anglican theologian and historian of science, has written of the positive effects of Anglican theology upon modern science. Most recently, Reijer Hooykaas, a Dutch historian of science, has capped a lifelong interest in this project by arguing for the positive support of Protestantism to the new science.[8]

Work of this sort, the present book included, must be sharply distinguished from a fairly distant and highly polemical background. At the turn of the century, a few historians set out to defend the progress of science against religious attacks. Andrew D. White's *History of the Warfare of Science with Theology in Christendom* (1896) is typical of these apologies for science, which in turn provoked a reaction by apologists for religion.[9] Not content to simply defend their turf, some "professors of polemic and didactic theology" set out to claim the new science as a direct result of Protestantism. Although deservedly forgotten by historians of science and religion alike, these apologists promoted a lingering habit of mind that regards religion and science chiefly as antagonists, locked in ultimate conflict. Perhaps more insidiously, they strengthened the tendency of subsequent historians, in turn impressed by the penchant for purity of positivism, to insist that religion and science, properly conceived, are mutually independent. My particular concern with the historical relationships between religion and science assumes not only that each is thoroughly historical, but also that history marks the course of their relationships.

Furthermore, the historical study of religion in the West remains deeply entrenched in long traditions of Roman Catholic, Reformed, Anglican, and Lutheran scholarship. This is prominent in the servant disciplines of church history that focus on histories of doctrine and dogma. Until recently, the Spiritualists, who frequently ignored Roman Catholic and Protestant boundaries, were neglected or dismissed as sectarians and mystics. Much of the Puritan story still remains untold. Efforts to distill the essence of purely Protestant Christianity (or some other variant) at the expense of larger realities have resulted in extravagant cultural claims. This history of parochialism echoes and reinforces the conflict voiced by the apologists.[10]

Fortunately, the combined pressures of more scientific modes of the study of religion, and ecumenism are gradually changing this situation. The nineteenth-century discovery of the development of Christian doctrines points beyond ecclesiastical polemics. One result is a more modest and ecumenical conception of the "history of Christian thought" and philosophy in late medieval and medieval times. There are also concerted efforts to understand the thoughts of sixteenth-century left-wing Spiritualists, who were made visible by Marxist and other social historians.[11] Nevertheless, these beginnings are only beginnings. This is clear upon comparing highly sophisticated and extremely developed historical-critical studies of the Bible, ranging from minute philology to sweeping phenomenology, to the underdeveloped discipline of church history. My inquiry rests on the conviction that long traditions of parochial Christian historiography must be overcome.[12]

On the other hand, if genuinely historical study of religion labors under an immense burden of history, historical study of science labors under the modern refusal to regard science as subject to history. Indeed, compared to the venerable traditions of religious study that often plague historical study of religion, history of science is young and relatively innocent. As such, it is vulnerable to prejudices that regard science as essentially unhistorical.

Nevertheless, in addition to the careful but limited work of narration noted above, the history of science is marked by extraordinarily promising developments. Most visible is the advent of historically informed philosophical reconsiderations of scientific growth. Kuhn invokes and seeks to discipline social meanings of revolution in the critical proposals of his influential *The Structure of Scientific Revolutions*. Toulmin invokes the promises of ecology in his effort to show the rhythmic yet rational course of science in his *Human Understanding*.[13] Despite important differences, these philosophical conceptions of science in history share a sensitivity to multiplicity that enhances the earlier work of Burtt and Koyré.[14] Equally significant is their common conception of the course of scientific growth inseparable from contemporary intellectual contexts.

In contrast to such broad efforts of historical understanding and explanation, other recent intellectual historians and historians of science have pursued a more modest path. Indeed, there is an impressive production of original inquiries by R. S. Westfall, A. Debus, J. E. McGuire, C. Webster, P. M. Rattansi, F. Oakley, and others, which is chiefly characterized by an effort to elucidate the incredibly complex character of science and religion in the seventeenth-century. Pointedly critical of established views of their relationship, these studies are somewhat less extensive in constructing new arguments relating science and religion.[15] Although I am happily dependent upon much of this work, one feature may distinguish my inquiry: the drive to explain more fully, albeit partially, the coming of the new science in a fresh account of its religious context.

Thus, I am particularly interested in the explanations of those scholars ranging from Whitehead and Collingwood to Merton and Hooykaas. Unfortunately their arguments, notwithstanding the promise of their attempts to show the historical significance of religion for science, do not constitute a well-defined or fully developed scholarly tradition. Not only are there deep differences of methodology and choice of subject matter, but so little mutual debate and discussion has taken place that most of the central issues remain unidentified. Moreover, even the advent of considerable inquiry into Puritanism and the new science has not produced clear theses around which scholars can fruitfully rally or over which they may profitably divide.[16] Nevertheless, two of the best arguments, those of Merton and Collingwood, raise three clusters of issues that deserve careful attention.[17] At the heart of these issues are the grasp of religion relevant to the new science, the understanding of that science, and the connection held to obtain between these cultural spheres in history.

Merton on Puritanism and Modern Science

Central to the work of some historians is the conviction that science is part of a definite cultural and historical milieu. Edgar F. Zilsel stressed socio-economic conditions that furthered the growth of science, for example, and Christopher Hill has long focused attention on the significance of revolutionary political and religious conditions in the sixteenth and seventeenth centuries. Similarly, although not indebted to Marxist thought, Robert K. Merton, guided by Weber's classic thesis on Protestantism and capitalism as well as his own general theory of science and society, set out to show the positive bearing of socio-religious conditions upon modern science, particularly in seventeenth-century England.[18] He terms the religious factor which was influential in the advance of the new sciences the "Puritan *ethos*," and, having identified the important sciences in the growing institutionalization and professionalization of seventeenth-century natural sciences (physics, mechanics, and chemistry), he shows by statistical analysis that a large majority of the figures in these new fields (and a majority of the members of the Royal Society) were Puritans even though the Puritans were a minority of the English population.[19]

To specify what may be called the distinctive life style of Puritanism, Merton draws attention to the intramundane asceticism of the disciplined life exemplified in Richard Baxter's *Christian Directory*. He contrasts the "immanent mystic" characteristic of the Puritan ethos to the "transcendental mystic" typical of Roman Catholicism.[20] He fleshes out his account of this disciplined life style by describing the social reality of the Puritan doctrines of justification and predestination. Justification appeared as the Puritan way of making the end of life the glorification of God, an eminently practical and utilitarian task. The doctrine of predestination, Merton holds, elicited "good works" to prove divine election; this gave divine sanction for diligence in labor.[21] In addition, the Puritans' general praise of reason, their refusal to oppose it to faith, coincided with their promotion of utilitarian educational reform.

To trace the relation of this ethos to the new science, Merton argues that Puritanism inspired the vocational discipline and penchant for experiment of the new scientists. Describing a very general influence ("Experiment was the scientific expression of the practical, active, and methodical bent of the Puritans") he argues that the scientific legacy was an unintended result of tendencies latent in the attitudinal set of Puritanism.[22] In effect, the Puritan ethos was a condition mediated by a new sense of disciplined vocation that promoted the new science.

Merton's grasp of modern science is largely implicit in his conception of the Puritan ethos as a condition for the new science. That is, his argument that the discipline intrinsic to the Puritan life style generated a new sense of vocation conceives of modern science chiefly as an experimental venture. This equation of the new science with experimentalism is, I believe, severely limited. It sheds little light on the vast intellectual scope and pregnant conceptual strength inherent in the new science and its respect for reason.

Merton also specifies economic and commercial pressures, chiefly in the fields of transportation and military technology, that stimulated discovery and created needs which the new science sought to satisfy. Noting the practical projects accepted by the Royal Society or recorded in Bishop Sprat's *The History of the Royal Society of London,* he concludes that between 30 and 60 percent of the researches of the Society were influenced by socio-economic needs. Throughout this argument Merton is aware that "needs" have often gone unsatisfied for generations. Accordingly, he writes that "need is an elliptical term which in this context always implies realization or consciousness of need."[23]

Although Merton claims that both the Puritan ethos and economic needs influenced the new science, he does not identify one factor as more determinative than the other (and both were evident in most cases). Thus his account is extremely general in relating the new science to Puritanism. His arguments raise severe questions of how one should weigh a plurality of conditions relevant to the new science. For example, how much was the new sense of vocation indebted to economics rather than religion? Zilsel's argument solely from socio-economic conditions is directly relevant to this point. Even more pertinent is Hooykaas' argument that Protestant religious practice overcame a traditional economic split of head and hand that precluded the unified and disciplined sense of vocation needed for the new science.[24]

Apart from these socio-empirical issues, and even granting Hooykaas' success in resolving them, a more nagging question remains. By failing to establish the link between Puritanism and modern science, Merton does not penetrate into the vast intellectual reaches of the new science. From a different angle, his major claims on Puritanism do not carry very deeply into the new science. His demonstration of the relevance of socio-religious conditions is no mean achievement, yet there appears to be a limitation built into a method content with conditional explanation. The structure of such an explanatory model stops short of exposing a common link between an initial condition and subsequent developments. In Merton's case this dualism of structure is apparent in his general theory of science and society, which separates the former as theoretical from a strictly practical conception of society.[25] Nevertheless, Merton at least points toward the intellectual significance of religion.

Nearly all of Merton's critics have noted that he labels a number of English thinkers "Puritan" whose sympathies were with the Crown as much as with Cromwell. Boyle, Ray, and even Wilkins after 1660 tended to identify themselves as Anglican, and Boyle, one of Merton's major subjects, explicitly distanced himself from precisely the sharp and distinctive features of Calvinist Puritanism reflected in the stern doctrines of justification and predestination. Thus, the rubric of the "Puritan religious ethos" must either be abandoned or virtually rebuilt in a stronger general argument that will take account of the many and diverse divines and lay religious figures influential in the new science.[26]

Merton correctly notes that Puritanism expressed an understanding of order in nature which facilitated new scientific development, but, unfortunately, he does not develop this suggestion. His tendency to contrast religious *ethos* with *dogma* works against systematic realization of the rubric of religious ethos. Apart from thoroughly probing basic beliefs, estimates of their social cash value are historically deficient. One ironic result of this weakness in Merton's argument is a serious overloading of the unavoidable but highly distinctive doctrine of predestination.[27] More seriously and broadly, he fails to ascertain the vast intellectual fallout of the varied and common doctrines dearly defended by Puritans, Anglicans, and radicals. Merton fails to unfold the potential of his rubric of religious ethos. Just as he slights the intellectual reality of science, he also misses it in religion. However much contemporary academic theology may be divorced from the religion of the common Christian, it is clear that in the seventeenth century religious and theological beliefs were taken so seriously that they often led to controversies in the University — and on the battlefield. Thus, in dealing with the materials of this period, one may assume that its theology is a relatively accurate index of seventeenth-century religion and culture.

In sum, Merton's contribution goes well beyond any direct causal explanation of modern science in relation to religion. His more modest conditional view is also more enlightening than explanations that assume the shape of a single narrative of science, society, or religion. For Merton does not force relationships, even though his contentment with relevance lacks the extraordinary comparative richness that renders Weber's two entities in search of a relationship — the Protestant ethic and the spirit of capitalism — so intriguing. More seriously, Merton's actual conceptions of religion and science, as well as their relationship, are severely limited and thus do not disclose the riches of the vast intellectual reaches of the phenomenal rise of modern natural science or its manifold and significant contexts.

Collingwood on Theology and Modern Science

The most crucial element in R. G. Collingwood's methodology is the concept of presuppositions which function as contexts. While this approach is less bold and more complex than causal explanation, it is also more fruitful than merely conditional explanations. And the presence of narrative interpretation is discernible in an adequate contextual mode of explanation. In brief, Collingwood's approach proposes a mode of systematic historical inquiry. This distinct methodology will be considered after a critical discussion of Collingwood's actual argument concerning the rise of modern science.[28]

Whereas Merton specifies the religious and theological background of the new science by attending to distinctively Puritan elements, Collingwood identifies the relevant theological background in much wider and bolder terms. Seeking to lay bare the common theology of the modern epoch within which the new science was born, he does not fall prey to so narrow a construction of religion or theology that key figures, such as Bacon, Boyle, and Newton, could be included only in an arbitrary fashion.[29] Yet like Merton, he sees a general congruence of religion and theology. He avoids reductive accounts of either component as psychic rationalization or social ideology.

Collingwood finds the historical beginning of modern scientific thought in the context of theological thought. He discerns a common theology of modern times in the actual thought of principal modern figures at the basic levels of their intellectual work. His argument does not move from the highest levels of modern philosophical reflection to less universal consequences of scientific theory; it employs but does not rest upon the effectiveness of highly individuated and often rarified philosophical achievements.[30]

Collingwood finds one decisive theological presupposition in the modern belief that the Creator-God is omnipotent and therefore does precisely and exactly what He does and not something else. He argues that the Platonic view of mathematics which Galileo, the "father of modern science," inherited presupposed that the world of nature was a mere approximation to the world of pure mathematics. Galileo's pronouncement "that the book of nature is a book written by the hand of God in the language of mathematics" was a basic modification of Platonism in the newly emerging science of nature. Collingwood's boldest claim may be that

> The possibility of an applied mathematics is an expression, in terms of natural science, of the Christian belief that nature is the creation of an omnipotent God. This belief is what replaced the Greek conception of nature as the realm of imprecision with the Renaissance conception of nature as the realm of precision. The Platonism of Renaissance natural science is not fundamentally Platonic, it is fundamentally Christian. Christian thought is adapting Platonism to its own ends, or begetting upon Platonism an idea which Platonism proper would never have originated or even tolerated. . . .
> Christianity, by maintaining that God is omnipotent and that the world of nature is a world of God's creating, completely altered the situation. It became a matter of faith that the world of nature should be regarded no longer as the realm of imprecision, but as the realm of precision. . . . Galileo, the true father of modern science, restated the Pythagorean-Platonic standpoint in his own words by proclaiming that the book of nature is a book written by God in the language of mathematics. . . . Galileo is deliberately applying to nature the principle which Augustine laid down with regard to the Holy Scriptures, the book *par excellence* "written by the hand of God"; that whatever doubts may arise about the meaning of this or that passage, it has a meaning, and the meaning is true (*Confessions*, XII, 23-4).[31]

Collingwood further explains that the pervasive theological presupposition of precision gave rise to scientific questions in the form of How? rather than Why? A new "principle of limited objective" was built into the way modern science asks its questions and poses its problems.[32] He argues that such a truly basic change strongly indicated that the supports for and even the pressures behind the questions had changed.

Collingwood goes on to identify another chief characteristic in the modern view of God — His transcendence as the Maker of a machine-like world — and argues that, in addition to precision in natural and mathematical inquiry, the new Christian theology also gave rise to a new cosmology that guided modern science. The distinction which is the "key to all the main differences between Greek and late Renaissance natural science" is that the Greeks saw nature as intelligently ruling itself, whereas the late Renaissance thinkers saw an omnipotent Creator other than nature. Correspondingly, nature as a whole was seen as an organism for the Greeks and as a machine for late Renaissance thinkers.[33]

Collingwood's argument for this new cosmology is set in an overall frame according to which the Greek organic view of nature gave way to Renaissance mechanism, which was, in turn, succeeded by the historical-evolutionary view that has been dominant since the eighteenth century. Yet his dynamic and comprehensive account focuses upon two stages in the advent of the modern idea of nature, dramatizing the passage from the organic to the mechanical. The animism of early Renaissance thought, which was recessive rather than dominant as with the Greeks, was partly overcome by Copernicus and Bruno preparatory to the mature statement of Galileo, who stood at the apex of this development. His principle of inertia, which opposed the Greek and early Renaissance theory of natural movements (as tendencies), joined with Kepler's suggestion to replace vital energy with mechanical energy (*anima* gives way to *vis*), resulted in a new outlook of systematic clarity. In Galileo the triumph of a mechanical view of nature was achieved.[34]

For Collingwood the disclosure of nature as a machine includes basic shifts in major categories. It means that quantitative rather than qualitative differences specify natural objects, change becomes a function of structure rather than tendency, causation is formally and efficiently immanent rather than teleological, laws formerly limited to earth now apply to the heavens, and matter is not the primeval and formless stuff from which all things are made, but ". . . the quantitatively organized totality of moving things."[35] In the advent as well as support of this comprehensive new view of nature Collingwood finds theological presuppositions. Just as the first stage of Renaissance cosmology presupposed animism in nature, so its theology ran together God and the world in such a way that nature itself was seen to be divine and self-creative. An immanent force actively drove and directed all things (against the teleology of Aristotle) within the passive complex of change and process in nature. Thus, presupposing an elaborate pantheistic cosmology, Bruno argued against Aristotle's external Mover and envisioned an

> . . . all-embracing and unchanging substance, the matrix of all change, [which] is at once matter, in its capacity as extended and moving, and form or spirit or God, in its capacity as self-existent and the source of movement; but it is not a transcendent unmoved Mover like the God of Aristotle but a Mover immanent in its own body and causing movements throughout that body. Thus every particular thing and every particular movement has, in Bruno's language, both a principle, or a source within itself, and a cause, or source outside itself; God is both principle and cause, principle as immanent in each individual part of nature, cause as transcending each individual part.[36]

Against Aristotelian thought, the presupposition of nature as divine induced late Renaissance thinkers to look at natural phenomena

> with a respectful, attentive, and observant eye; that is to say, it led to a habit of detailed and accurate observation, based on the postulate that every thing in nature, however minute and apparently accidental, is permeated by rationality and therefore significant and valuable. The Aristotelian tradition, regarding nature as a material imitation of a transcendent immaterial model, implied that some things in nature were accidental.[37]

Noting similarities between pantheistic Renaissance cosmology and late Ionian thought, Collingwood goes on to remark that

> just as the pantheism of Anaximander gave way, as Greek thought developed, to a doctrine according to which the world is not God but God's creature, so Bruno's pantheism gave way to a doctrine according to which the world is not divine but mechanical, implying therefore a transcendent God who designed and constructed it. The idea of nature as a machine is fatal to monism. A machine implies something outside itself. The identification of nature with God breaks down exactly when the organic view of nature disappears.[38]

Although Bruno did not really move from an organic to a mechanical view of nature, Galileo did. Collingwood argues that Galileo definitely presupposed the quantitative and mechanical character of nature vis-a-vis man the transcendent knower and God the transcendent Creator:

> Both God and man are regarded by Galileo as transcending nature; and rightly, because if nature consists of mere quantity its apparent qualitative aspects must be conferred upon it from outside, namely by the human mind as transcending it; while if it is conceived no longer as a living organism but as inert matter, it cannot be regarded as self-creative but must have a cause other than itself.[39]

Thus, in addition to the theological shift from pantheism to theism, which was deeply involved in the shift from an organic to a mechanical view of nature, an equally decisive new presupposition of knowledge came to the fore. Collingwood argues that the key difference between Greek and modern epistemology is that the Greeks saw the mind that knows thoroughly involved in nature (hence to know was to conform to nature), whereas for Galileo the mind that knows transcended nature and could manipulate it theoretically in mathematical formulas and practically by experiment.[40] The divine transcendence of the Creator-Maker and the transcendence of man as knower reinforced each other in the modern epoch.

Bold and impressive as Collingwood's argument is, it raises several questions. For example, given that God's omnipotence and transcendence are traditional Western affirmations, why were these presuppositions so effective in the rise of modern science? Or, given these presuppositions, why did not modern science appear earlier — say, in the beginnings of Christendom? Collingwood answers the second version of this question in his *Essay on Metaphysics*, arguing that Augustinian theology was presupposed in subsequent Western natural science. He claims that there are perennial if not permanent theological presuppositions in Western science and interprets the rise of modern science as a renewal of a more classic Augustinian-Platonic outlook.[41] In brief, Collingwood's background argument is that the Augustinian presupposition of the Triune Creator reformed the inadequacies of classical Aristotelian metaphysics. Aristotle did not presuppose the existence, unity, and movement of the natural world, for he believed that they were disclosed by sense experience. Hence, nature was presupposed as self-derived, living, and potentially intelligent. Collingwood holds that this led to a breakdown of Greek science. However, Augustine's Catholic presupposition of the existence of a single divinely created world, with the source of its motion in the Triune God, was a restoration of the supposition of a unified natural world crucial to the advance of Western science.[42]

But even if this argument is judged fairly accurate, one can still question whether the distinctive theological characteristics presupposed in the modern epoch should be seen chiefly as a renewal of Christian (Augustinian) Platonism.[43] Is it historically adequate to advance an epochal sketch that jumps from the Greeks and early Christian Fathers to the Renaissance? Was no contribution to modern Renaissance thought made by the medieval and late medieval views of nature, creation, and God? What of the many revivals of Augustine in Renaissance and Reformation times, including the mystics, Luther, and Reformed Christianity? Of what significance is the late medieval advent of nominalism in theology and natural philosophy? In Collingwood's estimate, Galileo emerges as a father in line with the ancient Church Fathers.

Collingwood's reconstruction of the distinctive theology presupposed in modern science primarily as a renewal of Christian Platonism is at best one-sided. His work is not sufficiently historical in discerning many theologies at work in modern thought. Without underestimating the modern theological presuppositions of creation, omnipotence, and transcendence, one can call for a more accurate and adequate account of them. Collingwood's main argument, as it stands, is not sufficient to bear the weight of the immense consequences he claims. He has not specified the distinctively modern theological presuppositions fully or sharply enough to yield the desired consequences.

Yet, even with a stronger constructive argument, it is by no means certain that the theology presupposed by Galileo amounted solely to a renewal of Augustine. Galileo was as adept in the employment of diverse theologies as he was innovative in

advancing alternative hypotheses in natural science. To vali-
date Collingwood's claim, one would have to conduct a
thorough inquiry into Galileo's science, natural philosophy, and
theology.

Nevertheless, despite its real limitations, Collingwood's
broad specification of common theological presuppositions in
modern thought goes far beyond the parochial accounts partly
represented by Merton. Furthermore, he appreciates both the
drama and the integrity of theism and pantheism, seeing their
activity in the magnanimity of change in modern thought. On
both of these counts, Collingwood's argument remains significant for this study.

Turning to Collingwood's appropriation of modern science,
the centrality of the idea of nature in his argument allows him to
discern continuity and discontinuity between modern,
medieval, and ancient scientific thought. He develops this central emphasis with sensitivity to two images of nature, as an
organism and as a machine, as well as a number of major
categorical components. He articulates a new comprehension
of nature, stressing its structural totality, as well as the priority
of quantity to quality and efficient to formal causality. Focusing
on such widespread images and structural components of nature, his argument avoids the weakness of many explanations of
the new science which constrict the larger phenomenon by
stressing (and reading in) particular natural sciences (and con-
sequent ideas of nature) which developed much later. Collingwood's argument also takes seriously the drama of conflicting natural philosophies.

Despite these virtues, however, Collingwood's account is
ultimately inconclusive, not only because his specification of
religious/theological presuppositions is inadequate, but also because his understanding of the new science is so broad that it
tends to disregard many particulars. His tendency to subordinate presuppositions of the power of mind and method to the
idea of nature, most evident in his grand developmental scheme
of eighteenth-century views of mind succeeding earlier views of
nature, is reinforced by the internal development he stresses in
organic, mechanical, and evolutionary views of nature. This
oversimplifies sixteenth- and seventeenth-century thought, and

especially the significance of experimental method in English thought.[44]

Although Collingwood's general account of the dramatic emergence of the new science is rich in many respects, it tends to stress the simple succession from organic to mechanical notions of nature, overlooking many obvious and profound spiritual, legal, and literary images in the rise of modern science. His impressive sketch of epochal change brings together seventeenth-century continental intellectual history and the thought of Galileo, but this is not matched by an equally intense inquiry into Galileo's thought.

The Methodology of this Study

Collingwood's contextualist mode of explanation goes well beyond Merton's conditional approach. Although Merton's method stands out by allowing the socio-historical reality of *both* religion and science, Collingwood's is distinguished by its *relation* of matters religious and scientific. His approach compares well with the methods employed in arguments that seek to explain modern science in relation to cultural spheres other than religion and is applicable to many other complex historical problems. It is the distinct integrity as well as the wide scope of Collingwood's approach that warrants my borrowings, interpretation, and adoption of it in this multi-disciplinary account of the new science. However, I shall give detailed attention to particular figures and prominent texts in modern science and religion. It is not enough to invoke a Galileo or a Calvin, much less the Holy Trinity. Attention to texts as well as contexts is crucial in a contextualist approach. Each claim, particularly in the difficult areas of understanding religion and its relationships to other activity, must be nailed down if one is to move beyond the realm of suggestion; perhaps the most prevalent fault in studies of this sort is exactly this failure to achieve specificity. Even Collingwood's argument does not escape this weakness, but his surplus of overview is not due to a fault in his methodology.[45]

Two assumptions constitute the explicit limitations of this inquiry. The first and broadest is that the phenomenon of the rise of modern natural science may receive a true, although far from complete, explanation by focusing on developments in mid-seventeenth-century English intellectual history. This period of creative thought, marked by the growth of the Royal Society, was characterized by the highly visible work of Bacon, Boyle, and Newton.[46] Although the phenomenon of the new science was international in character, and the epochal significance of earlier breakthroughs cannot be minimized, the period I shall emphasize is genuinely representative and will be related to earlier and later epochs.[47]

My second assumption is that the thought of one man, Robert Boyle, may illuminate the intellectual history of this period. Boyle's work is remarkably characteristic of much early modern natural philosophy, science, religion, and theology. E. A. Burtt's judgment is typical:

> Robert Boyle exemplifies in most interesting fashion all the leading intellectual currents of his day; every important or prevalent interest and belief occupied some place in his thinking and the conglomeration was harmonized with considerable success around the foci of his two most dominant enthusiasms, experimental science and religion.[48]

Boyle's many-sided but unified thought will be related in this study to the major English experimental tradition from Bacon to Newton, which includes religion as well as natural philosophy, and to Descartes and the general, reserved appreciation of Cartesianism in England. More specifically Boyle's thought will be compared to major competing orientations in seventeenth-century natural philosophy and religion, that is, traditional scholasticism and the renewal of Spiritualism represented in the ambitious work of Johan Baptist van Helmont. Thus Boyle will be studied neither as an isolated figure nor as a specialist, but as an opening to major currents of thought in and before the middle decades of the seventeenth century, a period in which he was a central figure.[49]

This contextualist approach involves an exercise of imagination directly inspired by Collingwood, who stretches the powers of empathy considerably in reenacting the thought of men, groups, and epochs. Collingwood's approach respects the way past events and actions happened and portrays their significance in a prominent mode through which they are accessible to us. Indeed, just as distinctive as his well-known view that historical inquiry reenacts thought is his virtually metaphysical passion for universality of imagination. For he asks nothing less than that the same universality which most historians presuppose in objective reconstruction should be manifest in imaginative reenactment.

This drive for universality in imagination is manifest in Collingwood's argument that the early Catholic dogma of the Trinity effected a reformation of classical Greek metaphysics. Going well beyond standard oppositions between Christian (or "purely Biblical") theism and Greek theism, he probed the careful formulas of trinitarian thought, comparing the outcomes of the classical view of the one and the many to those of the dogma of the Trinity. The striking results of this imaginative comparison are highly questionable — he read the paternity of modern science as a renewal of the reforming early Church Fathers — but the comparison opens up truly basic conflicts of great proportion within and between the traditions. Such a comprehensive contextualist inquiry cannot avoid the most moving presuppositions that characterize and distinguish whole epochs of culture.[50]

Furthermore, a widened imaginative quest for whole epochs of culture guards against subtle depreciations of a given epoch. Specifically, the integrity of early modern developments has often been slighted because highly visible eighteenth- and nineteenth-century gains and losses — the rapid proliferation of special natural sciences, the effects of deism, and secularization — have been read back into the earlier era.

My demonstration of the neglected yet immense significance of Christian belief in creation as a presupposition in the new science will be developed by an imaginative effort to show the fallout of numerous conflicting orientations toward creation. It will not take the form of a more or less familiar history of dogma. Rather, it will attempt to grasp what the many profound orientations to creation meant to those who were engaged in the pursuit of amorphous natural philosophies by means of an imaginative reenactment of their thought. Imagination of this scope is needed simply to marshall into some coherent shape the huge welter of conflicting religious traditions and movements bearing upon the new science.

As one examines the thought of a tradition including its own disciplines, one becomes able to distinguish the problems that a particular group recognizes it can handle and those it cannot. Moreover, recognition of a wider problematic which calls a group, tradition, or discipline itself into question generates pressure to locate changing positions characteristic of a whole epoch and its outstanding individuals.

Collingwood's approach calls attention to change which is so intensive that it redirects individuals, so extensive that it realigns epochs, and so radical that it may well involve the creation and destruction of particular intellectual traditions (or groups). His comprehensive contextualism, which sets out to understand the broadest, deepest, and sharpest of changes, is profoundly attuned to the strains, swells, beginnings, and endings of history. For example, his brilliant map of the adventure of the idea of nature shows that, although it often issued in dead-ends, protracted traditions, and enthusiastic visions (and regressions), it also raised in dynamic terms novel problems, questions, and answers.

Similar attention to change is evident in Collingwood's concept of absolute presuppositions. In his *Essay on Metaphysics* he holds that some strained absolute presuppositions of one epoch may be carried over as seeds into another. This developmental image of change is complemented by the more dialectical view that organic absolute presuppositions of nature are succeeded by mechanical and then by evolutionary absolute presuppositions in the overall development of the idea of nature.[51] Characteristically, he argues that what may be called perennial absolute presuppositions of natural science from early medieval times (e.g. the existence and order of nature as a single system) persisted in later changes in natural science. In short, absolute presuppositions for Collingwood were subject to historical change, yet the continuities as well as discontinuities were respected.

Although Collingwood's sensitivity to change is less evident in his account of particular individuals, and even more deficient in his tendency to oversimplify theological (and some cosmological) developments, these particular failures do not disqualify the way his general approach facilitates comprehension of change and conflict. Not content with static portraits of epochs, snapshots of individuals, or sequences of a tradition, this approach aims for an entire moving picture. It is committed to understanding change that courses through dimensions of history that are frequently, and systematically, separated.

Historical inquiry marked by imaginative reenactment and attention to radical change may, despite efforts to be specific, seem in danger of a lack of discipline. This danger can be overcome by respecting a definite structure of inquiry. At one (sustained) moment of inquiry this may mean adopting a dual perspective. Religion may serve as a context for the new science, which in turn may become a context for religious developments. Ultimately, this approach seeks to reveal the power of both religious and scientific presuppositions within the arena of their seventeenth-century meeting ground, the realm of natural philosophy, in which ideas of nature, creation, and history (among others) figured prominently. Apart from the fact that within seventeenth-century Christian intellectual culture religion usually appeared to be ancient and science novel, there is no a priori methodological reason for understanding nature as an exclusively scientific province, or even creation as an exclusively religious province. Initially, various possibilities must be respected, for only in this light does a further determination of a larger, more effective context of particular developments become credible. Moreover, relative suspension of judgment at one moment of inquiry also enables one to disclose the power of novel developments in such perennial beliefs as divine creation. Merely to assume that typical seventeenth-century intellectuals took creation for granted, and then to break off inquiry, is to miss the more dramatic and productive fallout of this theological staple.

Further, in the perspective adopted here, one must not only look over the shoulder of religious and scientific subjects (frequently joined in one person) to grasp distinct meanings, but also view the broader subject matter both historically and systematically. Change must be imaginatively reenacted to arrive at an understanding that amplifies but does not destroy the initial understandings. Thus, the search for presuppositions is structurally linked with other components in a common frame.

At this level, contextual inquiry is deepened, for it must confront the question: How should empathetic imagination, at once specific and prone to universality, be disciplined in the interest of a sound and systematic historical reconstruction? Collingwood's proposal is that the disciplined inquirer should initially consider statements as answers to questions. This assumes that the provision of answers (for men cannot live by shared presuppositions alone) is integral to the notion of an epoch, and that the pressing of timely questions is integral to the notion of uniquely conscious individuals. Therefore, the imagination, in reenacting radical change which is epochally extensive, radically intensive, and productive and destructive of new disciplines, may be further disciplined by mapping or reconstructing the peculiar interplay of problems, questions, answers, and presuppositions. The discernment of answers will point to a more limited number of more compact questions. A question which receives high and common articulation is likely to promote a diverse series of theoretical (and experimental) problems and sets of answers which hold for a time. Some questions may well go unanswered, or at best be indirectly answered in times of great change. Yet, when a particular question elicits many answers which fail to comport with the question, then one may find either that another question is involved or that the very presuppositions that give rise to the most fruitful and interesting questions can be disclosed and reconstructed.[52]

The interplay of questions and answers, and their presuppositions in the proposal just sketched, provides unusual scope for inquiry, but not at the price of disciplined historical disclosure and reconstruction. For that interplay is rooted in the deepest senses of bodily dissatisfaction and psychological frustration as manifested in the processes of problem-solving. Moreover, it characterizes such intellectually sophisticated activities as experiment, hypothesis, and theory construction.[53] As a disciplined way of grasping all these activities in and with their rich and diverse contexts, a Collingwoodian method promises an adequate and fruitful common language that does not predetermine any specific explanation.

But structures per se are not enough. Collingwood proposes that historical inquiry disciplined to disclose the structural interplay of questions and answers should end in the search for absolute presuppositions. While relative presuppositions may be converted into questions, and vice versa, absolute presuppositions require further elucidation. Collingwood points out that it is much easier to disclose the absolute presuppositions of another age and its subjects than of our own. Indeed, Collingwood argues that one cannot get in touch with present presuppositions without first disclosing those of the past. The historian cannot, therefore, read his own basic presuppositions back into an earlier age. However bold his historical reconstruction may be, he must ultimately respect whatever he may find.

This position is no denial of the integrity of absolute presuppositions. They are not merely functions of the mind of the historian. Although Collingwood's statement that absolute presuppositions have "logical efficacy" might suggest that they are purely formal premises, as in traditional logic, they are best interpreted as constituting an informal logic.[54] Insofar as absolute presuppositions have general priority and superiority in the complexes of questions and answers disclosed in highly disciplined historical inquiry, they may be likened to Kant's notion of regulative, rather than constitutive, ideas. Yet, by holding that questions follow presuppositions, Collingwood incorporates the insistent pressure of both into a view of the vicissitudes of genuinely historical rather than pure reason.

This informal logic rests on the efficacy of absolute presuppositions. While Collingwood did not liken such presuppositions to the direct power of causes, he did claim that they give rise to questions. If the classical notion of "first principles" could be purged of its ontological import, it would serve to point up the actual priority or potential of situation (if not always of chronological time) on which Collingwood sought to focus.[55] Any reading of absolute presuppositions as substances misses their simple strength as suppositions.

Collingwood's statement that absolute presuppositions are usually taken for granted, although to a lesser extent in times of social strain, has led some to the conclusion that presuppositions are social conditions. The point, however, is that the maintenance of absolute presuppositions is rooted in diverse social strains and pressures.[56] Such presuppositions may include but cannot be exhausted by social conditions or physical causes. Collingwood's care not to exclude the presuppositions of individuals, groups, or epochs invites an articulation of the influence of society upon historical thought. Although he does not spell this out, apart from warning against determinism, any inquiry capable of disclosing the integral significance of symbols for historical consciousness complements his approach. For example, Robert Bellah's modest probes into the development of cultural symbol systems in history can serve to flesh out the necessary sketchiness of epochal presuppositions.[57]

In order to render the conception of absolute presuppositions more useful, their central and positive meaning must be further clarified. Collingwood points out that such presuppositions are not premises yet they are the foundation for a definite structure. Taken with his insistence that although they are not causes they are efficacious, this amounts to a conviction that logic and reality are ultimately linked. A basic conviction of unity is manifest in Collingwood's very expression of "absolute presuppositions" (and of "logical efficacy"). Accordingly, in arguing that such presuppositions are not mere conditions or purely abstract reflections, his example of the widespread presupposition of precision specifies a significant coincidence of background and foreground, a pervasive context more penetrating than conditions and more effective than reflections. Collingwood is indicating a unified beginning point of (historic) questions and (historical) inquiry. That is why he sees the discovery of absolute presuppositions as the final lure and goal of systematic historical inquiry. They are working unities of mind and historical reality. In support of this, Collingwood's argument that such presuppositions are taken for granted, or by "faith," is not made to highlight their often unconscious and deeply motivational strength (although such roots are not denied), but to indicate the unity of power and structure that characterizes them.[58] He might have said that such presuppositions are held in *trust* by men, groups, and epochs, for the basic affection of trust unifies power and order for the mind. Trust positively allows the risk of a question. Hence the efficacy of basic presuppositions is rooted in their trustworthiness over time.

On this basis of interpretation, and with an understanding of man as a thinking, acting, and feeling creature, one may regard and expect to find basic presuppositions in at least three forms.[59] As the chief contexts of thought, they lend situation and control to the positions and problems pursued by diverse figures, and define the limits of particular lines of questions. Viewed as wholes rather than premises or causes, such intellectual contexts promote some problems and not others. Thus basic presuppositions may appear as general intellectual intuitions about the particular order, direction, and so on, that thought should take. Particularly when analyzing the pressure of limiting questions, the historian may locate basic presuppositions. For example, the limiting question of self-identity does not rest before a true answer, "I'm an American," but calls for greater unities of the questioner and his true, but incomplete, answers. Similarly, limiting questions of the constitution of nature call for estimates of ever larger contexts.[60]

Second, as paradigmatic events for human action, basic presuppositions give concentrated articulation to the specific examples deemed most significant for diverse lines of human action and thought. For example, Kant's invocation of the Copernican revolution in relation to his own effort to comprehensively reorder philosophical critique presupposed that earlier change — not, of course, as a detailed model, but as the most significant way of raising a whole new set of questions in the philosophy of experience. The Copernican revolution was a paradigmatic event for his architectonic program of philosophy.

Third, basic presuppositions may take the form of pervasive moods which govern human feelings, affections, and even passions and instincts. They set a tone of harmony or chaos which has its own significance. The presupposition of chaos, for example, has functioned for many as a kind of terrible unity to shake loose normal uniformities (and habits) of feeling and affection. Those pressing questions generated by the presupposition of deep turmoil have often had a kind of urgency bordering on desperation. In general, such deeply sustained moods or tones as chaos or, more typically, order have been expressed in images, which are as intrinsic to thought as is metaphor. For example, the formal clarity of basic presuppositions, such as God and nature, would fall short of concrete persuasion and coercion without such images as Author and the machine. However difficult it may be to disclose the relationship between proliferating or conflicting images and the lesser number of ideas that regulate understanding, the power and even epochal significance of such images, which are basic to perception as well as thought, can be disclosed.[61]

Collingwood's contextualist approach is a disciplined way of interpreting radical change both extensively and intensively. For during periods of such change men are most open to the widest contexts, greatest events, and the most pervasive moods in and of their times. My argument here will be mainly limited to the bearing of religious and theological presuppositions upon the new science. But it is not intended as a simple piece of history of religion or history of science. Rather it is an effort to transcend these fields of study and yet not lose their more limited, distinct perspectives, an attempt to articulate the larger unities of our past. To bring a measure of discipline to this multi-disciplined inquiry, this study makes use of imagination, attention to epochal change, and specificity. The overall structure of the inquiry culminates in the search for basic presuppositions. In this case, my chief purpose is to show that belief in creation was a major presupposition in the rise of modern natural science as it occurred in seventeenth-century England.

Chapters 2 and 3 are largely devoted to elucidating diverse orientations to creation in a broad historical perspective. Subsequently, Chapters 4 through 6 disclose the bearing of competing theologies of creation presupposed by the major figures, and the influence of these presuppositions in the ideas of modernity, knowledge, and nature prevalent in the advent of modern natural science. However, this gross two-fold order of composition could be reversed with equal justification. Such a presentation would begin with Boyle's diverse discoveries (in the midst of questions, problems, and positions) and reconstruct their presuppositions in a more logical fashion. However, I have chosen to map the more informal logic of history.

CHAPTER TWO:

The Development of a Voluntarist Theology of Creation

My attempt to trace the rise of modern science in its mid-seventeenth-century intellectual context must fall short of a full account of all Western religious and scientific thought that preceded its manifestation. But one earlier orientation to creation is of particular interest. The voluntarist theological presuppositions that developed in late medieval and Reformation thought were eventually extended to epochal proportions in seventeenth-century English thought. Not only was belief in creation presupposed by virtually all the diverse figures in the rise of modern science, but voluntarist orientations toward divine creation had especial significance.

Historians have generally interpreted Christianity as a religion of redemption, largely on the basis of its vigorous New Testament manifestation.[1] Beginning in the third and fourth centuries, however — from Constantine's conversion and Augustine's consolidation of Christianity in the West — Christianity can with equal validity be viewed as a religion of creation. From the advent of Christendom until its nineteenth- and twentieth-century demise, Christianity was part of the criticism, destruction, construction, and maintenance of culture. Indeed, deep cultural involvement has been integral to the Christian belief in divine creation. As a guardian of divine aseity and creaturely dependence, Christianity has articulated belief in creation in response to the ancient Gnostic threat of an alien Creator and creation pervaded with evil, the perennial question of Jewish theology—whether Christianity is beyond morality — the lingering Greek establishment of an eternal *kosmos*, the Enlightenment challenge of autonomous Reason and Nature; and more recent proclamations of human self-

29

creativity. In the main, Christian theology has maintained the goodness of creation as a basis for ethics, the temporal course of creation under God, and the priority of the Creator to reason, nature, and man.

Such a summary barely indicates the positive meaning of Christian belief in creation. Unfortunately, the critical intent of the main dogmatic rubric, *creatio ex nihilo*, provides little additional help. The complex rubrics of man as *imago dei*, and the *orders of creation* would be more pertinent. Yet, incredible as it may seem, there is no comprehensive scholarly history of the Christian doctrine of creation as a whole.[2] Hence, any analysis of the main tradition of medieval thought on creation must remain sketchy.

With the advent of Christendom, Christian theologies of creation focused on created and uncreated being: they became explicitly ontological. Augustine's prayerful and original probing of his own being in the *Confessions* personally expressed a theology of created being; his meditation on God's eternal Being in the *De Trinitate* turned on his presupposition of the contrast and real analogies between uncreated and created being; and his map of corporate Christian existence over against and in relation to that of civil temporal order in *The City of God* was a truly grand statement of his theology of created being and culture. Henceforth the Christian drama of Creation, Fall and Redemption acquired universal cultural significance in the West. It remained for Anselm and Thomas to state in careful detail a theology of the hierarchy of created being ranging from divine, angelic, and human being down to the lowest reaches of prime matter. The great Christian chain of being was partly borrowed from classical Greek ontology, but it was secured in that divine ground of being which was, in turn, variously reflected throughout diverse levels (densities) of created being.[3]

This hierarchy of created being was manifest in hierarchies of ecclesiastical and secular order. Classic medieval natural philosophy, derived largely from Aristotle, was gradually integrated into and expanded in the institutions of medieval culture. Thus Aristotle's doctrine of four elements, and his concepts of law, motion, causality, and purpose, became parts of a great, if loose, synthesis. The presupposition of created being provided a context in which the natural world was taken as a single system; its order, in the last analysis, was dependent upon the eternal Being of God. Even the rise of modern natural science, facilitated and promoted by later theologies of creation, did not call this presupposition into question.[4]

Until the eighteenth century, when the Creator was conceived as a dispensable hypothesis, all serious Western thought presupposed God as Creator, the act and/or relation of divine creation, the order of creation at large, and man as God's special creature. These four components are systematically apparent in the historical unfolding of quite diverse orientations to creation.

It is difficult to overestimate the significance of the whole family of presuppositions indicated by these components, for it characterized classic Christian belief in creation, partly by nurturing a comprehensive, highly rational genre of religious expression peculiar to Western Christendom. The patristic beginnings of systematic dogmatic theology allowed for a critical appropriation of many ancient pre-Christian cultures. Such an encompassing (if not imperial) belief in the whole of divine creation (along with *logos* christology and the ontological Trinity) differed profoundly from the ancient Jewish presupposition that divine creation was the stage and very beginning of the only history of ultimate redemptive significance. For the Old Testament creation was history, preeminently the history executed by Yahweh in which Israel was chosen for a unique redemptive destiny.[5] But systematic theology, coincident with Christendom, transposed the old story-telling of Genesis, so appropriate to ancient Jewish religion. Of course, the new mode of Christian discourse was metaphysical. But that was only one aspect of an extremely bold mystical-rational religious philosophy rooted in the hierarchical structure of creation. Beginning with Augustine, Christendom's belief in creation gave intellectual and cultural shape to Western life. It so captured the religious imagination that it was even more potent than its romantic denomination, the great chain of being, suggests.

The demeaning of this grand achievement by the main thrust of nineteenth-century scholarship in historical theology, i.e., the interpretation of the rise of Christendom as a sell-out to speculative Greek metaphysics, was in fact based upon an epochal loss of belief in creation. At worst it was an expression of the monumental hubris of nineteenth-century German intellectual culture.[6] Whereas classic Christian thought always respected creation as an original divine mystery, the eighteenth-century exchange of the Creator for a mere Maker scuttled the mystery and ushered in the great nineteenth-century reduction of belief in creation, anticipating its near total eclipse in the twentieth century. Schleiermacher, the father of much nineteenth- and twentieth-century theology, did hold that creation was presupposed in the Christian's consciousness of redemption, of sin and grace.[7] But the creation to which he referred was like a perennially receding *ding an sich*, systematically akin to Kant's non-view of reality. It was a poor offspring of the rich family of presuppositions which shaped the classical belief. As such, belief in creation functioned only as a critical principle, a guardian of the absolute dependence of things finite. Yet even this formal critical power was endangered, for the belief had lost not only its content (for example, the historical-political orders of creation) but also its richly structured scope and dramatic style to move imagination. History and evolution (and even "absolute causality" for Schleiermacher!) truly captured nineteenth-century imagination, and the epochal effectiveness of belief in creation was the victim.

Aware of this overall development, the rise and demise of Christendom, the historian can gain a more adequate grasp of highly significant seventeenth-century developments by attending to the four components mentioned above. They indicate that a whole family of presuppositions, ranging from Creator to creature, are systematically apparent in the historical unfolding of the ontological, voluntarist, and Spiritualist orientations to creation within many diverse disciplines.

Beginnings of Voluntarist Thought in Late Medieval Criticism

Many historians of Christianity have tended to slight fourteenth- and fifteenth-century theology in favor of the achievements of high medievalism and the sixteenth-century Reformation. The very Catholic-Protestant polemics that were indirectly conducive to modern historical inquiry have tended to promote neglect of late medieval as well as seventeenth-century theology. Thomists, Calvinists, and Lutherans alike have not found their heroes in these periods. However, other historians have long noted the contributions of late medieval thought to epistemology, the problem of universals, natural philosophy, and doctrines of natural law. And, more recently, suggestive revisions in the history of Christian thought, particularly by Oberman and Vignaux, have disclosed the integrity of late medieval theology.[8] Works of this sort, partly supported by that of Gilson, counter the older interpretation of these times largely as a disintegration of the medieval synthesis. The achievements of late medieval nominalist or voluntarist theology are beginning to receive the fresh scholarly attention they deserve.

The advent of late medieval voluntarist theology marked the beginning of an orientation to creation which, partly derived from a nominalist rejection of universals, refocused the work of the Creator in terms of His supreme will rather than the divine intellect. In relation to the Creator's will, the contingency of creation was emphasized in contrast to more rational relations of participation. The older proposition that the will moved according to the last dictate of understanding was fundamentally called into question, along with the confident search for types and archetypes. The order of creation became the law imposed by God, and man, God's creature, was identified by his free and voluntary obedience to the ordinances of God, which set the boundaries of his existence, action, and inquiries. These ordinances marked the path of his union with God.

Of course, this new theology of creation did not appear overnight. It was the accomplishment of numerous late medieval theologians and natural philosophers such as Ockham, Biel, d'Ailly, Gerson, Buridan, and Oresme, spanning at least two centuries. The theological statement of this tradition acquired some official prominence in the Paris and Oxford Condemnations of 1277, directed chiefly against the Averroist-Christian thought of Siger of Brabant, but also partly against Thomas' synthesis of Augustine's theology and Aristotle's natural philosophy. As part of a general renewal of Augustine's stress on the freedom of God (as in the work of Hugh of St. Victor, Bonaventure, *et al.*), there was widespread protest against necessary relations between God and the world and against such relations in mundane affairs.[9]

Although the Condemnations do not allow a full reconstruction of the basic view of the world they oppose, it is clear that Siger of Brabant's fusion of the classical Greek view of the natural world and a thoroughly ontological orientation to creation was read as a dangerous sign. Such a complete union of Christian belief in creation and Aristotelian natural philosophy called into question the basic direction of Thomas' achievement. At stake were not only presuppositions of a temporal vs. an eternal world, but the entire Greek view of the world as organic, for not only philosophical propositions were indicted, but also the rationale and practice of necromancy.[10] Ever since Thomas, Aristotle's natural philosophy had acquired theological sanction and had been elaborated in a highly sophisticated system which featured intelligences, elements, purposes, motions, and immanent laws of the natural world. In this imposing edifice, based on a hierarchical if not necessary joining of God and nature, philosophy distinguished between naturally circular movement in heaven, in which the fifth element obtained, and the built-in corruptibility of all terrestrial motion, whether ascendent or descendent.[11] Yet the *telos* of all motion involved a basic bond of natural intention and purpose, an inner connection between the attraction of divine Being, heavenly intelligences, and earthly movement.

The Paris theologians condemned the affirmation of perpetual movement of the heavens.[12] Siger was the principal offender here, but Thomas also held that the "nature" of heaven demands, according to its inner law, perpetual movement even though its realization requires God's will. The critical point of the Condemnations was that God's will should not be restricted to naturally perpetual motion.

This interest in the freedom of divine will was further presupposed in the condemnation of the Aristotelian thesis that it is impossible to affirm a plurality of worlds. Here the official theological weight of the Condemnations allowed that the natural philosopher is free to hold a possible plurality of worlds. Although Thomas, who may have been implicated here, did not flatly deny the possibility of other worlds, his commitment to a single universe on the grounds of his more rational ontology and theology was clear.[13]

Three other condemnations bore directly on the defense of

the divine act of *creatio ex nihilo* over against the eternality of the world. The eternity of species was condemned and the possibility of a void affirmed. In further defense of the contingency of the world, those propositions affirming the control of heavenly intelligences were denied. Perhaps the best summary of the interest in God's freedom and the contingency of creation was the condemnation of the view "that God necessarily produces what immediately follows from him."[14] The initial critical achievement of the Condemnations was to heighten the contingency of natural creation.

A relatively new departure, correlated with contingency, was the affirmation of the freedom of the Creator's will. Best expressed in the chief mark of late medieval theology, the dialectic of God's *potentia absoluta* and *potentia ordinata*, this belief acquires increasing prominence throughout the thought and life of the period. While anything short of violating the law of noncontradiction fell within the range of God's absolute power, He had freely committed Himself to a definite order, of which creation, fall, and dispensations of redemption were the rudiments. According to God's ordained power, His work was a series of historical acts, not "within" the course of history but veritably establishing that course.[15] Yet, because by His absolute power God could suspend His ordinary work, the contingency of creation was at once established and dramatically reinforced by the dialectic of His *potentia ordinata* and *absoluta*.

Although this distinction was not original to Ockham, or late medieval theology, it was particularly in his theology that the marginal *potentia absoluta* came into the foreground. As Oberman puts it, the *irrealis* of what could have happened became a *realis*.[16] The *potentia absoluta* became God's power to reverse the natural order in miracles, for example. God was not held obliged to obey natural or moral law, and creation itself, including its order, came to be regarded as miraculous. An increasing awareness of the eschatological openness of such a radically contingent creation emerged, and Ockham sharpened the focus on divine will. Opposition to the older theology of divine ideas (or essences), which Scotus had criticized, was extended when Ockham rejected even the Scotistic *formal* distinctions in Deity, highlighting not only the freedom and will of

God but also His simplicity, which became a special concern of this new theological orientation.[17]

Gabriel Biel, the disciple of Ockham whose nominalism influenced Luther, further denied that God may alternately act in an ordinate and inordinate way, since God's actions *ad extra* could not be divided. Nor could God act sometimes with and sometimes without order, for that would contradict His being.

> But the distinction should be understood to mean that God can — and, in fact, has chosen to — do certain things according to the laws which he freely established, that is, *de potentia ordinata*. On the other hand, God can do everything that does not imply contradiction, whether God has decided to do these things, or not, as there are many things God can do which he does not want to do. The latter is called God's power *de potentia absoluta*.

At one point Biel (and d'Ailly) extended Ockham's teaching. Regarding the exercise of human capacities, Biel

> shows that, *de potentia absoluta*, natural laws can be suspended to such an extent that a created cause can produce effects radically different from what they can now, *de potentia ordinata*. Miracles are the reminders that nature is not a self-contained reality — nature is creation.[18]

Thus necessary connections between causes and effects were ruled out, for both were more closely, if mysteriously, related to the dialectical power of God. A recent comment on d'Ailly summarizes the relatively new view of God in late medieval theology: "The basic tenets of [d'Ailly's] thought, as of Ockham's, are the unity, freedom, and omnipotence of God."[19]

Within this dialectical orientation, the order of creation was conceived in terms of law, and entities subject to law, rather than in terms of symbols with varying degrees of mind and soul which participated in the divine Logos. Fully developed, this shift from *logos* to law acquired epoch-forming proportions, for law in this tradition had its own character. In principle, law was dependent chiefly upon God's will rather than His reason, although the latter was not neglected. Since there was no easy or natural transition from God's power to the created order, obedience reinforced the sense of a transcendent Lawgiver. Like the ancient Jewish understanding of law, the voluntarist view presupposed God distinct from His creation, which He orders by law.[20]

Whereas natural law for Thomas was part of God's wise and rational sovereignty, the voluntarist orientation, typified by Ockham, related law to God's power of command. Since eternal and natural law are ultimately matters of divine reason for Thomas, the whole universe, but especially man, is governed by rational structure. But Ockham emphasized that the chief mark of law is obligation rather than a relatively immanent built-in regularity. Thus law was externally imposed upon a subject creation. God acts not because something is good, but because He acts it is good. Although Ockham's position, including his "rule ethic," verged upon arbitrariness, his decisive, even formative argument held that God can, *de potentia absoluta*, suspend particular rules but has condescended, *de potentia ordinata*, to establish a natural and moral order, the common course of nature.

The stock example of God's miraculous work — the preservation of Daniel's friends in the furnace of fire — was also a witness to the strange work of God in choosing a people for his own. In effect, the voluntarist notion of natural and moral law fell back upon the mysterious, but highly active will of God.[21] The general position that the binding power and order of imposed natural law presupposes a dialectic of God's ordained and absolute power was shaped in opposition to the long tradition of immanent natural law which expressed the built-in tendencies of nature.

Turning to anthropological considerations, whereas classical scholastic thought located the image of God in man's rational soul and understood the will to move according to the last dictate of understanding, the Paris theologians of 1277 condemned the propositions that will must necessarily follow insight, that the will necessarily follows what reason accepts, and that right will is subsequent to right reason. This encouraged a voluntarist understanding of man as God's special creature.[22]

The intensive depth of this new voluntarism can be seen in the distinctive mysticism of such late medieval nominalists as Gerson and Biel. As Oberman has shown, nominalist *pietas*, man's private relation to God, is quite different from the intellectual contemplation of God, i.e. the transcendence of time, pluriformity, and corporeality in creation as in Meister Eckhart. The willing union with God implied great respect for His transcendence. Oberman notes that the nominalist cannot go beyond God's actual revelation: "At the point where human reason finds its limitations the soul meets the divine will and is united with it in love, not through conformity of intellect, but *per voluntatis conformitatem.*"[23]

Respect for the disproportion between God and man in this piety gave first place to the virtue of humility. This was manifest in what Oberman calls "penitential" rather than "transformational" mysticism. The self did not participate in the divine ground, as with Eckhart, nor was it transubstantiated on the model of the Mass. A sense of eschatological futurity was proper to that type of piety which outfitted and disciplined the life of the *viator.*[24]

Finally, this entire budding voluntarist orientation to creation raises an intriguing question of its significance for the knowledge of nature. If the context represented here of the comprehensive aspirations built into the voluntarist theology of creation is sound, then both various suggestions that it enhanced empirical inquiry and promoted a relatively independent natural philosophy may be amplified together.[25] That is, as the virtue of humility enhanced empirical respect for fact, the *viator's* obligation to construct his life nurtured reason. Moreover, as the contingency of creation promoted *a posteriori* rather than *a priori* questions, the belief that creation was ordered according to divinely imposed laws encouraged lawful answers or explanations to the questions of natural philosophy. Again, if late medieval thought in general gave more weight to experience than reason in the activity of knowing, e.g., by shifting the natural knowledge of God from Anselm's *necessitas* to probable opinions,[26] it also promoted a more liberated exercise of reason in the judgment of such opinions. If the epistemic meaning of stressing God's *potentia ordinata* was the nurture of empirical respect for inquiry into the given, then the meaning of God's inseparable *potentia absoluta* was the promotion of powers of reason released from the logic of being, now beholden only to the law of noncontradiction.

To substantiate this suggestion would, of course, require a full-scale inquiry into nominalist logic, epistemology, and natural philosophy in the context of voluntarist theology. Yet, although our textual demonstrations below into such matters pertain to early modern figures, the latter were closely linked to their late medieval forerunners. In any case, the suggestion ventured here does have genuinely epochal proportions for inquiry, irregardless of late medieval realizations. That is, it is commonly recognized that modern thought subordinated ontology to epistemology, thereby reversing the medieval orientation. The question (at once historical and systematic) is how this came about. If our suggestion above is true, then the shift occurred not simply because of liberation from the demands of scholastic reason, and not simply because of the advent of secular epistemic pursuits, but rather because of liberation from the demands of ontological reason, logic invested with being, or better, the *logos* of being which presupposed the ultimate Being of God.[27] Liberation of this vast scope required a new principle, a moving beginning point of thought and life. For natural philosophy and science the late medieval bud bloomed in the seventeenth century.

Voluntarist and Aesthetic Orientations to Creation in Calvin's Theology

Voluntarist and nominalist traditions continued in English universities, particularly Oxford, and in the work of many Anglican divines who nurtured the historical succession between English Protestantism and medieval thought. Equally important, an altered voluntarism was mediated to English thought through the Reformation thought of Calvin, whose general significance for English religion is well known.[28] Although many proponents of the general argument on religion and modern science appeal to Calvin's significance, there is very little agreement as to which aspects of his thought, or the doctrines of Calvinism, are relevant and influential in the new science. The general scholarly neglect of Calvin's theology of creation necessitates a fresh inquiry in this context.[29]

Calvin built no theory of being, no system of ethics, and no general anthropology to soften the straight edge of God's will. Presupposing the existence of creation, he saw it as simply contingent upon the power of the Creator. Given the miracle of creation by the Word through which God called and commanded this world from chaos, and presupposing man's link in conscience to the Creator, he stressed the transcendent obligations of man. Presupposing man's original integrity of soul, he stressed the depth of man's fall and the glory of God which he seeks.

The radical contingency of creation was a central point of Calvin's definitive exposition of divine Providence.[30] Throughout his attempt to convey the richness and realism of the biblical images of creation, he never relaxed his ultimate point that God is in charge of creation and that its contingency is universally extensive as well as intensive. Yet, in Calvin's thought the entire world is no more insulated from mighty vicissitudes than an individual's life is free from historical suffering. His lengthy discussion of Providence pits God's power against that of fate, chance, and blind determinism. He portrays a remarkably enigmatic power-filled picture of the world. The particularity of providential care overcomes all other powers, but never without considerable dramatic, and historical, tension.[31]

Calvin's conviction that all creation was egalitarian because of its ultimate dependence upon God's power further undercut traditional presuppositions of the hierarchy of being.[32] Far from being closed to God, creation was opened to His power. Hence, as the late medieval thinkers had set aside the influence of the heavenly intelligences, so Calvin argued against astrology. The point that all things hang directly upon the sufficiency of the Creator's will was further underscored by Calvin's strictly instrumental doctrine of angels, in contrast to Thomas' view of angels as higher created entities.[33]

Moreover, Calvin saw a relatively direct relation between God and creation. In no small part that relation consisted of the work of God and of man. While many have noted that his doctrine of God is remarkable for its absence of a theory of divine attributes, few have recognized the definitive and formative significance the category of works acquires in his theology of power and will. Calvin elaborated a theology of God's work, not His being. Although, given God's total work of redemption, he stringently opposed salvation by human works, Calvin insisted not only that man's response to divine redemption should be a lifetime of work ordered by God's law (the third use) and motivated by gratitude, but also that man's proper work as a creature was to enjoy and rightly use God's creation. Thus his theology of God's work was also a theology of man's working responses.[34]

This emphasis is evident in the primacy Calvin gave to practical virtues and disciplines rather than contemplative ones. At one point, having written of the bright display of creation, he does not stop with either a common appreciation or a pious adoration of the theatre of creation. Instead, he insists that ". . . there is need of art and more exacting toil in order to investigate the motion of the stars, to determine their assigned stations, to measure their intervals, to note their properties."[35]

Calvin's affirmation of the contingency of creation, which is inseparable from his theology of Providential work, raises the question of the nature of God as Creator. This is the subject of the first book of the *Institutes*. Having begun by noting that "spirituality" is one of two "epithets" sufficient to convey what is proper to Deity, Calvin establishes the framework for his *magnum opus* by stating a doctrine of the Trinity, which is most noteworthy because of the full personal Deity ascribed to the Holy Spirit.[36] The doctrine of "Spiritual Providence," for example, explicitly rejects the Thomistic *concursus generalis* and insists that the whole of creation is directly present to God. The physical, material world is not reduced to the last link in the chain of being, for *creatio ex nihilo* is a work of the Spirit as well as the Father. Creation is in principle egalitarian, presupposing that man remains a spiritual creature who, despite dualist tensions, is always responsible for his actions and knowledge, the latter by virtue of wisdom and the former by virtue of conscience.[37] Even Calvin's emphasis on the accusing finger of God in his doctrine of man in sin and the regenerating Spirit in his doctrine of redemption presupposes the concrete work of the Spirit in creation at large. In holding that by the power of His Spirit, God inspires the whole of creation, that the universal motion of creation is one direct manifestation of God's spiritual work, Calvin is critically interpreting the Renaissance Platonic tradition, according to which creation is the body of God.[38]

Calvin insists that creation is the objective revelation of

God, even though man may not be able to perceive God's revelatory publications in creation. "The Knowledge [or Revelation] of God Shines Forth in the Fashioning of the Universe and the Continuing Government of it," is his title for Book I, Chapter 5 of the *Institutes,* which argues:

> [God] . . . revealed himself and daily discloses himself in the whole workmanship of the universe . . . wherever you cast your eyes, there is no spot in the universe wherein you cannot discern at least some sparks of his glory. You cannot in one glance survey this most vast and beautiful system of the universe, in its wide expanse, without being completely overwhelmed by the boundless force of its brightness.[39]

Creation is not simply a revelation of God but also a showing forth of its own order (or brightness in this case). Since God's Spirit is expressed individually and as a whole in the creation, as in a painting, theater, or edifice, all men are invited and attracted to the work of the Creator.[40]

While Calvin found more than faint traces (footsteps) of God in creation, he was neither concerned with degrees or kinds of being and causality (as was Thomas), nor with finding and aligning types and archetypes. Creation was an open book, not an outer garment or extension of God himself. Revelation in creation was not the unveiling of God and the unveiledness of creation. Nor was it an infusion or impartation of God himself. Calvin vigorously resisted any kind of "confusing" relation between creation and Creator; the Spiritual work of God and the spiritual work of man remained distinct. Creation was a spectacular theater and a moving edifice, revealing its Author and the order given to it by Him.[41]

Calvin's forthright articulation of God's "infinite" power and will, the second of two epithets sufficient to communicate Deity, served to discipline his "high" doctrine of aesthetic creation by the Spirit of God. The boundary between Creator and creation, which no creature can overcome, was as important as the bond between Creator and creation. Calvin was so insistent upon the supreme and sole prerogative of God's will that if a choice had to be made between God's powerful will and the efficacy of second causes, he was willing to scuttle the latter. The constant and particular will of God was not merely "permissive" agency but an active willing. Calvin's rejection of any *idle* Deity strongly affirmed God's governorship down to the very last detail. It was precisely by virtue of this universality that the rule of God was asserted over that of any law of nature without God.[42]

Calvin's dialectic of ordinary and extraordinary Providence reasserted earlier distinctions in more particularistic and spiritualistic terms, even though he rejected the terminology of *potentia absoluta* because of its dangerous suggestion of an idle Deity.[43] From Calvin's continual reference to the secrecy of the divine plan into which no man may inquire, which is later developed in the distinction between God's decretive and preceptive will, it is clear that the primacy of God's powerful will is so strong that the latter may become an inner abyss.[44] Thus the distinction between God and the world which had been muted in Renaissance aestheticism is here affirmed.

In articulating the fundamental order of creation and man's task along broadly aesthetic and specifically voluntarist rather than hierarchical lines, Calvin eschewed both systematic discussion of the traditional orders of creation and an exegesis of the six days of creation in the *Institutes*.[45] His forceful style was a literal attempt to communicate the divine beauty and design of creation which, he insisted, also manifests an unalterable lawful order. Proclaiming and defending what he called the "signs of divinity" in creation, parallel to the "seeds of divinity" in man, he opposed the Epicurean substitution of "nature" and its order for God. Arguing against a similar "confusion" of Creator and creation in Lucretius, he declared, "As if the universe, which was founded as a spectacle of God's glory, were its own creator!" Then he continued:

> See, of what value to beget and nourish godliness in men's hearts is that jejune speculation about the universal mind which animates and quickens the world! . . . This is indeed making a shadow deity to drive away the true God whom we should fear and adore. I confess, of course, that it can be said reverently, provided that it proceeds from a reverent mind, that nature is God; but because it is a harsh and improper saying, since nature is rather the order prescribed by God, it is harmful in such weighty matters, in which special devotion is due, to involve God confusedly in the inferiour course of his works.

Having set aside such errors, he gave his own statement of the design which the Divine Author displays.

> With what clear manifestation his might draws us to contemplate him! . . . by his nod alone sometimes to shake heaven with thunderbolts, to burn everything with lightnings, to kindle the air with flashes . . . . Belonging to this theme are the praises of God's power from the testimonies of nature which one meets here and there especially indeed in the Book of Job and Isaiah. . . . This way of seeking God is common both to strangers and to those of his household, if they trace the outlines that above and below sketch a living likeness of him.[46]

In many similar passages Calvin praises the power, wisdom, and goodness of the Creator in creation. But a theory of divine attributes is at best latent in such descriptions, which celebrate not so much particular events in creation as vivid total displays. Indeed, Calvin's suggestion that the "signs" are "lively images" shows that he regards the Spirit of the Creator present in the beautiful order of creation.[47] While he does ascribe mildly argumentative weight to created design in showing forth Deity, the prominent feature of his "argument" is the delight and attention he gives to the presence of God's Spirit in all things that manifest divine glory and invite creaturely praise and respect.[48]

Lawfulness is equally prominent in Calvin's conception of the order of creation. Carefully distinguishing Christian teaching from any fateful law of nature, he writes that "we do not, with the Stoics, contrive a necessity out of the perpetual connection and intimately related series of causes, which is contained in nature; but we make God the ruler and governor of all things." Thus he incorporated the older natural law tradition as an expression of the regularity of God's own Providence and Law: the lawfulness of nature is acceptable when subordinated to the supreme rule of God.[49]

Calvin's view of man's intrinsic and extrinsic creaturely task comports with his aesthetic and legal conceptions of the order of creation:

> Heaven and earth being thus most richly adorned and copiously supplied with all things, like a large and splendid mansion gorgeously constructed and exquisitely furnished, at length man was made — man, by the beauty of his person and his many noble endowments, the most glorious specimen of the works of God.

Man is a beautiful, noble, and glorious specimen, not because the *imago dei* is identified with creaturely dominion, but because he is uniquely endowed with spirituality and wisdom. The underlying attention to the Spirit in creation is also manifest in Calvin's view of man's creaturely task. "If we regard the Spirit of God as the sole fountain of truth, we shall neither reject the truth itself, nor despise it wherever it shall appear, unless we wish to dishonour the Spirit of God." Truth, like motion, is part of God's creation. Since man is distinctive by virtue of his spirituality and wisdom, his orientation to truth, created and revealed at large in creation, is more than an extrinsic obligation; it is intrinsic to his religious life in the world.[50]

However, the intrinsic creaturely task must also be exercised extrinsically. Man's work as God's creature is not natural labor; it is rather a disciplined dominion of the earth. Commenting on Psalm Eight, Calvin indicates the extrinsic task of man under God's mandate:

> [Man] has a singular honour and one which cannot be sufficiently estimated, that mortal man as the representative of God has dominion over the world, as if it pertained to him by right, and that to whatever quarter he turns his eyes, he sees nothing wanting which may contribute to the convenience and happiness of his life.[51]

By the "law of creation" man is bound to the Creator; he stands under the mandate of God's "command by right of creation." The power and responsibility Calvin accords to man were evident in his disciplined revision of the microcosm-macrocosm relationship. Man as creature is not a microcosm of the world, but rather an image of God in His supreme relationship of control over and responsibility for the world.[52]

In sum, it is clear that Calvin strengthened the late medieval beginnings of voluntarist theology and enhanced that theology with a complementary aesthetic theology of creation. At the same time, he disciplined more exotic Renaissance aesthetic orientations to creation.

Voluntarist Theology of Creation in Seventeenth-Century England: An Introduction

Originally a highly dialectical theology of protest, voluntarism became a relatively well established orientation to creation in seventeenth-century English thought. Historically opposed to traditional ontological theologies of creation, the voluntarist orientation gradually acquired major constructive significance. Presupposed in the rise of modern natural science, voluntarism acquired epochal cultural significance. But it did not stand alone. For traditional ontological theologians, such as Hooker, a synthesis of Thomistic theology and Aristotelian philosophy, as well as Reformation elements, remained at the center. This orientation subordinated will to reason and interpreted the law of nature as the rule of reason; the Being of God secured the rationality of law.[53] Moreover, aesthetic theologies of creation were variously combined with voluntarist lines of thought, and Spiritualist theologies of many types flourished. In short, there was a lively arena of conflicting theologies of creation in seventeenth-century English thought.

Nevertheless, voluntarist views of creation, marked by belief in Providence, were particularly extensive. The voluntarist orientation cut across the ecclesiastical loyalties that divided many English divines. It was formative in conceptions of political, ethical, natural, and theological order. And it penetrated deeply into the personal life of believers. Systematically, these historic forces were reinforced critically and constructively by the scope of the new orientation, which included a relatively new understanding of the Creator, contingency and order in creation, and man's creaturely task.

Although the broad extent of voluntarist orientations to creation, which were manifest in many different spheres of culture by many different figures in seventeenth-century England, can only be sketched here, our following inquiry into the content of Boyle's fairly representative theology and that of others who understood nature as creation shows further its central importance. Moreover, despite the similarities between these seventeenth-century developments and Calvin's work, there were no less important differences. Most English figures went well beyond Calvin, not only in obviously stressing the attributes of God, but also, and more significantly, in developing belief in Providence and other beliefs related to creation.

The highly visible conflicts over the Calvinist doctrine of predestination and the frequent interpretations of seventeenth-century thought in terms of the eighteenth-century Enlightenment have long obscured the chief staple of Providence in seventeenth-century theology, especially in the voluntarist tradition. Central to this tradition was the insistence that the efficacy of God's will, His power in action, was more important than God's foreknowledge and final purposes in creation. William Ames, perhaps the most precise and systematic Puritan divine, understood Providence as the "efficiency" of God. Nothing was more basic to his influential theology than this conception.[54]

With all the many distinctions regarding Providence — direct and indirect, general and special, ordinary and extraordinary — the presupposition of God's manifold activity for man and creation was sharply voluntaristic. It relegated God's foreknowledge and final causes to a subsidiary position without simply discarding traditional ontologies. Whereas Providence understood chiefly in terms of divine foreknowledge and final purposes was often another version of older ontologies — stressing divine ideas and the hierarchy of being concomitant with that of causes — the voluntarist theology of Providence stressed not only that God was present in the totality of creation and in its structures, but also that He cared for all particular creatures. The power, will, and Spirit of God were focused and concretized in voluntarist belief in His providence. In effect, the reality of the Creator loomed so immensely that there was little need for ontology.[55]

Both Puritan and Anglican divines taught that the Christian life should be formed under the rule and care of God's providence. Flavel typically lectured that the individual should keep a record of God's providences and meditate on them as well as on those of his fellow saints and martyrs. Others celebrated the "spiritualizing" of events, including order in natural creation, in order to discipline the good life. In this development, Providence, the content of the Creator's work for man and creation, supplied a real context and supplemented the nurture of sacraments and edification of preaching. This systematical recommendation of Providence as a moving norm for disciplining individual life went far beyond Calvin.[56]

The concept of Providence not only cut across ecclesiastical divisions, but was regarded as integral to the political, ethical, and natural order. The Puritans seldom limited Providence to the spheres of theology or church. Natural law was subsumed under its power, and the rule of magistrates and the responsibilities of subjects were also understood on this presupposition.[57]

The appearance of the rubric of God's *potentia ordinata* and *absoluta*, often articulated as ordinary and extraordinary Providence, is a further indication of the scope of voluntarist theologies of creation. This conception was influential in such definitive Puritan theologians as John Preston, William Perkins, and William Ames. Anglican divines such as the influential Robert Sanderson, and John Wilkins, and also Nathaniel Culverwell, Walter Charleton, and John Locke, took it for granted.[58] Moreover, this way of identifying Providence with the dialectic of God's power (and will) heightened theological tension in the English voluntarist tradition. That tension arose from a renewed emphasis upon God's transcendence and mystery as well as on His will. In effect, the bold and positive affirmation of God's universally efficacious Providence was joined to an equally strong critical affirmation of His transcendence, a position akin to that of the late medieval theologians.

The tendency of earlier Calvinism, if not of Calvin, to collapse the integrity of the created order was not shared by many of even the most rigorous English Puritan divines.[59] They stressed both the dependability of God's work of creation and His supreme right to reorder that creation as a whole or in any of its parts. In the later case, miracles were cited as witnesses to God's *potentia absoluta*. With regard to the order of creation itself, this tradition emphasized its contingency on the one hand, and a conception of divinely imposed laws of nature on the other hand.

Praising God's law as in the Psalms, Culverwell rested the chief mark of law in general, i.e. obligation,

> partly in the excellency and equity of the commands themselves but they principally depend upon the sovereignty and authority of God Himself, thus contriving and commanding the welfare of His creatures and advancing a rational nature to the just perfection of its being.[60]

This statement makes clear the universality of law based upon God's will. Likewise for Ames, law is promulgated in the form of commands: its distinguishing mark is obligation.

Oakley has demonstrated that this understanding of divinely imposed natural law in creation was fundamental to both seventeenth-century and late medieval political philosophy. In contrast to the classical tradition of immanent natural law, the voluntarist conception stressed both the transcendence of law, created and maintained by the Creator, and the dependability of that law in the common course of creation.[61]

To trace the significance of the voluntarist traditions for the pursuit of natural philosophy will require an equally detailed analysis of their power as presuppositions. For the voluntarist (and to a lesser extent, aesthetic and Spiritualist) "theologies" of creation acquired widespread prominence (and significance, as we shall see) partly because they articulated what was common and distinctive to English "religion" in the seventeenth century. In contrast to continental religion (Lutheran, Reformed, and Roman Catholic), it was distinguished by a vigorous interest in creation and new creation.

The common interest of Anglicans, Puritans, and Spiritualist groups was presupposed in the conflicts among them as they attempted to found different designs of ecclesiastical and political order. The relatively long and mild conflict of civil war in England, as compared to the intense religious wars on the continent, was due in part to the fact that the parties were deeply interested in shaping the created order. The stakes in England were high between those who wanted to improve, reform, or usher in a new society, but they were not as high as on the continent, where the issues of redemption itself and political life or death coincided.

Limiting attention to the English scene may appear trivial, but the English religious interest extended to new creation and was perhaps more basic than the overwhelming religious interest in redemption on the continent. Continental Calvinists were no different from the Lutherans and Catholics in their desires to compromise with the establishment of nation-states; their interest was securing a stable order of political and ecclesiastical institutions that would protect or embody God's work of redemption rather than creation. In England, Calvinism, however, was transformed into an effort to reform creation in the entire course of individual life and social institutions. Puritans boldly seized the power of the state because they were interested in bringing about a true Kingdom of God on earth. Spiritualist groups, often joined by transplanted continentals, boldly called and worked for new institutions of learning because they were interested in releasing the original Spirit and wisdom of God in new creation. Anglicans contributed to a distinctive common law tradition partly because they were convinced that reason and experience were goods of creation that should be extended throughout society. A common religious interest in the goodness and integrity of creation and its extension into a new society — notwithstanding the ravages of sin — set most English Protestants apart from the basic religious interests of continental Lutheranism, Calvinism, and Roman Catholicism.

Lutheran religion tended to subsume God's work of creation under His chief work of redemption. Thus the functions of law and conscience were to convict the believer of sin, to ready him for the redemptive grace of forgiveness.[62] But English Protestantism refused to make God's work of creation a function of his work of redemption. This meant that the law and order of creation, apprehended in conscience, not only enhanced the common law tradition but also promoted both Puritan and Anglican ethics of "cases" of conscience and degrees of reason in morals, in short, an elaborate distinctive system of moral casuistry.[63] Secondly, the law and order of creation was reflected in a different view of the redeemed life, namely, one characterized by the *ordo salutis*. The grace of sanctification and ultimately that of glorification served to stretch out the Christian life such that the function of law in ordering redeemed life equaled its function of preparing the believer for the grace of forgiveness. In short, the integrity and significance of God's distinct work of creation was stressed in English religion.

Continental Calvinism ordered God's work of creation to that of redemption in such a way that the latter was the restoration of the former. Thus, while law and conscience acquired greater positive significance than in Lutheran religion, they were not widely extended as instruments in the achievement of new creation. English Protestantism expressed a sense of eschatology, a sense of new creation, such that the entire course of common life was to be fashioned according to the image of both pilgrim and saint. From the Puritan schooling in sanctification, which was directed toward glorification, the end of the *ordo salutis*, to the divinization of reason in Cambridge Platonism, the religion of new creation was rigorously optimistic. It did not dwell upon the pervasiveness of guilt and the corruption of sin, but sought to work through it.[64] The Spiritualists believed in the perfectibility of men and such institutions as universities, the Puritans worked for a godly discipline of man and government, and many Anglicans believed in the "improvement" of the human estate through a reformation in learning. In short, a fairly common English belief in eschatology spread throughout the culture.[65]

The contrast of this religious orientation to the continental Counter-Reformation is also instructive. Whereas classic Lutheranism tended to subordinate creation to redemption, this Roman Catholic movement regarded the existing hierarchy of orders and powers as the very creation of God. Given a natural framework within which the religious life of the corporate body of Christ existed, the commitment to ontology and natural being was so primordial that optimism, perfectionism, and interest in new creation seldom emerged, particularly in society. Appeals to the Creator supported the *status quo* and worked against the reform of political, university, ecclesiastical, or scientific life.

Although a distinctively pious interest in God's great handiwork of creation was manifest in many religious traditions in the sixteenth and seventeenth centuries, the belief that such attention provided spiritual instruction gained unique strength in English religion. Creation piety of this sort was at the moving center of the development of "natural religion" and "natural worship," concepts that were articulated in English accounts of "natural theology." When a few continental philosophers largely ignored revealed religion and fashioned great systems of rational theology (Descartes, Spinoza, Leibnitz), their English counterparts crafted a more empirical natural theology built upon God's general providence. Indeed, at the close of the seventeenth century, in some rarified English circles, the religious involvement in redemption was reduced to that in creation.[66]

In sum, although the English religious interest in creation was never strong enough to bring unity on issues of redemption and polity, it was powerfully articulated in voluntarist theologies. This interest in creation and new creation stood in contrast to continental forms of religion and culture. Widely extended throughout many spheres of English culture, this distinctive religious interest generated a common arena in which a fruitful conflict of competing theologies of creation was to have profound importance for the reform of natural philosophy. In this arena voluntarist orientations to creation and Providence were most prominent.

CHAPTER THREE:

Spiritualist Theology of Creation and Natural Philosophy

In seventeenth-century natural philosophy, voluntarist opposition to traditional ontological orientations to creation was often intertwined with a relatively amorphous yet influential cluster of ideas, practices, and ideals which may be called a Spiritualist orientation to creation. The many roots of this orientation included the radical Protestant Reformers — who were as critical of Luther and Calvin as of the Roman Catholic tradition — as well as varieties of Renaissance Platonism; mystical strains in Catholic, Protestant, and Jewish thought; alchemy; and, not least, the alleged writings of Hermes Trismegistus.[1]

The extent of Spiritualism was particularly great in England, where it ranged from Rosicrucian sects to the sophistication of the Cambridge Platonists. Drawing on the resources of Spiritualism, magic and alchemy thrived as never before. Comenius and Hartlib proposed reform in the universities and an ecumenical union of all Christians under the wisdom and inspiration of the Spirit.[2] Especially during the brief Puritan rule, enthusiasts envisioned numerous utopian projects. Even non-Spiritualist Puritans as sober as Perkins and Ames cultivated a new form of pilgrim piety in which true life was life in the Spirit, a way of "living to God."[3] Natural philosophers such as Robert Fludd and John Dee combined the lore of Cabala, Gnostic insight, and various numerological and psychic patterns to explain the universe. Thomas Browne's *Religio Medici* sought the wisdom of the Spirit in the Philosopher's Stone.[4] The posthumous writings of Paracelsus were disseminated in England, and the medicinal, theological, and natural philosophical works of his critical disciple, Johan Baptist van Helmont, were championed by Charleton and Boyle for a brief time in the middle decades of the century.[5]

Spiritualism in this context raises difficult problems for the historian not simply because of its immense diversity and extent, but also because it did not closely adhere to fairly compact or relatively well-known traditions, as did the voluntarist and ontological orientations to creation. Even Spiritualist theologies were part of a movement which rose and fell, flamed and dimmed, rather than a tradition characterized by relatively measured growth and decline. Indeed, for many alchemists secrecy was intrinsic to their work. Moreover, the scholarship devoted to the movements of Spiritualism is relatively recent, and has merely begun to map out its cultural significance, especially for the rise of science.[6] Accordingly, my brief initial account of Spiritualism will be followed by a close but comprehensive study of Helmont's impressive and attractive blend of natural philosophy and theology.

Helmont has been chosen not only for reasons of economy but also because his thought was fairly representative. It fell between that of the extremely secretive and philosophically sophisticated figures in the continuum of the Spiritualist movement. More importantly, Helmont's thought was a truly major alternative for natural philosophy in the middle decades of the seventeenth century in England. Not only did it exert major influence upon Boyle's early work, but the issues and contrasts between Helmont and Boyle resemble those between other Spiritualist and modern figures — e.g. Fludd vs. Gassendi, More vs. Descartes, and Leibnitz vs. Newton.[7] In addition to his attraction as a pious natural philosopher, Helmont's alchemical interests, medical projects, and experimental work have brought him some well-deserved attention.[8]

Helmont blended natural philosophy, medicine, theology, religion, and chemistry in a coherent and immensely attractive statement which clearly reveals the immediate bearing of "religious" presuppositions upon a definite kind of seventeenth-century "science." My extended case study of his fusion of theology and natural philosophy foreshadows the critical differences between Boyle and Helmont to be discussed in later chapters. It anticipates the epochal conflict between largely voluntarist early modern, traditional ontological, and Spiritualist orientations to creation. In this three-sided conflict, Spiritualist orientations were directly and indirectly influential as targets, catalysts, and partial bearers of the emerging new science.

Spiritualism: A Premonition

Twelve years after Walter Charleton had translated three of Helmont's treatises on medicine, natural philosophy, and the immortality of the soul, John Chandler published an English version of Helmont's major work, the *Oriatrike* (1662) which called for a reformation of medicine and natural philosophy based upon "Christian Phylosophy."[9] Chandler's introductory "Premonition to the Reader" shows the attraction of Spiritualist presuppositions, which promised simultaneous unity of virtually everything. It opens with an interpretation of the creation story in Genesis; man as natural philosopher "having experimentally known evil" by eating of the Tree of Knowledge must now "come to know himself and his Creator in the Unity of the Spirit, *and all other things in that Unity.*"[10]

This presupposition of unity is evident throughout Chandler's statement, which moves back and forth from prayers and scriptural exposition to claims about the constitution of nature and the efficacy of various medicines. It is manifest in a simultaneous sense of history, past, present, and future. It voices profoundly wholistic convictions of the Creator as Spirit, self-knowledge in the Spirit, and the knowledge of all created things in the whole context of the Spirit. Heretofore, according to Chandler, natural philosophy, theology, and scientific practice have been eating from the Tree of Knowledge of Good and Evil; that is, they have participated in the Fall by holding to the corrupted theology, natural philosophy, and medicine of Aristotle and Galen which currently infests the universities and medical establishment. Natural philosophers should return to the original Tree of Life, regenerating natural philosophy and medicine by fully restoring these endeavors to their original Spiritual vitality.[11]

This vision of the renewal of natural philosophy led to intense Spiritualist opposition to all "pagan" natural philosophies, especially those of Aristotle and Galen. Also under intense attack were scholastic theology, logic, and medical diagnosis. Such heresies, derived from Aristotle, were held to proceed from a sinful ignorance of the Creator and a defilement of His gifts to mankind. It is difficult to overestimate the critical force of this wholistic condemnation of classical and medieval natural philosophy. Some Spiritualists advocated a return to an Adamic knowledge of nature modeled upon the Mosaic Law and Genesis, while others sought to reappropriate secret knowledge begun in Egypt. But such a return to the original wisdom of creation was not enough for Chandler and the Spiritualists. Natural philosophy was to be reshaped now in the light of the Christian philosophy of the Spirit. Knowledge of the "self," the "Creator," and "all other things" in the Unity of the Spirit would realize a vision in natural philosophy in which all knowledge would be permeated by wisdom and the Spirit.[12]

To know the Creator together with His creation, only knowledge through the Spirit of God would suffice. Indeed, for both true natural philosophy and good medicine, Jesus Christ, the wisdom of God in creation at large and man's understanding, was essential. The cosmic and epistemological dimensions of Christ for Spiritualism appear in Chandler's claim that Christ is the "Archetype" of the physician, ". . . true wisdom, i.e. that which alone tends to the healing of the Maladies of man's Spirit . . . is *The Lamb of God*, and *a quickening Spirit*," and the "true Handmaid" of divinity, philosophy, and medicine. Jesus Christ, as the true or Spiritual Handmaid of God "reflects" and "refracts" God, the "Father of Lights," in the whole visible creation and particularly in the creature who manifests true Spiritual understanding. The true Handmaid

> is the Son of God, by whom the World was made, and all living souls created, . . . in whom they all subsist, who filleth all in all: This Son of God is the Eternal Eye of the Father, which runs through the whole Creation.[13]

Although not all Spiritualists introduced Christology as fully into natural philosophy, Chandler's claim that Christ is the "Eye of the Father" was one of many witnesses to the Creator as "Father of Lights." This rubric was as central to Spiritualist theologies of creation as Providence and God's *potentia absoluta* and *ordinata* were to the voluntarist tradition. Chandler (and Helmont) favored this name as an index of all the mysterious and Spiritual ways of God in himself (as Father, Son, and Holy Spirit) and divine ubiquity in creation and man. All the works of God were merged in an equivalent designation, "Unity of the Spirit."[14] Speaking of knowledge in this context, Chandler wrote that the ". . . Father knows all, and insofar as we are in the Son who alone reveals the Father we too gain right knowledge." This knowledge is like

> a reflex act [which] goes forth with a pure clear ray or Beam, towards particular things or objects, apprehending or looking through them, according to their particular natures or properties placed in them by the Word, the Creator: This kind of knowledge is not the fruit of the forbidden tree, but of the Tree of Life; for Life is at its Root, and Love is its Branches; first extended towards God the Creator, in the measure of whose Image, the Understanding doth apply itself by an intellectual act, unto the particular thing understood, and so in that Image adoring his Wisdom and Power therein. Secondly, towards the Neighbor, in directing such a particular knowledge or knowledges, unto the use, service, benefit, necessity, and health of the same, in this mortal life.

Here natural philosophy rooted in The Tree of Life is a Spiritual process of understanding expressing God's own Image. Flowing from the Father of Lights, Spiritual understanding is a Beam which apprehends created particulars. Acknowledging the multiplicity of creation, Chandler argues that the Spirit constitutes the true unity of created entities. This original and simple goodness reveals the falsity of apparent plurality. "It is not Words but Things, not Names but Natures, not Resemblances but Realities, not Sublimities but Simplicities, that the Sons of Truth do seek after."[15]

The predominant image of processes of life and light serves as a root metaphor for the entirety of creation in Spiritualism. Despite Spiritualism's opposition to Aristotle and scholasticism, this basic image is far more organic than mechanical, legal, or political. More precisely, since life and light are so totally grounded in the wholistic divine Spirit as the Father of Lights, creation itself is seen as a *Spiritual process* expressed concretely in these dominant metaphors.[16]

The rich passage quoted also shows an order of thinking characteristic of Spiritualism. The knowledge of God is of the first importance, followed by that of the self and then, in this light, of all created things. At best pagan natural philosophy confuses and at worst reverses this approach. The passage concludes by articulating the two proper ends of natural philosophy: adoration of the Creator and service or benefit to the Neighbor.

The Spiritualist vision for natural philosophy was more than a renewal of original creation and more than a Spiritual apprehension of God's Spiritual creation in the present. Advancing Christian natural philosophy with great eschatological fervor, the Premonition joyfully proclaims that

> The hour is coming and the day hastens, wherein all things shall be seen and enjoyed in the root which beareth them, *that all the Pots of Jerusalem may be holy to the Lord, and Holiness seen even upon the Horse Bridles: and this was the Word of the Lord to Daniel concerning the last time.*[17]

The text from Daniel is not cited as a "sign" as in voluntarism; it is celebrated as a full presence in which the truth of all times past and future comes to fruition. Under the aegis and power of the Spirit both the past and future can be realized. This simultaneity of time and history, and of all kinds and orders of genuine thought, vision, and practice, is the distinguishing mark of Spiritualism. Although deeply involved with creation, the Spiritualist orientation differs profoundly from more linear (and modern) estimates of creation and the future as history. Spiritualism was enthusiastically apocalyptic.[18]

Helmont on God the Creator as Spirit

In a primer on creation which serves as a Preface to the *Oriatrike,* Helmont's son, Francis, a friend of More, addresses God as the All in One and One in All. The massive *Oriatrike* itself begins with a prayer in which Helmont offers himself and his work to God. "O Lord, I am nought but nothing, nor any thing besides, but as it hath pleased thee, that I may pertain unto Thee. O All, of All, and my Desire. . . ."[19] This prayer to God as the All pervades Helmont's work. To put it categorically, God is the inclusive All rather than the exclusive and transcendent One. In speaking of the Unity of divine Spirit, Helmont refers to the basic presupposition of Spiritualism, which other Spiritualists call the "omneity" of God.[20]

Helmont's immediate rejection of pagan astrological influences in the name of God present in all created entities bespeaks the Spiritual inclusiveness, the ubiquitous power of God. ". . . I profess, that he who by the only word of his good pleasure, made the Universe of nothing, is All in All, and at this day also, the way, original, life and perfection of all things." The key point is that all created entities are forms of the divine Spirit. Although second causes cannot be denied, God

> Always remaineth, as the totall cause, continuing the perpetuall parent of things, the framer of nature, and its governour by creation: Therefore I profess, that as in the beginning, nothing was made without him; so also, that at this day, the creation of every form is a thing made of nothing, by the very same Creator.[21]

God's inclusiveness is the source not only of His unity, but also of His relation to all creation. He is the "totall cause" and "perpetuall parent of things."

Within this presupposition of the Creator as the All in All, Helmont affirms a perpetual creation, *ex nihilo*, of the way, life, and perfection of all things. Theologically, this immediately implies that the titles and works of God are run together in an undifferentiated way. The understanding of God as the continual Creator of free and specific entities does not deny original creation but stresses the processes of life, generation, and light in divine creation.[22] The work of the Redeemer is inseparable from that of the Creator. Redemption is not a distinctly spoken Word of forgiveness but a purification and enlightenment of the mind such that true or Spiritual understanding rests on nothing other than cosmic Wisdom and the clemency of Christ. Christ, who is in the mind *and* "run thorrow all creation," is none other than that Wisdom and Word through which all things are created and sustained.[23]

The view of God as the principle of light and life in creation, always manifest in Helmont's favored name for God, the "Father of Lights," pervades the opening prayer of the *Oriatrike*, which affirms that "thou onely are All, unto whom every wish of sanctyfying Love doth properly belong." Rather than a feeling of uncleanness before the transcendent purity of God, this prayer expresses a sense of emptiness which is, in turn, filled by the overflowing Spiritual light and life of God who is in

him and all things. Given this abundance of the sanctified life
filled with the Spirit, Helmont calls upon God not as the
". . . God of our fathers, as in times past but now as a God
declared to be our Father . . . as God, the God of Mary our
Mother, and who art made our Brother in the Love of thy
grace."[24] From this it is a short step to man himself as a creature filled by the Spirit:

> The Kingdom of God, doth as it were, come to us, and is
> received, or doth spring again, as often as we in faith do intel-
> lectually and presentially adore the goodness, power, infinite-
> ness, Glory, truth of God, etc. *in the Spirit:* And thus it is unto
> God a delight, to be with the Sons of men. Surely it is thus.[25]

For Helmont man in the Spirit participates in God; and He
delights in us!

As Light the Creator is the principle of mind. As Life He is
the principle of the world and its motion. As the principle of
mind He is the enabling context of true knowledge. Helmont's
chapter on knowledge in the sciences begins with the maxim,
"know thyself," but ". . . the manner of knowing the soul is to
be begged from the Father of Lights, and not from elsewhere."[26]

The Father of Lights is also the principle of true knowledge
of the world. When man relies on Spiritual understanding, the
"candle of the Lord," he rejects the vanities of Reason "because the hidden knowledges of things are infused by the
Father of Lights into us, by means of this Candle." This is not
simply a polemic against "empty" scholastic epistemology;
Helmont claims that certainty in empirical knowledge can be
attained. But the Spiritual gift of clemency steadies the inner
act of Spiritual understanding and dispels darkness in this
search. "I saw," wrote Helmont upon his conversion to Christian philosophy, ". . . that the searching into all things which
are under the Sun, was a good gift, descending from the Father
of Lights, into the Sons of men."[27]

In short, Helmont holds that God as Spirit, the Father of
Lights, is presupposed in all knowledge, including empirical
inquiry in natural philosophy. Mysticism supports empirical inquiry because understanding in the Spirit is equipped for that
task. The category of Spiritual understanding or revelation has
been so greatly expanded that Helmont regards the science of
medicine, like all sciences, as a sure *gift* of the Father of

Lights. It comes from divine Wisdom and is not a "traditio" handed down through Aristotle and Galen.[28]

As the immediate principle of all created things, the inclusive Spirit contains the world as well as the mind:

> Although a fleshly Father doth give of his son, whence the name of Paternity or fatherliness is given unto him: yet because he is not the giver of vitall light, or the Creator of Forms, the name of vital Fatherliness is forbidden to be given to the Creature. Therefore God is the Father of Lights, or of vitall Forms. . . .[29]

Natural philosophy was intoxicated both subjectively and objectively by Helmont's Spiritualist theology of creation. The thorough pervasiveness of Spirit in concrete created things lays bare the deepest reason why his "mysticism" called for penetration into, rather than flight from, the world.

Spiritual Natural Philosophy: From Water to Gas

Helmont's view that the Creator Spirit is constitutive of and the key to nature allowed for no boundaries between the use of the mind in worship and medical practice. Nor were there any barriers between natural philosophy and theology. This profoundly wholistic view of the mind was bound up with a view of nature as process opposed to hierarchy but open to organic motifs in the traditional Greek and medieval view of nature. It resisted Paracelsus' ascription of mind to nature (and the microcosm-macrocosm rubric) by finding Spirit in the process of nature. It stood directly over against modern legal and mechanical views of nature, although it was open to their aesthetic motifs. For Helmont, the Whole dwells abundantly in each part.

A Biblical Doctrine of Matter as Water

Helmont's Spiritualist natural philosophy was obvious in his actual use of Scripture. He regarded the creation story in Genesis and passages in the Old Testament Wisdom literature as normative in Christian as opposed to pagan natural philosophy. It was normative, not in the sense of an external standard, but in that Scripture, particularly in the creation by Word and Spirit, expresses the very same life-giving power which is in the universe and human understanding. As Helmont puts it, the Scriptural Word is One with the unutterable Word dwelling within the Spirit itself.[30] In short, Scripture has a direct authorizing power; it is not a court of appeal. In the *Oriatrike*, extensive references to Scripture (like prayers and confessions) are at the moving center of inquiry.

Helmont's use of Scripture also explains his peculiar employment of the book of Scripture and the book of nature or creation, which were traditionally distinguished from each other. In Spiritualism the two books were read together and each had authorizing power for the other. Through a direct or immediate passage from one book to the other, Scripture entered into the very constitution of natural philosophy and vice versa. The presupposition was that Scripture bespeaks the same inclusive and pervasive Spirit of creation. This typically Spiritualist way of running the two books together was challenged by Bacon and Boyle.[31]

To support his cosmology based upon "Christian philosophy" and Scripture, Helmont passionately objected to "The Ignorant Natural Philosophy of Aristotle and Galen." In the chapter bearing this title, he argues that Aristotle defines nature as ". . . the Principle, or beginning of motion, as also rest in Bodies, in whom it is in, by itself, and not by accident." Helmont counters, "But, I believe that Nature is the Command of God, whereby a thing is that which it is, and doth that which it is commanded to do or act. This is a Christian definition taken out of the Holy Scripture."[32]

A number of key points are involved in this confrontation. First, Helmont is protesting the reduction of nature to the principle of motion (or rest) in things. "But Christians are held to believe, Nature to be every Creature, to wit, a Body, and accidents, no lesse, than the beginning of motion itself." The whole of nature is creation, accidents as well as substances, and matter as well as motion. Secondly, Helmont attributes the order and motion in nature directly to God. Although he speaks here of command, which suggests a view of God and nature over against each other, he nowhere develops that image. Moreover, in the context of his theology of inclusive Spirit, the command here should not be interpreted as a Word from the outside, but as the moving regularity of nature itself directly related to God. Finally, Helmont's most vigorous opposition to Aristotle contested the notion of an Unmoved Mover who draws all things to himself. The very suggestion is antithetical to the free, creative, and pervasive Spirit he presupposed.[33]

In setting forth his presupposition of nature as a whole process, Helmont compared the creation to the chemical art. The entire real process of creation was a kind of expanded chemistry. Simultaneously, pyrochemical preparation, analysis, and synthesis were seen as a re-enactment of divine creation, separation, and order.[34] Helmont's commitment to this grand *process* qualified the organic motifs of his thought.

Against Aristotle, Helmont argued that there is no preexisting mysteriously disposed matter which the natural philosopher must simply accept. His more lively view involved spiritual Agents, seeds, and ferments. Aristotle was deceived in "that he determined every natural Agent to *require* a disposed matter: when as otherwise, the Agent in Nature doth dispose of the matter that is subject unto it." Continuing the argument, Helmont wrote ". . . that all tangible bodies do immediately proceed out of the one only Element of Water: by what necessity I pray you, shall the Agent require a fore-existing disposition of the matter." In contrast to a pre-existing disposed matter, Helmont proposed a single, universal, and simple element, water, as the basic matter from which all things proceed and to which they return. Of this "one only Element" he wrote that the

> universal beginnings of Bodies which is the water, is the onely material cause of things, as the water hath the Nature of a beginning, itself, in the manner, simpleness, and progress of beginning, even also in the bond of dissolution, unto which, all Bodies, through the reducing of the last matter, do return.[35]

This is the key point of his famous and influential willow-tree experiment, which demonstrated the measurable dependence of plant growth on water.[36] On another level, his exegesis of "heaven" held that it signifies primordial and simple water:

> In the beginning . . . the Almighty created the Heaven and the Earth. . . . Afterwards in the first day, he created the Light, . . . Secondly, he created the Firmament, which should separate the inferior Waters from the waters that were above

itself, and named that, Heaven. Therefore it is hence plainly to be seen, that before the first day, the waters were already created from the beginning, being partakers of a certain heavenly disposition, because they were hidden under the Etymologie of the Word, Heaven . . . all the waters above the Heaven, being conjoyned to ours, upon the Earth, did make an Abysse of incomprehensible deepness, upon which the Spirit (whose name is Eternall) was carried, that he might with his blessing, replenish his new Creature of water.[37]

In sum, the Spirit broods upon water, the first creature, blessing and replenishing that which proceeds from and returns to that fundamental matter.

This doctrine, supported by the willow-tree experiment, had real appeal in England shortly after the middle of the seventeenth century. It gained special significance when Boyle attacked it in his *Sceptical Chemist*. Despite the implications of that attack, it is noteworthy that Helmont's vigorous rejection of Aristotelian matter in the name of the Spirit was a move toward a more simplified understanding of matter. While a simple appeal to the ultimacy of water served to check the proliferation of various material entities, it affirmed material causation. Boyle and other modern natural philosophers moved much further in this direction as they too entered the lists against Aristotle.

The Efficiency of Seeds in Creation

A second fundamental in Helmont's natural philosophy was his doctrine of seeds as seminal beginnings which perdure in things. This conception of particulars also expressed their efficiency.

Therefore there are two chief or first beginnings of Bodies, and corporeal Causes, and no more, to wit, the Element of Water, or the beginning, [of which] and the Ferment of Leaven, or seminal beginning, [by which] that is to be disposed of; whence straightway the seed is produced in the matter: which (the seed being gotten) is by that very thing made the life, or the middle matter of that being, running thorow even unto the finishing of the thing, or last matter.[38]

This concept pointed to the irreducible and continuous specificity or identity of created things. Moreover, that specificity of things was held to be manifest in terms of the life they bear.

Helmont underlined the *unique* specificity of created seeds by criticizing Aristotle's easy acceptance of the rhythm of life and death in a theory of generation and corruption which threatens identity. "Therefore let it be an erroneous thing: *that the corruption of one thing is the generation of another.*" He added:

> Therefore no privation happened in things that have life, and so neither can privation, there, have the force of a Principle: Seeing that from the seeds, even unto the vitall being, there is but *one* progress, promotion, and ripeness; about the end thereof, the form is given.[39]

Against a view of matter with built-in corruption, generation, and disposition, Helmont sought to locate the continuity as well as the uniqueness and specificity of things in the divine seeds.

This is not as primitive as the language might suggest, for Helmont also denominated the seeds as "forms." Against Aristotle's view, however, such forms must be not only in things but *in act.* Thus, the smallest units of nature are processes, to which Helmont ascribed a kind of eternal duration. This interpretation was reconciled with the temporal specificity and uniqueness of those processes by the view that the seeds or forms are hidden.[40]

Helmont's cosmology attempted to locate the reality of particulars primarily in terms of material and efficient causes, for ". . . matter, and also the efficient cause do suffice to every thing produced." It rested on a distinction between seeds as "immediate active principles in things," and ferments as "background generating causes."

> Therefore, the Ferment holds the Nature of a true Principle, divers in this from the efficient cause: that the efficient cause is considered as an immediate active Principle in the thing, which is the seeds, and as it were, the moving Principle to generation, or the constitutive beginning of the thing: but the Ferment; is often before the seed, and doth generate this from itself.[41]

Thus, there is a double efficiency in created things, an outer and inner power in specific creatures. Such a focus ruled out the dominance of Aristotle's teleological causation:

> Since the efficient containeth all ends in itself, as it were the instruction of things to be done by it self, therefore the finall

externall cause of the schooles, which only hath place in artificial things, is altogether vain in Nature. . . . Because in the efficient natural cause, its own knowledge of ends and dispositions, is infused naturally by God.[42]

Helmont summarized his argument against Aristotle's final causes by arguing from the Unity or Allness of God and efficient seeds in His creation.

Truly, I have not studied to imitate Aristotle in this thing, who teacheth that the End is the first of Causes: For I have elsewhere plentifully demonstrated, that Aristotle was plainly ignorant of whole Nature: Wherefore that his Maxime, as well within, as out of Nature is false. Because if we speak of God as the First Mover, the Archetype of all things, and of the invisible world; be it certain, that with him there is not any priority of causes, but that *they all do co-unite into Unity, with whom all things are only one*. Likewise, seeing whatsoever is made or generated in Nature, is made or generated from necessity of the Seeds, and so that Seeds are in this respect, the original Principles, and natural Causes of things, and do act for ends, not indeed known to themselves, but unto God alone: From a necessity of Christian Phylosophy, a Final Cause hath no place in Nature, but onely in artificial things.[43]

Helmont's Spiritualist theology involved a positive as well as critical presupposition of the concept of seeds. For "God is also at this day, the immediate principle of things, everywhere present, working all the perfection of all things." But God is not only the perfecting power of "internall essentiall forms" (or seeds). Helmont adds: "For that most glorious Mover [i.e., the Spirit] hath given powers to things, whereby they of themselves, and by an absolute force may move themselves, or other things."[44] In short, Helmont holds both that God is the immediate principle of seeds and that seeds have their own "absolute" force. Helmont sees no contradiction because the Creator is the inclusive Spirit rather than an individual agent.

Helmont's conception of seeds or forms was conducive to the more modern views expressed by Boyle and other thinkers who shared his attention to particulars and their efficiency. Even though Boyle moved in another direction, he and Bacon shared an interest in God's "hidden" ends in things. The critique of Aristotle was no exclusive province of the more visibly modern; it was basic to Helmont's mystical thought.

The Elements, Air, and Spiritual Discoveries

The third fundamental of Helmont's natural philosophy, his teaching on the elements, is ambiguous. His rejections are clearer than his affirmations. But the Spiritualist presuppositions of his elemental theory, particularly Air, nurtured some interesting discoveries.

Helmont joined with many Spiritualists in rejecting the traditional four-element theory. He adopted a tone that, like Paracelsus', was partly polemical:

> For they who before me have thought that to all Generations of Births of Bodies, four Elements do co-mix, have beheld the Elements after the heathenish manner, and have tried by their lies, or devices, to marry the Elements, and obey them.

Helmont's rejection, however, was explicitly based upon Scripture.

> Therefore the juggling deceipts of Pagans, being cast behinde me, I direct my experience, and the light freely given me, according to the authority of the Holy Scriptures, at the beholding of which light, the night-birds do fly away.

Interpreting the Genesis story as a highly spiritual text Helmont focused upon the Creator Spirit which hovers over the waters and the Wisdom which guided their division in the subsequent days of creation. ". . . the Waters . . . did make an Abysse of incomprehensible deepness, upon which, the Spirit (whose name is Eternall) was carried that he might with his blessing, replenish his new Creature of Water."[45] The Creator as Spirit is seen at work in an enlivening way both at the beginning and subsequently. Thus, the Aristotelian philosophy epitomized in the four-element theory was the very opposite of what Helmont and the Spiritualist tradition envisioned as true natural philosophy.

In his more measured objections, Helmont argued that insofar as there is no mention whatsoever of fire in the biblical truths of creation it is palpably pagan to regard fire as a basic nontransmutable "element":

> But nowhere anything is read of the Creation of the fire; neither therefore do I acknowledge it among the Elements, and I reject my honour or esteem with Paganisme. Neither also, may we with Paracelsus, acknowledge the fire, by the name of Lights,

and Stars, to be a superlunary Element, as neither to have been framed from the beginning: the which not withstanding, it should needs be, if it ought to resemble or partake of the condition of an Element.[46]

Going further, Helmont sensed that the four-element theory presupposed an entire organic or hierarchical view of nature, even though the Aristotelian view admitted contrarieties among the elements. Helmont's strong attack on this entire complex sees that with the omission of fire as an element the entire Aristotelian system is shaken. Against the view that the four qualities associated with the four elements are primitive agents which may in various things either be like or contrary to each other, Helmont brought the weight of his doctrine that God creates specific seeds. "For indeed, whatsoever is made or born in nature, is made from the necessity of efficient seeds." These seeds are not conscious; instead, they are specifically what they are by virtue of being "created gifts" of the Lord. In general terms, the relationship of seeds ". . . is altogether seated in the most full, or innermost substantial principle of forms or seeds itself, wholly incapable of contrariety. . . ." In short, the radical specificity and perpetuity of the seeds is such that even their relations are built into their particularity. Given the creation of such entities, to speak of likes or contrarieties is, at best, superfluous. At worst, contrarieties lead to multiple "relations of relations," a concept that tends to assume a mundane mentality in nature. Pressing his point against the Schools, Helmont insisted that "at length they must confess with me that there is no contrariety in nature, except among free and elective Agents."[47]

Such a vigorous opposition to the Aristotelian conviction of contrariety was also undergirded by a presupposition of the Creator. "But if thou considerest these things even as supernaturally, and in God, they are not also therefore made contraries; and so neither shall they flow from God into nature, as contraries. . . ." In a world of the Spirit if there are no contrarieties in God, there are none in nature. Helmont's point was that God is the "lover of Peace;" and as He is good, so too is his creation.

For truly, in the first place; we believe it by faith to be true, that God is the daily Author and Governour of Nature; and that every where his own creature doth as much as it can, express and witnesse him in goodnesse. In the next place, that God is the fountainous Beginning of Love . . . and peace; also that he hateth discords and contrarieties, so that if he could have framed the Universe without brawling and contrarieties, there is no doubt but he hath done it.

Helmont affirmed Spiritual unity at all levels — qualities per se, and whole "Systems or collections of things." On the basis of that framework he judged the scholastic teaching of the "fighting" of heat and cold to be pagan, whereas in truth and ". . . subject of the aire, [they] do mutually suffer each other."[48]

Helmont's denial of the general Greek view of nature as a delicate balance of elemental powers undercut the interpretation of health as a balance of the four humours and of disease as an imbalance of such humours brought about by contrariety. He wrote that ". . . it is vain, that the fire doth materially concurre into the mixture of bodies. Therefore, the fourfold kind of Elements, Qualities, Temperaments or Complexions, and also the foundation of Diseases, falls to the ground." Pagel notes rightly that Helmont thus discovered the "modern" concept of diseases, which are efficient causes or "seeds."[49] His polemic against Galen and the Schools for having missed the true causes of ills in focusing upon disease (in the singular) led to an understanding that diseases (in the plural) need to be combatted and the more chemical remedies the better.

More ambiguously, Helmont, like most alchemists, affirmed the *tria prima* of air, earth, and water, or alternatively, salt, sulfur, and mercury. In agreement with a restatement of this tradition by Paracelsus, Helmont did not regard the *tria prima* as the literal components of all things, but rather as principles which are constitutive of nature properly understood. However, in accordance with the primacy he gave to water, Helmont did speak of the *tria prima* as modes of that basic element. Moreover, he clearly argued that earth is not primary, for it may be turned into water. Air, however, could not be accounted for with such simplicity. Arguing from the creation story in Genesis, Helmont closely associated water and air. "I call these two Elements Primogeniall, or firstborn, in respect of the Earth. . . ."[50]

The noteworthy "first-born" place given to air calls for further elucidation. It seems to be both a special locus and agency

of the Divine. In his chapter on "The Causes and Beginnings of
Natural Things," Helmont distinguished the external yet effective generation of the Father with respect to seeds from an inner
power. "For in the Seed, which fulfills and contains the whole
quiddity of thingliness of the immediate efficient, that is not the
Father himself: but the Archaeus or chief workman." This Archaeus, an immediate and inner efficient principle, contains all
ends in itself. Accordingly a final cause ". . . is not to be considered in a distinct thingliness from the efficient itself." Helmont adds that in all "efficient" natural causes ends are
". . . infused naturally by God." Thus there is ". . . a seminal,
efficient, disposing, directing principle, the inward one of generation." The mention here of ends infused into efficients and
the many functions of the "inward" principle of generation,
especially "disposing and directing," suggests an aerial agency
(the Archaeus) in efficients, yet it does not deny their specificity,
spontaneity, or perpetuity. The function of the Archaeus seems
to be that of the governor of growth or life.[51]

In his chapter on "The Chief or Master-Workman," Helmont identified the Archaeus or Master-Workman in all things
as air. "In some things this Air is loose and plentiful, in others
pressed and juicy, and in others homogeneously thickened.
There is one gift of Air, which contains the fruitfulness of generations and seeds, in all things." Arguing that such air is
present behind the "husk" of the "visible Seed" Helmont wrote
that the ". . . chief Workman *consists* of the *conjoyning* of the
vitall air, as of the matter, with the seminal likeness; which is
the more inward spiritual kernel, containing the fruitfulness of
the Seed." The chief Workman not only effects a union of
matter and seeds, but it is, "consists," of that union.[52]

Air (the Archaeus) may well be a third fundamental of Helmont's natural philosophy because of its special unifying power
in things. In any case, the significance of Air is underscored in
Helmont's interesting chapter entitled, "The Gas of the Water." Helmont argued that air, ". . . the spirit or breath of life,
is materially the Gas of the Water." At the same time, he was
careful to distinguish aerial spirits from the "vapour of water."
Thus, Helmont's extensive reflections on the powers of air led
him to propose a gaseous reality in nature which is not to be
confused with steam, nor to be reduced to water. Pagel and

others have rightly hailed this as a discovery of the "modern" conception of gas: a nonreducible fundamental state of reality with its own integrity.[53]

Quite apart from the fact, or accident, that Helmont's discovery of gas was a successful modern conception, it is remarkable that it was part of his working out of what he took to be the power of air and of Spirit. Accordingly, Helmont concluded his chapter on gas with a "demonstration from creation" showing that God creates the Heavens (air) which govern the separation of the waters.

> Therefore the holy Scriptures do name the air, the separater, but not the destroyer or annihilator of the waters. Nor is it right, that the air should be drawn to other offices, than those which are enjoyned to it by the workman and Lord of things.[54]

In direct succession, Helmont moved from the divine Spirit hovering over the waters as their Creative Lord to the air which is "primogeniall" but does separate the waters, and finally to the gas (Archaeus) which specifies and directs seeds. Significantly, this gas is freed from vapours just as the Spirit separates the primordial waters. Through the power of the Archaeus, the Spirit is effective and present in things as gas. This is a truly fascinating blend of Spiritual theology, cosmology, and "hard" scientific discovery.

Finally, it should be noted that Helmont's Spirit-based and Scripture-inspired discoveries and doctrines, although intimately related to their divine sources, did not always issue in such "modern" discoveries as gas and diseases. On the basis of the hidden Spiritual power of efficient seeds and air, he also promoted the infamous weapon-salve cure.[55] But the key point is that in Helmont's largely undifferentiated view of Spirit and natural processes neither the successes nor the failures could be easily resisted.

Spiritual Understanding in Conversion, Empirical Inquiry, and Cosmic Chemistry

Whether Helmont is studied theologically, cosmologically, or scientifically, the confluence of his thought into an inclusive whole is paramount. This is also true of his view of knowledge, which he called "Spiritual understanding" and whose universal scope was indicated in the first of two texts on the title page of the *Oriatrike*. Drawing upon the Wisdom tradition in Spiritualism, Helmont quoted Job 32:8, "There is a Spirit in Man, and the inspiration of the Almighty giveth Understanding." The second text quoted these words of Spiritual Wisdom: "I Wisdom dwell with Prudence, and find out knowledge of witty Inventions." Thus, true knowledge both thrives in the Spirit of God and seeks empirical exercise.

Any talk of Spiritual understanding in natural philosophy or chemistry raises spectres of secrecy, private revelations, and general mental chaos. But Spiritual understanding for Helmont was neither a secret path nor a way in which discoveries were sanctioned by private revelations. A wholistic Spiritual orientation to creation, rather than chaos, was directly presupposed in the theologically saturated empirical inquiry he promoted. His vision had direct implications for a novel chemistry and natural philosophy rooted in his view of knowledge as being simultaneously mystical and empirical.

Visions, if not the conversions to which they often point, have received meagre historical examination in the history of theology, and less in the historical study of natural philosophy. Even less attention has been given to the similarities of conversion accounts in both "religious" and "scientific" traditions. The similarity of Helmont's account of his vision and conversion to those in a long tradition of theologians from Paul to the seventeenth century is remarkable.[56] Such accounts almost always occur as the high point in a specific literary recital of the errors of the past and the promise of the future.

Reformers in natural philosophy as well as theology frequently indicate by means of a narration of their conversions or visions, often written later in life, the central message of their respective reforming efforts. They often include an address to Deity and/or the call of God to the reformer, which is of central significance in estimating the view of God in each vision. Finally, each vision or conversion account may specify the errors of the past and describe how a new and glorious future may be achieved.

Although such stylized conversion accounts may be understood psychologically, such interpretation requires a major reconstruction of the inner life of a reformer. The written account usually expresses the end of a long struggle.[57] Historically, such conversion accounts, particularly by natural philosophers, often witness various forms of creation piety. One of their major purposes appears to be that of recording the reformer's own special vocation in order to involve others in a task of reformation.

In theological tradition, Luther, relatively late in his life, recounted his conversion from the justice to the graciousness of God. And he specified the central message of his reforming efforts as justification by faith in opposition to works-righteousness. The central message of Calvin's conversion was *docilitas*, which he held necessary for the edification of a wayward Church. As Oberman has shown, similar conversion accounts appeared in many of the major late medieval thinkers — Gerson, Biel, Ockham, and others.[58] The same phenomenon appeared in the visions of and attempts to reform natural philosophy in the sixteenth and seventeenth centuries, usually within the context of skepticism and a correlative search for certainty in newly perceived problems of knowledge. Descartes' distinctive answer to skepticism was the relatively late *Discourse on Method*, which recounted his personal journeys away from early scholastic training at La Fleche, and advocated a method which turned upon clear and distinct ideas. Descartes' method was thoroughly mathematical, yet he believed that it was expressive of reason, the "light of nature," and he even sought to demonstrate the true existence of divine substance which united mind and external reality. His optimism, based on rational relations and perfectibility, was clear throughout.[59]

Helmont's visionary conversion account forms the first chapter of the *Oriatrike*, entitled "The Author's Confession." Brief references to it are also found in the second chapter entitled "The Author's Studies," in which he recounts his conversion from Stoicism to mystical Christian philosophy. It was after (the standard) departure from the schools, that he turned to Thomas à Kempis and Tauler. Helmont's account of his vision concludes with a call to reform medical natural philosophy.[60]

Citing a "Dream" or "intellectual vision," Helmont saw his soul in the light of God. Invoking the "Thrice glorious God" and the "Father of Lights," Helmont wrote that ". . . therefore the soul determined to examine itself in the Image set before it, according to that saying, 'For who knowes the things that are of man, but the Spirit of a man that is in him?'"[61] For Helmont, the light and spirit in the illumined soul is none other than God himself.

The central message of the vision is that henceforth truth must be sought empirically, by inquiry into the nature of "things themselves":

> For hence have I learned, that it happens, that we do not perceive that we do understand any thing, so long as the chief Agent of this wretched and frail understanding, hath not turned its force even to the bounds of sense. Wherefore also, neither do we remember that we do understand, unless the same action be propagated or planted into us by a sensitive order or Government.

Simultaneous with the conversion to sensible empirical understanding is the way the mind comes to depend completely upon God:

> For then I saw, that the searching into all things which are under the sun, was a good gift, descending from the Father of Lights, unto the Sons of men, for a diligent study, and a certain serious ascending of forepast ignorance, otherwise the danger of a vain complacency, or well-liking, would sometimes vex by the By.[62]

This point is further highlighted by Helmont's rejections of the way of reason and the method of analysis and synthesis. In sharp contrast to Descartes' trust in clear and distinct ideas, Helmont confesses that he formerly trusted the being of Reason rather than the sound truth of "things." He regards the way of pure reason as religious idolatry and morally assertive "selfishness" against God. It is Spiritual "charity" and "humility" in the understanding that enable the natural philosopher to search into the truth of things empirically. Spiritual understanding unifies all modes of knowledge (philosophical, scientific, religious, and moral) in a moving service of God and the neighbor.[63]

Earlier in the seventeenth century, Bacon provided a somewhat similar conversion account. This is apparent from his unpublished *Masculine Birth of Time* (1605), subtitled *The Great Instauration of the Dominion of Man over the Universe*. This autobiographically charged short piece was prefaced by a prayer frequently repeated in his works. This early piece, decisive in Bacon's changing strategy in pursuing natural philosophy, shows that he believed his special vocation as a writer was to reform the arts and natural philosophy for the benefit of mankind. Bacon contrasted this new-found vocation to his temporary abortive forays into administrative reform.[64] The telling prayer "To God the Father, God the Word, God the Spirit" petitions

> that our human interests may not stand in the way of the divine, nor from unlocking of the paths of sense and the enkindling of a greater light in nature may any unbelief or darkness arise in our minds to shut out the knowledge of the divine mysteries; but rather that the intellect made clean and pure from all vain fancies, and subjecting itself in voluntary submission to the divine oracles, may render to faith the things that belong to faith.[65]

It is clear that Bacon saw religious/moral conditions which must be met before the mind can attend clearly to the path of the senses.

The *Masculine Birth of Time* goes on to spell out in detail the necessities of humility before God and charity toward man, if the prideful and idolatrous ways of Aristotelian speculation as well as Paracelsian fancy are to be overcome. The philosophy of Aristotle and the alchemists is seen to be an ancient and corrupting deviation from the religious and scientific integrity of Adamic man who was called to subdue the earth in the original creation. In short, all the elements of the conversion accounts are present.

Boyle's conversion account appears only in fragments. Moreover, his conversion has a more explicit religious than natural philosophical character. One autobiographical statement interrupts Boyle's youthful two-year academic stay at Geneva. Writing of himself in the third person he notes that ". . . at *Geneva*, there happened to him an accident, which he always used to mention as the considerablest of his whole life." Because of his fears before storm and thunder which terrified but did not "blast" him, he swore an oath of diligence. In particular he notes that ". . . piety was to be embraced, not so much to gain heaven, as to serve God with," and this included the duty of examining religion itself. In short, the central message of Boyle's conversion is that life consists of service to God. The piety manifest in this conversion was evident in Boyle's lifelong religious and scientific thought.[66]

Despite certain common motifs in these more or less stylized conversion accounts — stressing the senses, rejecting Aristotle, and specifying a divine and human purpose for the new philosophy — there are epochal differences between Bacon (and Boyle) and the Spiritualists. This will become clear upon further examining the content of self-consciously modern programs diversely related to conversion accounts, for no conversion can be understood simply by itself. In any case, the Spiritualists clearly expressed their conversions in "visions" that were accurate indications of the simultaneity that marked their thought. Thus Helmont's conversion account is a microcosm of his thought in general, particularly his view that true knowledge is a whole unity of Spiritual understanding in relation to God, man, and things.

Specifically on the relation of man as knower to God, Helmont presupposes that spirit rather than will or reason marks the *imago dei* in man. He speaks of God as the Archetypal Light and Word of the soul and conceives of Him as more than a model. The *imago dei* in man is defined in terms of the "efficient Creator," the efficacy of Spirit.[67] Given the eternity and unity of God, the soul of man is immortal and also a unity.[68] This leads Helmont to reject Augustine's alleged "tripartite" soul and the dualism of Tauler, which affirmed a spiritual soul but a gross material body. Helmont's insistence on the unity of the soul will not allow him to divorce understanding and life. He writes of God being "bred in us" and the "melting of the mind into God."[69]

Helmont's presupposition of the Spiritual unity of the soul is equally apparent in his opposition to voluntarism. The discussion of the *imago dei*, which he holds is more intimate to the soul than the soul is to itself, concludes with the claim that will is only an accidental reality, at best an "added talent" in true, that is Spiritual, understanding. The contrast with the voluntarist tradition could not be more striking. Helmont adds that there is no will in Heaven.[70]

Against Aristotle, who was "plainly ignorant of creation,"

and subsequent scholastic definitions of man's "rational essence," Helmont protests that ". . . the world is everywhere miserably misled, and deluded by thinkings. And first, indeed, because everyone thinks Reason to be the Image of God, and our best Treasure, etc." Reason is not only prideful, evil, and subtle, but also manifold.[71] In the name of the wholistic Spiritual unity of God and man, Helmont argues that the scholastic tradition not only ignores the original gifts of charity and humility from the Father of Lights, but has also lost the unity of Spiritual understanding in the multiplicities of reason. Religious pride, moral evil, and scientific falsity coincide in Aristotle's legacy of the Fall. To the manyness, activity, acquisitiveness, and pride of rational man Helmont opposes the union, passivity, suffering, and humility of the Spiritual man who understands.[72]

For Helmont an empirical knowledge of various concrete processes was inseparable from their Spiritual truthfulness. This advancement of empirical spiritual understanding was apparent in his "Authour's Promises" which precede his "Confession." Helmont sets the general limits of heathen knowledge and indicates that the general object of knowledge in Christian natural philosophy is the created seeds:

> The Heathenish Schooles, indeed, may have an Historical knowledge, the observer of things contingent or accidental, of things regular, and necessary: which is a memorative knowledge of the thing done: They may also get learning by demonstration, which is the knowledge of applying things unto measure. And lastly, they may promise rational knowledge which is derived from either of these, by the fitting of discourse. . . . But to *understand* and *savour* these things (i.e. natural causes) from the spring of the first cause, is granted to none without the special favor of Christ the Lord . . . *they have of necessity been ignorant of created things, and the Seeds, Roots, and knowledge of these.* Therefore the knowledge of nature, hath indeed been attempted by the Heathen, through childish conjectures; and very little even obtained.[73]

In short, heathen knowledge, ignorant of creation, is unproductive and superficial. But to know the seeds is a different story; to "understand and savour" things is the way of the Spirit.

One characteristic of this empirical Spiritual understanding emerges in Helmont's vigorous rejection of *ratio*, which derives from the Fall. Such prideful reason cuts the thread of life in its imperial tendency to dominate the soul. Helmont finds religiously, morally, and scientifically objectionable its almost limitless capacity to generate more and more thoughts. Reason displays a manifold activity of fabrication. It ". . . doth generate nothing but a dim or dark knowledge, or a thinking . . . because it is that which is properly nothing else, but a wording faculty of discoursing, cobred with us as mortalls, from sin." In contrast, understanding is essentially humble. It is marked by its receptivity to Spirit and matter. As Helmont puts it, ". . . I may not believe the Agent to be more perfect than the Patient." Resting in the unity of divine Spirit, the understanding perceives the true nature of things chiefly by attending to them.[74]

A second empirical characteristic of Spiritual understanding is its immediacy. Again, the antagonist is reason:

> I have seen and learned, Reason to be a naked thing, because Reason, for every event, did bring forth nothing but a thinking of truth, by which meanes, it did bury the intellectual understanding. . . . For truly, Reason is by no meanes, a cause, part, or essence of the thing caused, much lesse doth the rational faculty in man, reach into things. . . . But reason is a mental, problematical, or intricate Being, onely appearing. . . . Reason . . . is nothing else, but a disposition . . . found by discourse, with the shapes, or Ideas co-bred in the Imagination. . . . So of necessity, it ought to be unstable, from the nature of the Subject of its inherence.[75]

At best merely mental and at worst crassly imaginative, reason is so far out of touch with the Spiritual truth of things that it can only proliferate uncertainty.

In sharp contrast to such a frail faculty, Helmont turns to the trustworthiness of understanding:

> In the understanding, truth is immediate because truth being understood, is nothing else, but a suiting of the intellect to the things themselves. Indeed, the understanding knows things as they are; and therefore likewise, the understanding is made true concerning the things themselves.

Spiritual understanding is trustworthy not only because it thrives securely in God, but also because it is "made true" by concrete things. At one point he speaks of our knowledge "transfigured" by concrete things. Yet the active side of such knowing is not neglected, for "in the Spirit" the ". . . intellect it self *doth transform it self, by passing over, or thorrow, into the thing understood.*" In the presence of God, a true communion with and understanding of *things* — concrete seeds — is accomplished.[76]

A third empirical characteristic of Spiritual understanding is discovery. Following the Scripture that faith without works is dead, Helmont has it that ". . . if I teach things that are profitable it is a Command, not to bury one's Talent renewed in the Earth." He develops this point in an attack on the lack of "inventiveness" of traditional reasoning in a chapter entitled "The Unprofitableness of Logick":

> To sum up all, the knowledge which we have by demonstration, was already before in us, and onely is made a little more distinct by a Syllogisme: Which thing indeed, is not the inventive office of Sciences: but a certain following order of discourse, to that which was found out. Lastly neither doth anything so made, any way have respect to Sciences: but onely to words. But Wisdom, the Son of the everlasting Father of Lights, onely gives Sciences or Knowledges. But the means of obtaining Sciences, are onely to pray, seek and knock.

Throughout his work Helmont attacks merely accumulated knowledge with the frequently repeated motto that one should search into "things, not words." "To pray, seek, and knock" signifies the empirical thrust of his Spiritualist orientation.[77]

Within this wholistic presupposition of the Creator — and for Helmont there was none other — chemistry itself was redefined and practiced with a renewed urgency of purpose. Its inherited forms were expanded into a natural philosophy at once cosmic and divine in scope and practice. Not content with joining the traditional alchemical arts to medicine, itself newly understood as a gift from the Father of Lights rather than a human tradition, Helmont expanded such iatrochemistry into a grand philosophy, which he called, variously, "natural," "chemical," and "Christian."

Maintaining that "Aristotle and Galen are ignorant of nature" because ignorant of creation, Helmont rejected Galenic medicine as a theoretical subdivision of natural philosophy. At the same time, he extended the long tradition of practical chemistry to the breaking point by propounding a comprehensive and coherent theological orientation based upon the

Genesis story of creation and separation, which in turn was present in alchemy. This universal chemistry, coextensive with the processes of nature, became the new realm of medicine, which was ruled by the efficacious model of the Great Physician (Jesus Christ). Against the current medical establishment, such practice involved charity for *all* neighbors.[78] The vocation of the natural philosopher, the profession of the physician, and the more practical arts of the pyrochemist were all blended together in a grand Christian natural philosophy presupposing the Spiritual Father of Lights. The entire process of nature was presupposed as a divine and chemical process of creation, separation, and perfection.

Thus Helmont arrived at a new definition of chemistry not simply as analysis nor simply as a synthetical art, although both were included. Chemistry became a reappropriation of the original perfection of all things; it was man's Spirit-filled performance in thought and deed of the work of the Creator himself:

> Finally, and finally, Chymistry, as for its perfection doth prepare an universal Solver, whereby all things do return into their first Being, and do afford their native endowments, the original blemishes of Bodies are cleansed, and that their inhumane cruelty being forsaken, there is opportunity for them to obtain great and undeclarable restoration and purification.[79]

To practice chemistry is to realize God's own work of restoration and new creation, for purification and perfection are one.

Nicholas Le Fevre, a follower of Helmont and the author of a textbook in chemical natural philosophy, gives an even clearer definition. "Chymistry makes all natural things extracted by the omnipotent hand of God, in the Creation, out of the Abysse of the Chaos, her proper and adequate object." Similarly,

> Chymistry is nothing else but the Art and Knowledge of Nature itself; that is by her means we examine the Principles, out of which natural bodies do consist and are compounded; and by her are discovered unto us the causes of their sources of their generations and corruptions, and of all the changes and alterations to which they are liable.

For Le Fevre, as for Helmont, this grand practice and philosophy is the "true Key of Nature."[80]

This new definition was connected with a new sense of purpose — namely, that God may be honored and man benefited. The initial confessional chapter in the *Oriatrike* calls for the renunciation of self, the attribution of all glory to God, and the practice of chemical-medical natural philosophy for the "common good," for "... the use of my Neighbour." This purpose, obvious throughout the *Oriatrike*, was anticipated in the Dedicatory Epistle of Helmont's *Opuscula Medica Inaudita* (1644), a collection of four short medical works.

> I have written these Paradoxes, for a Pledge of a bigger section promised; wherein I will lay open the Beginnings of Natural Philosophy, and new Maximes of Healing, for a publick good; to wit, that the Schools may learn, and repent. Let them learn indeed ... from the Giver of all Good. But I have endeavoured so to manifest my Talent received, for the profit of my Neighbours.

Helmont attributes the humane ends of medicine to the whole of natural philosophy. "For the whole faculty of natural Philosophy is committed to man," Helmont writes in his Promises. In short, the purpose of Christian natural philosophy is the glory of God and the benefit of mankind.[81]

This sense of purpose has long been recognized in Boyle's work but has not been sufficiently recognized in Bacon's.[82] His call for a science productive of works is expressed in a way that is paradigmatic for the rest of his program. His illuminating *Thoughts and Conclusions on the Interpretation of Nature as a Science Productive of Works* (1607) begins in a typically critical fashion. Physicians are faulted for having no purpose outside their own guild; their "... art escapes condemnation in a court where it is itself the judge." Natural philosophy can make no headway in human power over nature for it is wrapped up in its own *perfection*. The alchemical pursuit of novelty results in no ordered science. The magician falls prey to the "wings of his imagination." Finally, the mechanic is limited to improving his old inventions thus reproducing what is old on a larger scale. In short, for Bacon "the goal has never been defined."[83]

Bacon, however, was not simply negative on all these efforts. Indeed, he was disposed in *Thoughts and Conclusions* to see "signs" in these efforts toward a science with power over nature. This science, strictly parallel to true religion, as seen in

Jesus' parable of the talents, must be ruled by the purpose of showing faith in works:

> For in nature practical results are not only the means to improve well-being but the guarantee of truth. The rule of religion, that a man should show his faith by his works, holds good in natural philosophy too. Science also must be known by works. It is by the witness of works, rather than by logic or even observation, that truth is revealed and established. Whence it follows that the improvement of man's mind and the improvement of his lot are one and the same thing.

It is a short step from this doctrine of works in religion and science to Bacon's view of the power and utility of knowledge. For Bacon this is the concrete value of the end of service to God and man.[84]

In sum, Helmont's Spiritualist orientation was profoundly wholistic. Temporal simultaneity and spatial fusion were wheels within an even larger wheel of Spiritual omneity. No matter whether Helmont's work is opened up in terms of his prayers, theology, doctrine of nature, or "hard" scientific discoveries, the result is the same. Presupposing the Creator Spirit as an inclusive and pervasive whole, he moves with immediacy from God to nature and vice versa. Objectively, the power-filled realities in Helmont's largely undifferentiated universe flow together. The vital processes of nature and the ubiquitous Spirit of God coalesce. The same is true for the subjective activities of worship, experiment, and a combination of speculation and reflection in cosmology and theology. Spiritual understanding unites these activities. Moreover, the purpose of empirical inquiry is divine, and God's purpose is no less than infusing His Spiritual light and life into created minds and seeds. Indeed, the common purpose of both activities is that they may be manifest or reveal themselves together. Chemistry is cosmic, divine, and human, and any separation here would deny the grand unity of creation.

Externally, as well as internally, the basic tendency towards total judgments in Helmont's Spiritualist theology of creation reinforces the same point: all or nothing. Spiritual understanding was opposed to reason; the *imago dei* as Spirit was stressed against will and reason. Natural creation as a vast process overcame scholastic hierarchies and theories of elemental balance.

God as Spirit and continual *creatio ex nihilo* superseded the orthodox interpretations of a distinct *creatio ex nihilo*. In relation to other theologies of creation the Spiritualist orientation tended to be as wholistic in its judgments as in its position.

Although Helmont's profoundly wholistic orientation was more anti-rational than that of some philosophically sophisticated Spiritualists, it was much less esoteric than that of many alchemists. More importantly, his empirical as well as mystical and philosophical views were conducive to the emergence of modern science. In addition to his hard discoveries, he opposed Aristotle and scholastic natural philosophy, directed study to the particulars of creation, championed experimental inquiry, and stressed the humane as well as divine purpose of natural philosophy. Nevertheless, the espousal of wholistic judgments severely weakened Spiritualism as compared to voluntarism, which was capable of many kinds of discriminating judgments. Thus it could develop an epoch-forming critical and constructive orientation even with respect to Spiritualism. This development, rooted in early modern differentiation, is the subject of the remaining chapters.

CHAPTER FOUR:

Theology and Modernity

Against the background of traditional ontological orientations to creation, a growing voluntarist theology of creation, which originated in late medieval thought and was strengthened in the thought of Calvin, acquired widespread prominence in seventeenth-century England. Equally, if not more, opposed to scholastic tradition, an immensely attractive Spiritualist theology of creation was represented in the thought of Helmont. These theologies of creation were powerful presuppositions partly because of their rootage in a widespread religious interest in creation and new creation that marked English culture.

Insofar as the rise of modern natural science was manifest in the middle decades of the seventeenth century, it presupposed both the voluntarist and Spiritualist theologies of creation. But in the vigorous conflicts and compromises that marked the epoch, voluntarist presuppositions were dominant because they gave rise to a thorough critique of tradition and at the same time contributed a relatively new understanding of God to the formation of modern culture. Less locked into a total opposition to tradition than Spiritualism, the voluntarist position was more discriminating, positively and negatively; it was able to select critically and constructively from both the traditional ontological background and the all-or-nothing foreground of Spiritualism. Also, in contrast to the wholistic strength of Spiritualism in both theology/religion and natural philosophy, which was also its weakness, the voluntarist orientation successfully employed perennial aesthetic attitudes to creation.

In England the rise of modern natural science was marked by an epoch-forming sense of modernity, in terms of which new and old questions were raised and differing basic presuppositions came into play. A distinct theology was presupposed along with certain questions of method and knowledge and a new idea of nature. Although most interpreters have noted the pervasive sense of modernity in modern natural science, surprisingly few have remarked that it is the most striking aspect of the new science and philosophy. The ideas of nature per se and science per se were not original to the new outlook, but self-conscious modernity was. R. F. Jones' excellent *Ancients and Moderns* does recognize that the sense of modernity in seventeenth-century English thought was such a total cultural phenomenon that it called for change in institutions ranging from university to church and in disciplines as diverse as theology and natural philosophy.[1] But other interpreters have assumed that it was simply a conversion from theology to science. Concepts of revolution and secularization are often used to support this view, and eighteenth-century definitions of the "natural sciences" are frequently misread into the earlier records of writers who viewed themselves as natural philosophers and reformers.

To provide an alternative interpretation of the profound sense and structure of modernity which coursed through the new science and presupposed a relatively new theological orientation, this chapter begins with an account of change in theology per se, including theology of creation. It then shows the religious/theological grounds of the lively and epochal sense of modernity, particularly in Bacon. The final three sections map the structure of modernity and its presuppositions. This increasingly manifold structure, marked by differentiation (and individuation), appears in significant new ventures in human consciousness; it is exemplified in Boyle's thought, though it is also apparent in Bacon, Newton, and Descartes. A more detailed representative statement of early modern, largely voluntarist theological presuppositions and their constructive significance for understanding nature will be given in Chapters 5 and 6.

A Quiet Reformation

Critical analysis of diverse "theologies of creation" — highlighting the comprehensiveness of orientations to the Creator, His relation to creation, the general order of creation, and man as creature in various traditions and movements — does not exhaust the theology of those who spoke of Spirit, Father of Lights, First Cause, and especially Providence and God's *potentia ordinata* and *absoluta*. A more adequate understanding of the reality of God presupposed in early modern thought must consider the distinctive belief in God in this period. In particular contrast to medieval theology, the way in which the reality of God was conceived in sixteenth- and seventeenth-century thought may be understood in terms of a new understanding of *unity*. Conceptions of unity have been central to the perennial meaning of God in Western culture, but a new kind of unity of reality, thought, and experience was decisive theologically.

Seventeenth-century thought did not fundamentally call into question the *existence* of God or creation. Nor was its vigorous criticism primarily an experience of the loss and redemption of *being*. Although nominalist ontologies increased, the most fundamental change did not occur at the level of gaining or losing ontological consciousness. Not until the Enlightenment was there a fundamental alteration in Western ontology. Unlike Descartes, Kant no longer presupposed the reality (substance) of God in subordinating ontology to epistemology. Moreover, his standard argument for God's existence, the moral argument, no longer presupposed the objective revelation and order of God in creation. Those beliefs were fundamental not only to the cosmological argument typical of high medieval thought but also to the teleological argument typical in the sixteenth and seventeenth centuries. Historically, both of these arguments, paradigmatic in their times, presupposed created being. However, deism, in part an attempt to argue God's existence from nature without presupposing that it was His creation, signalled the ending of such presuppositions and introduced the moral-rational critiques and defenses of eighteenth-century Christianity. Despite its theological limitations, deism sufficed to break the hold of the mysterious sense of being intrinsic to classical Christianity. Deism exchanged the foreign mystery of creation for the domestic experience of making.

To be more precise, the basic seventeenth-century presupposition was the unity of *individual* reality. God, creation, and the self were regarded primarily as individual unities in contrast to both the *wholistic* unities of Spiritualism and the *hierarchical* unities of traditional Aristotelian and medieval thought, and each of these unities was largely understood to be externally related to the others. Such predominantly external relations conflicted with both the largely internal relationships of God, man, and world in Spiritualism, and the order of hierarchically related beings to Being in the classical medieval tradition. In any case, this different appropriation of unity was expressed in theological terms. Since no properly creative power was attributed to human reason, will, or affection, theological consciousness pervaded the writings of such obvious moderns as Bacon, Boyle, Newton, and Descartes, as well as such figures as Helmont and the Cambridge Platonists.[2]

The modern presupposition was anticipated in the late medieval voluntarist orientation to creation, where it was expressed in terms of the divine *potentia absoluta* and *potentia ordinata*. This rubric made more sense as the divine unity was seen in increasingly individual terms, for only an individual had such options. The frequent debates about what God can do, has done, and will do stemmed from this orientation rather than the less dialectical communication of causality and divine power in Thomas, which presupposed the hierarchical unity of Being.[3] For the moderns, however, the chief unity of God was neither the principle of Being itself nor simply His deity as highest Being (although this was seldom denied). Instead, the reality of God was focused and concentrated into an understanding of the supreme individual. A new sense of God's unity overcame the unity of Being itself. No less important was the opposition to the Spiritualist unity of Deity as inclusive All; the moderns presupposed God's unique individuality in contrast to the divine Whole.

This distinctive view was evident in the term "Author." When the major Protestant reformers spoke straightforwardly, if not literally, of God in biblical terms as Lord, King, and so on, and the seventeenth-century divines dwelt so long on Providence, they presupposed that God was an exalted and majestic individual. Indeed, the theological concept of Providence, so frequent at this time, was an extended systematic statement of modern orientations to God as an individual. A heightened awareness of divine transcendence is frequent in times of great religious change, but the modern orientation went beyond both the contemporary Spiritualist revival, which tended to equate transcendence with wholeness or universality, and the classic medieval view that to transcend was fundamentally to exceed something else. The transcendent individual unity of God meant that He was distinct and often over against His creation, just as His creatures were in turn highly distinct and set over against God and other creatures. In a word, otherness (although not closure) was the mark of modern transcendence.[4] (Concomitantly, the problem of relations between individuals — atoms, simple ideas, consciences, etc. — was acutely modern.)

The modern understanding of unity gave rise to radical differentiation, in contrast to the deliberate undifferentiation of Spiritualism and preservation of the chain of being in classical medievalism.[5] It was marked by a new appreciation of God as personal. The very issue of God's personhood, apart from special trinitarian considerations, was newly highlighted in the late medieval debate with classical medievalism on the primacy of divine will or intellect.[6] Seventeenth-century thinkers tended to favor the former alternative, advancing an understanding of God's personhood in tension both with the impersonality of Deity in classical medievalism and the systematic anthropomorphism of Spiritualism. Their new sense of God's power may have been only a change in emphasis, yet there is a striking neglect of the medieval preoccupation with divine love — and man's love for God — in sixteenth- and seventeenth-century theology. Faith, a decisive response to God's power and a person-forming claiming of His promises, became a more central category. This was especially evident in the rubric of divine *potentia*, which stressed His activity. Even Spiritualists as different as Helmont and the Cambridge Platonists estimated the love of God by practical work and an ethical rather than contemplative religious life.

With respect to creation as such, the idea of hierarchical orders of nature and causality gave way to an egalitarian understanding. Although many interpreters have recognized this shift, it cannot be adequately understood apart from the modern protest against Spiritualism. The wholistic unity of creation fully informed by Spiritual mind gave way to a clear affirmation of material creation. Matter was neither spirited nor eternally preexistent for modern thought. (Concomitantly, materialism became an acutely modern problem.)

The magnitude of change in this theology of creation was considerable. Although it did not match the primitive Christian presupposition of God in Christ, it was roughly of the same order as the epochal Patristic and Augustinian presupposition of God as Eternal Being. In degree of change it is perhaps more akin to the presupposition of dialectic and process intrinsic to Deity in nineteenth-century post-Hegelian thought.

One indication of epochal change in early modern theology of creation was its generation of a distinct kind of paradigmatic argument for God's existence. Just as early medieval Augustinian theology, presupposing rational participation in the divine Logos, generated the ontological argument, a hallmark of seventeenth-century thought was the teleological argument, which turned upon many individual works and designs evident in creation. Divine individuality was presupposed in inferences that celebrated created individuals. Such argumentation should be carefully distinguished from the favored cosmological proof of high medieval thought, which presupposed empirical causality mainly as an occasion for demonstrating the First Cause. The variegated design of concretely created individuals and their rich efficiency was central to the teleological argument, which interpreted the being of God chiefly in terms of His power.

Furthermore, the teleological viewpoint required lengthy statements which gave a sense of movement from one individual to another. This approach stood in sharp contrast to argumentation within the Spiritualist presupposition of the togetherness of God, self, and world. The heavy reliance upon divine illumination in "Spiritual understanding" favored the ontological argument, often in the form that every true thought is a proof of God. The coincidence of proof and vision was broken in early modern thought.[7]

Of course, the modern theology of creation did not simply replace either the medieval background from which it sprang or the Spiritualist foreground with which it struggled. Despite the prominence of voluntarist orientations, much compromise marked the diverse conceptions of Deity. Nevertheless, as an epochally new unity of reality and experience overcame the traditional hierarchical unity of being and the wholistic unity of Spiritualism, the systematic conservatism of an ontological theology of creation gave way to a new progressivism. A new sense of historical tension appeared in contrast to both classic medieval immanence and perennial Spiritualist presence. The modern "pilgrim" succeeded the medieval "saint," and *doing* God's will rather than *being* in His presence or *dwelling* in His Spirit was what counted. Outlooks preoccupied with the quest for immortality and dedicated to the virtues of contemplation gave way to a practical utilitarian spirit, which was, in turn, ruled by and drawn to the transcendent Jehovah who ruled in His own freedom and glory. The ties both between God *qua* Being and His hierarchical order and between God *qua* Spirit and His body of creation were stretched as a new religious and cultural unity of God *qua* individual Author of a subject creation was forged.

This quiet reformation in theology, overlooked in standard accounts which stress the alleged "scholasticism" of seventeenth-century theology, did much to unify early modern culture concretely as well as formally.

The Sense of Modernity in Bacon, Boyle, and Newton

Throughout the seventeenth century, and especially in its middle decades, English culture was marked by a lively mood that was something more than an openness to the change of experience and institutions. For the intense religious and political pressures exerted by various groups generated a climate which forced change upon many normally reluctant Puritans and Anglicans. Frequently defined as revolutionary, this pervasive and self-conscious mood of change was highly ambitious and programmatic. It is clear in retrospect, however, that many of the participants, especially at the level of intellectual culture, were influenced by the events of the Protestant Reformation and the Roman Catholic Counter-Reformation. In general, the paradigm of reformation was a more commonly held context for change than revolution. Earlier models of reformation were presupposed in the way much seventeenth-century culture conceived of and participated in change. Various religious and other views of reformation were taken for granted to provide direction if not details in many modern projects.

When Bacon, whose works acquired much influence in the middle of the century, sought in his *Advancement of Learning* to enlist contemporaries in a proposed reformation of learning, he wrote:

> We see before our eyes, that in the age of ourselves and our fathers, when it pleased God to call the Church of Rome to account for their degenerate manners and ceremonies, and sundry doctrines obnoxious and framed to uphold the same abuses; *at one and the same time it was ordained by the Divine Providence that there should attend withal a renovation and new spring of all other knowledges.*[8]

The presupposition of Providence invoked a largely Protestant spirit of reform which Bacon also found in the Jesuit Counter-Reformation. He held that this should apply to all branches of knowledge. Boyle and the Royal Society saw this sense of reform as the work of God in their own time as well as a task modern man should do to the glory of God. This attitude, present in Helmont, also reached such Spiritualists as Hartlib and Comenius, who proposed a reform of learning, and the Cambridge Platonists, who were deeply committed to ethical reform.[9]

Bacon also articulated a definite modern theology of reform in natural philosophy.[10] In opposition to both resurgent Spiritualism, which he attacked in Ficino and Paracelsus, and outmoded medieval ways, he expressed a self-conscious theology of creation as history. Whereas Spiritualist theologies stressed the simultaneity of the beginning and the end in the present fullness of time, which could be realized in the confluence of vision, inquiry, and art, Bacon saw past, present, and future as distinguished but not separated, related but not fused. History was tensed; a definite sense of historical progression gave shape and direction to the reform of natural philosophy.

This interpretation recalled the perfection of original creation, especially the mandate to Adam to command and control the remainder of creation subject to him. On the basis of that ancient mandate — finally articulated as the message that knowledge is power — Bacon called for a present use of man's powers. Thus he opened his early *The Masculine Birth of Time*

(1603), subtitled "The Great Instauration of the Dominion of Man over the Universe," with a prayer petitioning ". . . that our human interests may not stand in the way of the divine, *nor from the unlocking of the paths of sense. . . .*" Similarly, his *Refutation of Philosophies* (1608) was a call to men to study and command as Adam had.[11] Utility was grounded in the ancient event of creation. Bacon's outlook, unlike Helmont's, recognized the distance (as well as relation) between command and subject, God and man, past and present. This distance was mediated by the powerful will of God and by that of man; no inclusive Spirit could bridge the gaps.

While Bacon criticized the ancient Greek and medieval tradition, which he held derived from the Fall, he was careful not to issue a blanket condemnation. His judgment was critical of scholasticism but discriminating, historical but not apocalyptic. Adamic man was perfect in both a moral or religious sense and by virtue of his knowledge. Thus, perfection meant that man as God's creature has both the power to do the good and the power to know the creation as it is. In a double Fall, man lost not only his moral strength but also his power to know creation aright. Without the virtues of "charity" and "humility," man as knower is prone either to ignorance or to the fabrications of a "prideful" imagination.[12] The mind must be cleansed so that we can know. Bacon's view of moral preparation for subsequent knowledge is another critical contrast with the Spiritualist fusion of corruption and error, of humility and truth. Bacon argued that the double Fall had been continued in the legacy of moral and scientific errors of Aristotle and the scholastics. Hence, he urgently demanded a reform in the present as a recall of original creation and a vindication of its powers. In short, the modern thinker could achieve critical leverage against tradition by going past it to the creation. But a history-denying Spiritualist regeneration of creation was not necessary.

Boyle and Newton followed Bacon's lead. Boyle, who often stressed the necessity of the original virtues of humility and charity, went so far as to rediscover in his own time atomic matter created in the divine "original."[13] More interestingly, Newton appears to have remained more indebted to Spiritualism. Frank Manuel has convincingly argued that Newton's chronology of ancient civilizations, especially in regard to the arts and politics, was a sustained and dogmatic vindication of Israel's cultural inventions. Despite considerable strain in his view of history, Newton held that Hebrew culture was the original not only of Greek achievements and medieval failures, but also of the most ancient Egyptian accomplishments. It has become clear that he, like Bacon, the Cambridge Platonists, and others, searched among the ancients for original piety, wisdom, and knowledge. He found a remarkable diversity of notions among the ancients — not only various "active principles" but also (differing from More and Cudworth) anticipations of universal gravity and its mathematical appropriation as well as atomic matter.[14]

Newton's efforts to locate numerous cultural inventions and various philosophical discoveries in the ancient beginnings of creation led him, like most Spiritualists as well as Bacon and Boyle, to criticize the scholastic tradition by showing its roots and deviations from the original. Yet he was more radical and discriminating in his criticism than even the Cambridge Platonists. He did not honor the thought of Plato and Plotinus as the greatest wisdom acquired from Hebrew sources, and he also insisted, against More and Cudworth, that God's presence is not mediated through some second-level "plastic power." Nor was God the soul of the world. In short, Newton remained faithful to his classic statement in the General Scholium that God is the transcendent Lord of the universe. This modern affirmation of the Creator and Providence, stressing the will and freedom of the mighty Jehovah, was at the same time much closer to Israel's God as Lord of history than any Platonic or Cambridge Platonists' affirmations of divine Spirit. Presupposing a Lord of nature and history, creation for Newton was linear rather than cyclical, as it was for the Spiritualists.[15]

The modern sense of reform recalled creation but was aimed toward a new future, partly anticipated in a common and progressive task. Bacon's *Refutation of Philosophies* opens with a long critique of the ancients. "No man can measure the extent of the injury they do to progress"; and Bacon compared progress to the fruitful work of the bee, rather than the merely gathering work of the ant or the merely speculative work of the spider. Concluding with a deliberately prophetic reading of the signs of his time, he claimed that now was the time to fulfill the prophecy of Daniel 12:4.

> Distant voyages and travels have brought to light many things in nature, which may throw fresh light on human philosophy and science and correct by experience the opinions and conjectures of the ancients. Not only reason but prophecy connects the two. What else can the prophet mean who, in speaking about the last times, says: Many will pass through and knowledge will be multiplied? Does he not imply that the passing through or perambulation of the round earth and the increase or multiplication of science were destined to the same age and century?[16]

In his early works, Bacon's understanding of biblical prophecy as pointing toward the future reform of natural philosophy was supported by his chief image of Jesus. Most clearly in the parable of the talents, he argued, Jesus calls men to the production of works in both morals and science.

One of his most mature eschatological statements, *New Atlantis*, envisioned a College of Six Days Work. This would restore the original creation by calling on God and man as co-workers. Whereas Helmont's call involved a return to the beginning, Bacon, projecting a forward-moving process, speculated that future scientists would be the new priests of knowledge and its increase.[17] Bacon's eschatology in general, like his view of the past, differed considerably from the Spiritualist orientation. Going beyond a shared purpose of reform, Bacon's appeal to familiar eschatological passages, such as those from Daniel, was set in a more linear historical framework. Since the course of creation was tensed, his conception of scientific utopia lacked the radical heavenly (visionary and/or regressive) cast of Spiritualist mystical utopias. Bacon's way was free from romantic or militant nostalgia.[18] It eventually gave direction and reinforced a sophisticated structure of early modern developments to be discussed shortly.

Bacon's strongest witness was perhaps in the last part of *The Great Instauration*, which articulated the philosophy of inquiry "to which the rest is subservient and ministrant."

> All depends on keeping the eye steadily fixed upon the facts of nature and so receiving their images simply as they are. For God forbid that we should give out a dream of our own imagina-

tion for a pattern of the world; rather may he graciously grant to us to write an apocalypse or true vision of the footsteps of the Creator imprinted on his creatures.

Therefore do thou, O Father, who gavest the visible light as the first fruits of creation, and didst breathe into the face of man the intellectual light as the crown and consummation thereof, guard and protect this work, which coming from thy goodness returneth to thy glory.[19]

This was cultural and religious optimism of a high order. Bacon's faith in creation and new creation attempted to go beyond the Renaissance quest for antiquity and immortality as well as the medieval and Reformation hunger for salvation, both of which were to be surpassed in the modern effort to remake the world.

Toward the end of the seventeenth century Newton's participation in the sense of progress was less exuberant, partly because of his more disciplined historical inquiries. His posthumous *Observations upon the Prophecies of Daniel, and the Apocalypse of St. John,* argued that

the folly of Interpreters has been, to foretel times and things by this Prophecy [of St. John], as if God designed to make them Prophets. By this rashness they have not only exposed themselves, but brought the Prophecy also into contempt. The design of God was much otherwise. He gave this Prophecy [of St. John] and the Prophecies of the Old Testament, not to gratify men's curiosities by enabling them to foreknow things, but that after they were fulfilled they might be interpreted by the event, and his own Providence, not the Interpreters, be then manifested thereby to the world.

Presupposing Providence, Newton eschewed speculation yet remained remarkably open to the signs of his time. He prefaced his critique by writing that

in the very end, the Prophecy [of Daniel and John] should be so far interpreted as to convince many. *Then,* saith Daniel, *many shall run to and fro, and knowledge shall be increased. . . .* 'Tis therefore a part of this Prophecy, that it should not be understood before the last age of the world; and therefore it makes for the credit of the Prophecy, that it is not yet understood. *But if the last age, the age of opening these things, be now approaching, as by the great successes of late Interpreters it seems to be, we have more encouragement than ever to look into these things.*[20]

Unfortunately, Newton did not identify the "Interpreters,"

nor did he explicate the signs of the end.[21] However, the reality of his hope clearly presupposed God's work in the entire history of creation, from beginning to end. At the least, this faith prevented him from simply embracing Spiritualism; it also gave direction to the modern sense of reform.

The Structure of Modern Differentiation Exemplified in Boyle

The very structure of the epochal sense of reform in early modern thought reflected a largely voluntarist theology of creation. This is particularly apparent in the proliferation of differentiation.[22] The structure of this process can be set forth in three dimensions: the sharp distinction between the Creator and the creation, the clear differentiation of the works of God, and increasing differentiation of human consciousness, or more broadly, the works of modern man. A fourth dimension, the sharp distinction of the modern self from its environment(s), corresponds to the distinction between Creator and creation. These dimensions cannot be analyzed according to a purely logical scheme. Nor can they be recorded as mere process, for their structure locates basic modern presuppositions, questions, problems, and positions. This will be shown chiefly in the full range of Boyle's highly representative work.[23]

The Distinction Between Creator and Creation

At decisive turning points in Western thought, deeply felt conceptions of divine transcendence have had profound critical significance. Augustine's view of eternal immutability vs. temporality, which issued in a critique of the Roman empire, also deepened the Western understanding of personal and temporal reality. Centuries earlier, Isaiah's critique of the Jews' entanglement with other cultures in the name of God's majestic holiness expressed the beginning of a profound eschatological orientation in the faith and and life of Israel.

In early modern thought, the understanding of God as the supreme individual, which stressed willful personhood, power, and, not least, transcendent otherness, functioned in a deeply critical and constructive way, particularly in relation to traditional and Spiritualist orientations to creation. Bacon saw himself fulfilling a decisive role as a prophet of the critical and productive significance of modern religious beliefs. His highly polemical and political program for reforming modern learning sought to promote and proclaim the integrity and relative independence of natural philosophy among and along with other disciplines. Boyle, a less explicitly prophetic figure, actually carried Bacon's program much further. But Bacon's religious and theological effort, which spurred the modern orientation, expressed belief in the transcendent Creator and its critical significance by drawing a sharp distinction between God and His creation. In his early *Meditationes Sacrae* (1597), "Of the Works of God and the Works of Man," he contrasted the power and perfection of the Creator with the weak productions of His creatures. "God saw all that he had made and behold it was very good: But man when he turned to look on the works that his hands had wrought, found that all was vanity and vexation of spirit." The transcendent agency of the Creator was also accorded first place in the brief *Confession of Faith* (1603). Bacon wrote that, "I believe that God is so holy, pure and jealous, that it is impossible for him to be pleased in any creature, though the work of his own hands."[24]

One index to the meaning of this affirmation appears in Bacon's (and Boyle's) understanding of atheism, the apparent opposite of belief in God. While Bacon defines "simple atheism" as a rebellious denial of and mutiny against the mighty power of God, he quickly passes on to the "degrees" of atheism which he perceives as genuine dangers — namely, the opposition of good (divine) and evil powers as equally ultimate, or the opposition of a strange power of privation to divine power, or the limitation of Deity to merely foreknowing the course of things.[25] Boyle evidences a similar concern for the jealousy of God and regards the threat of atheism primarily as a kind of confusion of God and the world in which His power is compromised. This view of atheism, concerned more with the power than the simple existence of God, is an indication that the transcendent Creator was taken for granted. This presupposition provided formidable critical grounds against any confusion of God and the world. In the interests of the "transcendent excellency" of God, Boyle frequently articulated the typically modern attack against any and all confusion at this crucial point.[26]

Whereas Boyle's critique of the Spiritualists focused upon Helmont, although Paracelsus and others were not overlooked, Bacon's targets were Paracelsus, Telesio, and Ficino. Bacon alternated between a stinging critique of the schoolmen and a no less telling criticism of the Spiritualists. His charge against Paracelsus was typical:

> By mixing the divine with the natural, the profane with the sacred, heresies with mythology, you have corrupted, O you sacrilegious imposter, both human and religious truth. . . . [Whereas] the Sophists . . . deserted experience, you have betrayed it. The evidence drawn from things is like a mask cloaking reality and needs careful sifting; you subjected it to a preordained scheme of interpretation.[27]

Boyle extended Bacon's critique. Although initially attracted to Helmont's thought — and doubly so because of his lifelong interest in practical medicine—he soon developed his own decisive position:

> I think the arguments, which *Helmont* and others draw from the providence of God, for the curableness of all diseases, are not very cogent, and somewhat irreverent, (for God being not obliged any more to continue life or health to sinful man, than to beasts, that never offended him, we ought humbly to thank him, if he hath, among his creatures, dispersed remedies for every disease, but have no right to accuse him if he have not). . . .

In another early piece, *Discourse Against Swearing*, Boyle warned against oaths which presuppose a kind of divinity in creaturely things, on the ground that such idolatory denies the sole honor and worship of God.[28]

Perhaps more significant is Boyle's resistance to diffusions of Deity in the world. In his *Notion of Nature* he objected to Spinoza's seeming confusion of God and the world under the rubric of the *natura naturans* concept. He opposed the attempts of some Spiritualists to attribute life if not mind to nature and objected to the Cambridge Platonists' conception of God related to the world as a kind of "plastic power." Typically, Boyle also rejected Hobbes' implication that God can be re-

duced to a material principle. Generally suspicious of the
speculative cast of Hobbes' philosophy, which closely linked
metaphysics, theology, and cosmology, Boyle's deeply rooted
practice of discriminating argumentation is more telling in ob-
jecting to Hobbes' misuse of Boylean experimentation with air,
as well as Hobbes' general theory of air. Boyle argues that
instead of Hobbes' appeal to what God might have done, the
true experimentalist should begin with the corpuscular fluidity
of air, which is what God has done.[29] Thus, Boyle remains not
only a firm guardian of the distinction between Creator and
creation against both Spiritualism and materialism; he also
practices a general mode of criticism that differentiates theory
and experiment in keeping with a theology that features transcendence. All of this is evident here in the distinct significance
of Boyle's empiricism, which will be discussed below.

Newton also expressed the distinction between Creator and
creation by stressing God's will and naming Him as the Author
of the world. Although more indebted to ancient theology than
Boyle, he modified its highly malleable traditions to conform
with his anti-Trinitarian adoration of the One God. Rejecting
the primacy of ancient polytheism, he found monotheism to be
original.[30] Also, Newton did not go as far as the Cambridge
Platonists in finding God within nature. God remained the transcendent cause of gravity, not the power or spirit of gravity
itself. Such critical modifications show the deep modern presupposition of God's transcendent will in Newton's thought.

It is evident that Boyle's strictures against confusing the
Creator and creation extend to human knowledge of God, His
speech, and "arguments" for His existence. Implicit in his
critique of human affairs are several distinctly different ways to
speak of God and creation. His position is clear in the opening
statement of *The High Veneration Man's Intellect Owes to God,
peculiarly for His Wisdom and Power*:

> Upon this occasion I shall take leave to declare, that it is not
> without some indignation, as well as wonder, that I see many
> men, and some of them divines too, who little considering what
> God is, and what themselves are, presume to talk of him and
> his attributes as freely, and as unpremeditatedly, as if they
> were talking of a geometrical figure, or a mechanical engine.

Opposing those who reason directly from the mind of God to

that of man, Boyle argues that God may have an immense number of attributes — the "foecundity" of God — of which we have at best only the faintest awareness. Even Scripture allows us to know at best the counsels or will of God and not his nature. Moreover,

> there are some of those divine attributes we do know, which being relative to the creatures, could scarce, if at all, be discovered by such imperfect intellects as ours, save by the consideration of some things actually done by God.

Pressing his nominalist and theological criticism, Boyle virtually rejects the approach to God through an "idea," in addition to His works and word:

> I know it may be alleged, that besides the two ways I have mentioned of attaining the knowledge of God's attributes, there may be a third way preferable to both the others, and that is, by considering the idea of a Being supremely or infinitely perfect; in which idea it may be alleged, that all possible perfections are contained; so that no new one can be added to it. But though I readily grant, that this idea is the most genuine, that I am able to frame of the Deity, yet there may be diverse attributes, which, though they are in a general way contained in this idea, are not in particular discovered to us by it. It is true, that, when by any means whatsoever, any divine perfection comes to our knowledge, we may well conclude, that it is in a sense comprised in the comprehensive notion we have of a Being absolutely perfect; but it is possible, that the perfection would never have come to our knowledge by the bare contemplation of that general idea, but was suggested by particularities; so that such discoveries are not so much derived from, as referred to, the notion we are speaking of.[31]

The objection here is essentially theological, though it is also based on the limits of knowledge. Similarly, in a later work, Boyle argues that He can and does speak to man in ways that comport with His and not necessarily our intentions:

> And if God vouchsafes to disclose those things to us, since not only he must needs know about his own nature, attributes, etc. what we cannot possibly know unless he tells us, and since we know, that whatever he tells us is infallibly true, we have abundant reason to believe rather what he declares to us concerning himself and divine things, than what we should conclude or guess about them, by analogy to things of a nature infinitely distant from his, or by maxims framed according to the nature of inferior beings.[32]

In sum, it is clear that Boyle, Bacon, and Newton presuppose a sharp distinction between Creator and creation, and that this is no idle piety.

Differentiation of the "Works" of God

Systematic division of the "works" of God in relation to the world was highly valued in the middle decades of the seventeenth century. Boyle, for example, bracketed matters of redemption when he set about the disciplined study and celebration of God's work of creation. Without denying the former, he rejected Helmont's Spiritualist view that all God's works, including the *personae* of the Trinity, could be run together in such a way that Jesus Christ, the Son of the Father, understood as cosmic wisdom and spirituality, was essential to true natural philosophy, medicine, and chemistry.

Boyle also sharply distinguished the two terms in the traditional binary of God's two great books, that of nature or creation and that of Scripture essential to redemption, whereas Helmont deliberately fused them, as well as the whole of piety and science, in the *Oriatrike*. Having carefully differentiated the two, Boyle gave the bulk of his attention to the book of creation. The sharp separation of both God's works and books in deism should not be read into these earlier developments, however. Nor should the quite different view of the Reformers be confused with later developments. In general, the Reformation practice of testing truth against Scripture favored this book over that of nature — a position not far removed from classic hierarchical ordering.[33]

In the context of the early seventeenth century Bacon's differentiation was of great significance and influence. His *Confession of Faith* ascribed the work of creation to God's power and the work of redemption to His will. The *Meditationes Sacrae* were explicit in their distinct calls to "Search the Scriptures" and to "Behold and consider the creatures." Similarly, the early *Valerius Terminus* (1603) aligned science and religion, respectively, with the power and will of God.[34] In his seemingly less religious work, *Thoughts and Conclusions* (1607), Bacon adopted the mantle of a priest and offered a "meditation" intended to meet the problems of superstition, ignorance, and uncertainty.

> Next to the word of God Natural Philosophy is the most certain
> cure for superstition and the most approved nutriment to faith.
> Its rightful station is as the accepted and loyal handmaid of
> religion, for religion reveals the will of God, Natural Philosophy
> His power.

The thrust of his meditation was against scholastic theology,
which blocked progress in natural philosophy and also reduced
theology itself ". . . into the form of a manual," thus incorporat-
ing into religion the ". . . disputatious and contentious philosophy of Aristotle." Alternately, the problem in natural philosophy was that ". . . during all those ages up till now no single
individual made a profession of Natural Philosophy in the sense
of devoting his life to it. . . . The Great Mother of the Sciences
has been reduced to their handmaid," i.e., the handmaid of
either Christian theology or Greek moral philosophy. Equally
pernicious for Bacon were those Spiritualist opinions

> in such favour today as those which with solemn pomp seek to
> celebrate a legal marriage between Theology and Natural Phi-
> losophy, that is between Faith and the evidence of the senses,
> and which charm the minds of men with a pleasing variety of
> matter while producing a disastrous confusion between the
> human and the divine.[35]

A year later, in his *Refutation of Philosophies,* Bacon spoke as
a prophetic seer, opening with the exhortation that God

> did not give you reliable and trustworthy sense in order that
> you might study the writings of a few men. Study the Heaven
> and the Earth, the works of God himself, and do so while
> celebrating His praises and singing hymns to your Creator.

Pointedly omitting an analysis of Aristotle's doctrines, Bacon
chose to read his "signs." "But in his case, the 'signs' are not
good. He was of an impatient and intolerant cast of mind." Led
by pride into a didactic fashioning of the world with his
categories, Aristotle had failed as a ". . . researcher into
truth." Bacon went on to note that many of the new Spiritualist
sects in natural philosophy, in spite of their greater devotion to
the senses, further confused piety and science, God and the
world. These arguments fully anticipated much of his major
work, *Novum Organum* (1620).[36]

The modern differentiation of God's works was institutionalized in the Royal Society. John Wallis wrote of the "in-

visible college," a possible predecessor of the Royal Society, that its business was "to discover and consider of philosophical inquiries," meanwhile "precluding matters of theology and state-affairs." Hooke wrote that "the business and design of the Royal Society is — To improve the knowledge of natural things . . . (not meddling with Divinity). . . ." Yet the assumption that attending to God's work of creation was equally integral to the Society was clear, if extravagantly put, in Birch's record of Boyle's contribution to the Society.

> It appeared to those, who conversed most with him in his enquiries into nature, that his main design in that, on which he had his own eye most constantly . . . was to raise in himself and others more elevated thoughts of the greatness and glory, and of the wisdom and goodness of the Deity. This was so deep in his mind, that he concludes the article of his will, which relates to the Royal Society, in these words: *Wishing them also a happy success in their laudable attempts to discover the true nature of the works of God, and praying, that they and all other searchers into physical truths, may cordially refer their attainments to the glory of the great Author of Nature, and to the comfort of mankind.* [37]

The most obvious result and paramount issue in the differentiation of God's works was the liberation of natural philosophy from the hegemony of traditional and contemporary theologies and philosophies. Yet this liberation — and others to come — was itself deeply theological in Bacon's proclamations, Boyle's practice, and the purposes of the Royal Society. The structure and spread of modern differentiation should not be confused with secularization.

Modern Differentiation of the Self: Literary, Historical, and Religious

A further step or dimension of modern differentiation was that of human consciousness, or, more broadly, many works of the self. Just as a heightened awareness of transcendence was integral to the differentiation of God's works, so too a sharp distinction between the self, increasingly individualized, and its environment was integral to the differentiation of many works of modern selfhood. In more direct theological terms, modern man's newly differentiated forms of serving God presupposed obedience to a clearly transcendent Lord, a kind of obedience at a distance. A thorough account of this change would require careful study of the distinctive modes of early modern knowledge, action, and feeling, as well as a full philosophical-psychological inquiry into diverse conceptions of the self in modern, as contrasted to medieval and Spiritualist traditions — in short, a full anthropological inquiry. But three central points can be summarized.

The conception of man focused in terms of will rather than reason or spirit nurtured a sharp distinction between self and environment. Viewed as a rational creature, man participated in the hierarchy of being; regarded as spirit, he was virtually identified with spiritual reality at large. But for man conceived as individual will, ontological and spiritual relations to created reality were no longer taken for granted. Indeed, these relations acquired the status of a major problematic in modern thought.

The profoundly but not exclusively voluntaristic conception of man in Bacon and Boyle exemplified this view. Bacon sharply criticized the Paracelsian doctrine of microcosmic man: "As for man, you have made him into a pantomime." He was equally critical of the "idols" of the mind enslaved to tradition. Moreover, his positive conception of man as the master and lord of creation was widely shared in the seventeenth century.[38] Boyle also — although his metaphor of the scientist as priest, one whose inquiry mediates between God and creation, tempered Bacon's view — presupposed heightened awareness of distance between both God and creation and man and created reality. The tendency was to set such realities over against each other.

Descartes' dichotomy between thinking substance and extended or material substance was perhaps the sharpest statement of early modern selfhood. Quite apart from the issue of whether or not his appeal to divine substance, the guarantor of human perception, was successful, the Cartesian tendency to a dualism of mind and body, God and world, and man and external nature was resisted and countered by English thinkers as diverse as More and Boyle, who clearly expressed an aesthetic attitude toward creation. Their insistence upon a sharp distinction between self and created reality did not force them to regard the manifold richness of created reality, especially in its particulars, as simplified phenomena of thinking or extended substance.

In this general framework of new understandings of God, man, and the world, the impressive increase of early modern differentiation may be charted in new works — conceptions, disciplines, and genres — of history, literature, and religion, as well as knowledge of nature. The latter will be shown in the next section.

Roughly contemporary with Spinoza's early biblical criticism, Boyle's *Considerations touching the Style of the Holy Scriptures* was typical of the advent of modern historical consciousness. Whereas Spinoza's rational-historical criticism called in question the order of biblical events, Boyle represented a more empirical approach to history, which was articulated decisively in English thought by Locke's work on the New Testament.[39]

In his effort to discover the events of biblical history, Boyle was convinced that reality, and not merely consciousness, was historical. Like Bacon, he was bent on recovering what was original. He presupposed the creation as a definite yet tensed historical order established by the Creator and providentially directed.

Accordingly, he showed the liberation built into the modern presupposition of God's transcendence (and power) by criticizing those who bound the style and meaning of Scripture to rhetorical rules. He protested against such "frothy censurers," for ". . . it became not the majesty of God to suffer himself to be fettered to human laws of method."[40] Identifying God as a free and legislating sovereign, he pressed the point:

> Moreover, there being many portions of Scripture, as almost the whole four last books of Moses, wherein God is introduced as either immediately or mediately giving laws to his people, or his worshippers, I suppose it will not be thought necessary, that such parts of Scripture should be eloquently written, and that the *supreme legislator of the world*, who reckons the greatest kings amongst his subjects, should, in giving laws, tye himself to those of rhetorick; the scrupulous observation of which would much derogate from those two qualities, so considerable in laws, clearness and majesty.

This criticism was directed against not only classical Aristotelian rhetoric, but also the sixteenth-century Ramistic method, which had proved particularly attractive to the Puritans. Appealing to God's freedom and majesty, Boyle cleared the ground for a more empirical historical sense of the Scriptural text. [41]

Going beyond Bacon's preference for biblical texts as opposed to dogma, Boyle sought to recover the original text in the original biblical languages. He moved from Stallbridge to Oxford in 1652 not simply out of interest in the new natural philosophy and for financial reasons, but also to seek instruction in the Hebrew language. He cultivated this interest in his trips to the continent and his friendship with a group of rabbis in Amsterdam. [42] While his historical inquiry did not equal the more extensive chronological and exegetical inquiries of Newton, his *Style of Scriptures* did issue some reflective statements upon the nature and importance of distinct historical inquiry. This effort exemplifies the self-consciousness of early modern beginnings of historical study.

Boyle insisted that the study of Scripture must make at least three careful distinctions. First, one must carefully determine who is speaking and to whom the subject is speaking. Secondly, one must sort out the different kinds of material in the Scripture. Thirdly, and most significantly, one must distinguish between what is being said in Scripture and what the Scripture itself says. [43] It was precisely the latter search for the kernel of Scripture, the primitive historical sense, which became so significant in the course of the modern epoch. History became that which indicates individual events in the past, and not simply the witness of ancient luminaries.

Moreover, in his pursuit of the historical sense of Scripture Boyle stressed that Scripture was "everywhere written with as much eloquence as the chief author." The infinitely manifold design of God was evident in the rich variety of biblical texts, and in their adaptability for different religious uses.

> But as a skillful fowler . . . according to the differing natures of his game, so contrives and appropriates his stratagems, that some he catches with light, (as larks with day-nets;) some with baits, (pigeons) some with frights (black-birds) and some he draws in with company (ducks, sociable birds) so God knowing that some persons must be wrought upon by reason, others allured by interest, some driven in by terrors, and others again brought in by invitation, hath by a rare and merciful (if I may so

call it) suppleness of wisdom so varied the heavenly doctrines
into ratiocinations, mysteries, promises, threats, and examples, that there is not any sort of people, that in the Scripture
may not find religion represented in that form they are most
disposed to receive impressions from; God therein graciously
dealing with his children not unlike the prophet, that shrunk
himself into the proportion of the child he meant to revive.

This text is important not simply because it continued the
Augustinian and Reformation affirmation of divine accommodation, nor even because it gave such vivid evidence of the cre-
ational content with which Boyle understood that accommodation.[44] Most significant was the way the immense variety of
Scriptural material was tailored to fit individual needs of diverse Christians in particular circumstances. The distinctive
English development of the "uses" of Scripture was also apparent in the sensitivity to particular meanings of biblical texts in
diverse contexts shown in the common Puritan and Anglican
compendia of "cases" of conscience. In promoting Robert Sanderson's definitive *Cases of Conscience* (1678) as well as in his
own practice, Boyle manifested appreciation of Scriptural variety and individuality.[45] The particularities of history became a
distinct consideration for both reading and understanding the
writing of Scripture.

In sum, Boyle's critique of rhetorical traditions, his affirmation of a theology of creation as history, his instructions toward
determining the exact historical sense, and his emphasis upon
the variety of Scripture in its diverse uses, as well as initial
reflection about historical consciousness, amounts to a real
contribution to the unique differentiation of historical inquiry in
the modern epoch. It was not highly original, yet Boyle
exemplified and anticipated the more visible and substantial
contributions of Spinoza and Locke.

In literary terms, modern differentiation of consciousness
was eventually realized in the novel. Although the novel was not
established as a genre until the late eighteenth century, literary
historians have generally held that it appeared in the works of
Defoe and Richardson. Ian Watt, for example, argues that certain philosophical assumptions from Descartes to Locke and an
eighteenth-century middle-class social setting were essential to
literary elements of the novel. Others have found its elements
in earlier eighteenth-century popular fiction. In this context, it

is interesting that Dr. Johnson judged Boyle's *Martyrdom of Theodora and Didymus* as a predecessor of the novel.[46]

The appearance of the unique and formative religious genre of narrative history in the struggles between the ancient Hebrews and their many opponents presupposed the agency of Yahweh, the God who acts. This genre — e.g. Exodus — was as decisive for Old Testament literature as the unique genre of the gospel, which presupposed God's presence in Christ, was for early Christian life and literature. Similarly, early medieval Christendom, which presupposed the Eternal Being of God, was partly shaped by the (Augustinian) genre of confessional autobiography, a deepening of personal being in the context of divine Being.[47]

By the seventeenth century, however, the most basic and widespread presupposition of literary consciousness (and eventually of the novel) was the reality of particulars. Individual characters had their own memories, decisions, and projects, and careful attention to particular circumstances in time and space allowed for complex dialogues. The techniques of plot and 'point of view replaced an omniscient perspective. These elements stood in contrast to presentations of individuals as illustrations of general principles as in the medieval *Everyman*.

Although Boyle's *Martyrdom* is a didactic piece intended to exhibit the virtue of constancy and the duty of obedience, it does convey an impression of God as Author and Lord. Debating the morality of suffering, and attempting to decide his own destiny, Didymus says that,

> The sovereign author and absolute Lord of our lives having thought fit to employ us here in his service, we cannot, without violating our duty to him, desert it, until we have performed his errand, which is, to glorify him by our lives, till loyalty to his truth, or his commands, convince us, that we may better glorify him by our deaths.[48]

It is precisely in relation to this supreme Individual that the submission to martyrdom of Theodora and Didymus takes on real significance. After Theodora patiently accepts her suffering and impending death, Didymus must decide whether or not he should take her place, allowing her to escape, or follow the counsel of prudence. His choice of obedience to Christ is not assured, for even when he decides to take her place there is the possibility that God will intervene at the last minute, as He did with Daniel.[49] This emphasis on God's will, fundamental to Boyle, reinforces the notion that the literary characters are real individuals.

Moreover, in his Preface to the *Martyrdom*, Boyle proposed that his reconstruction of this ancient Roman legend aimed to go beyond mere recital or the chronicling "of a mere historian." He also sought to distinguish his piece from current revivals of scholasticism in "some better meant, than penned, books of theology and devotion."[50] This critical reflection upon the weakness of older genres may be interpreted as an early manifestation of that differentiation of consciousness which was realized in the novel. Linked with the anticipations of individuality in the characterization of the *Martyrdom*, this work is loosely representative of early modern differentiation in literary consciousness.

Boyle represented the early modern differentiation of religion much more fully than that of historical and literary consciousness. To see this, one must carefully distinguish the seventeenth-century attitude from both its sixteenth-century sources and eighteenth-century developments in the meaning of religion. Since Calvin saw religion as virtually coextensive with the entire edifice of Christian theology, he did not trace or develop the religious "seeds of divinity" he claimed were present in all men. Like Paul, he could simply cite such seeds to show that all men were ultimately guilty of sin against God. In the *Institutes*, where Calvin elaborated a full correlation between the wisdom (*sapientia*) of God and oneself, religion was very broadly understood. However, during the eighteenth century, after "other" religions had been widely discovered in primitive and new world cultures, religion itself became virtually coextensive with an entire human system of belief in God or the gods. This trend was most visible in deism and subsequent searches for the rational essence of religion.[51]

In contrast, religion in the seventeenth century was chiefly theistic. Yet it was clearly differentiated from the entire edifice of normative Christian theology (or philosophy). Henceforth, one could appeal to religion in either dogmatic or apologetic theology, for religion per se was, at best, coextensive with theism. Or, to put it concretely, religion was oriented to the

Creator and His work of creation rather than to *all* of God's works (Calvin), or *none* (deism). Strictly speaking, deism pointed to an original divine making which was then abandoned; in effect it gave up the continual working of God central to classic Christianity.

The theistic differentiation of religion from the hegemony of the Reformation heritage — not to mention its liberation from hierarchical medieval theology and the wholistic "Christian philosophy" of Spiritualism — was exemplified in Boyle. Although he did advance apologies for distinctive Christian beliefs, such as resurrection, his most frequent apologies were against "atheistic" Epicureanism. These arguments were apologies for theism, but they were also outright celebrations of the beauty and design of God's workmanship in creation.[52] Boyle's many elaborate statements of the teleological argument were diversely directed appeals to *religion*, which was neither divorced from nor wholly determined by theology. A similar differentiation was taking place in natural philosophy. Religion was the source but not necessarily the norm of theological systems in the seventeenth century, but it was not removed to one among many areas of human belief, as in the eighteenth century. Indeed, the sense of reform depended on a religion of creation and new creation that was a central presupposition of seventeenth-century cultural activity.

Yet religion stood at the center of seventeenth-century culture in a different mode from its presence in the sixteenth century. For Calvin, religion was "piety," which signified man's manifold yet inerasable relation to God as well as the chief locus (in conscience) of man's culpable idolatry. This, in turn, required the repair of redemption, relating man to the fullness of God as Creator and Redeemer. In contrast, the seventeenth-century differentiation of God's works of creation and redemption liberated not only "natural philosophy" but also "natural religion" (not from theology per se, but from traditional and contemporary forms of theological hegemony).

However, the conception of "natural religion" did not appear until after the 1670's — in later eighteenth-century usages, it was opposed to "revealed religion."[53] In the preceding decades, and indeed as early as Bacon, its emergence was gradually presaged by what we may call creation piety. As the inner side of the optimistic sense of reform, it inspired widespread cultural activity. It was not, however, freighted with the desire for salvation intrinsic to the Reformers' far more inclusive understanding of religion as piety. In short, theistic liberation also took place *within* religion. Henceforth creation piety was distinct although not separated from pious desires for salvation.

Of course, a conviction of the creature's desire to worship His Creator and both use and enjoy His handiwork was no seventeenth-century invention. Frequently manifest in Western Christianity, it was prominent in aesthetic orientations to creation expressed by many Renaissance thinkers as well as Calvin and Helmontian Spiritualism. In the thought of Bacon, Boyle, and many other seventeenth-century figures, however, this kind of piety acquired a distinct integrity and direction of its·own.[54] Supported by voluntarist anthropological presuppositions, the differentiation of God's works of creation and redemption, and a sharp differentiation between the books of nature and Scripture, a pronounced individualizing turn in Puritan and Anglican meditation shaped and was shaped by powerful religious genres which rendered the differentiation of creation piety very concrete. Crucial to the cultivation of practical religious life among Puritans and Anglicans was the attention given to individual piety in "spiritual meditations" or "Reflections." The process of their formation and repetition was known as "spiritualizing." Characteristically brief, Reflections began with a short protasis which served as the occasion for the subsequent apodosis or "improvement." Izaak Walton's Reflections, occasioned by angling, were typical, as were the biblically based exhortations of Boyle's friend, Bishop Hall.[55]

In part, these meditative Reflections were a popular extension of the practice of preaching, which was formalized by the Puritans into two steps. Doctrine was drawn from the biblical text and then applied to practical use. Whereas individuals had formerly been expected to come to an established (Protestant or Roman Catholic) Church to be faithfully fed, many churches now bent their efforts to the particular needs of diverse individuals. Despite Luther's appeal to conscience, the sixteenth-century Reformation had only begun this process; it was left to seventeenth-century Puritans and Anglicans to systematize personal Bible reading, keep diaries of God's providences, and practice specific meditations which outfitted the pilgrim's disciplined progress through earthly life. This represented a new atomizing of religious consciousness.[56]

Boyle's *Occasional Reflections upon Several Subjects*, a typical example of the relatively new genre, was first published with his *Discourse touching Occasional Meditations* and was more frequently reprinted than his visible works in natural philosophy. Advancing a two-fold employment of religious meditations, Boyle argued that the chief "religious use" of such meditations resided in their power to instruct men in what to imitate and what to avoid. Thus his observation that the moon was a conveyor rather than source of light afforded a comparison for human prosperity, preachers of the Gospel, and the bountiful person who receives his largess from the exuberant goodness of God.[57]

Generally, the protases of Boyle's *Reflections* expressed the ways of creation rather than incidents in biblical history. Although he went so far as to apologize for the lack of positive divinity in his meditations, he argued that the whole creation is a pulpit designed by the divine Author to nurture individual piety. Criticizing the "ancients and scholastiks" who, insofar as they practiced such meditation, quickly passed over the protasis into the apodosis, he urges the pious reader to dwell upon, adore, and be instructed by God's book of creation:

> He that can (as it were) make the world vocal, by furnishing every creature, and almost every occurrence, with a tongue to entertain him with, and can make the little accidents of his life, and the very flowers of his garden, read him lectures of ethicks or divinity; such a one, I say, shall scarce need to fly to the tavern.[58]

These meditations have a "religious use" as vehicles for creation piety differentiated from more complete meanings of piety.

Boyle also stressed their secondary use in improving the power and attentiveness of the mind. This is closely related to Boyle's recommendation of empirical attentiveness in natural philosophy:

> For, in the first place, it accustoms a man to an attentive observation of the objects, wherewith he is conversant. . . . The themes we undertake to handle, unperceivably ingage us to pry into the several attributes and relations of the things we con-

sider, to obtain the greater plenty of particulars, for the making up of the more full and compleat parallel betwixt the things, whose resemblances we would set forth.

Besides that though we should at first apply our headfulness to circumstances of only some few sorts of objects; yet the habit being once acquired, would easily reach to others than those that first occasioned it.[59]

Another description of the power of meditations to induce attentiveness explicitly goes beyond the Spiritualist fascination with hieroglyphics.

But the practice I have all this while been recommending, does not only dispose us to attention, in observing the things that occur to us, and accustom us to reflect on them seriously, and express them fitly; but does also, though insensibly, suggest to us ways and methods; whereby to make the object we consider informative to us.

For by example, analogy, or some of those other ways, which we may be invited, on another occasion, to insist on, we are, as it were, led by the hand to the discovery of divers useful notions, especially practical, which else we should not take any notice of. And indeed the world is the great book, not so much of nature, as of the God of nature, which we should find even crouded with instructive lessons, if we had but the skill, and would take the pains, to extract and pick them out. The creatures are the true Ægyptian hieroglyphicks, that under the rude forms of birds, and beasts, etc. conceal the mysterious secrets of knowledge, and of piety.

Such meditations also provide unanticipated instruction. Boyle noted the

unexpectedness of the things that please us. . . . We need not in this case, as in most others, make an uneasy preparation to entertain our instructors; for our instructions are suddenly, and, as it were out of an ambuscade, shot into our mind from things, whence we never expected them, so that we receive the advantage of learning good lessons, without the trouble of going to school for them, . . . the informations we receive from many creatures, and occurrences, are oftentimes, extremely distant from what, one would conjecture to be the most obvious, and natural thoughts those themes are fitted to present us.[60]

Finally, though Boyle used meditations expressive of creation piety for scientific discipline, he was not bound to that practice. Unlike Helmont, who derived natural philosophy from

Genesis, Boyle was open even to the instructive power of created design. Creation piety could have a scientific or a more specifically religious (and ethical) benefit.

In sum, Boyle's thought typified a complex transitional stage of the differentiation of religion. A specific creation piety mediated between a more complete Reformation piety and Enlightenment convictions of religion as human belief. An orientation to a distinct Creator succeeded earlier worship of the absolutely unavoidable immensity of the One Creator-Redeemer, preparing the way for later deistic venerations of Deity at a safe distance. The genre of "occasional meditations" was at the center of this development, which tempered the reign of established preaching and eventually led to the essentially moral-philosophical reflections of the deists.

Toward Natural Science:
Early Modern Differentiation of Knowledge

In mapping the spread of modern self-differentiation in the areas of history, literature, and religion, the parallel differentiation of natural philosophy has been noted. The driving modern tendency was to promote many differentiated works. Moreover, just as, for example, beginning differentiation in religious consciousness and disciplines proliferated, so too an increasing differentiation took place within natural philosophy. This involved the generation of increasingly complex and individuated structures of mind and discipline. Many "natural sciences" were the eventual outcome.

This particular phenomenon, the proliferation of differentiation within early modern natural philosophy, is exemplified in Boyle's work.[61] It is also a part, albeit a central part, of the widespread seventeenth-century structure and sense of differentiation which presupposed the distinctive efficacy of early modern theology. As the most common component in the advent of science — modernity — proceeded on this basis other relatively new components, such as ideas of nature and knowledge, also took hold. By focusing upon the component of knowledge, the significance of distinctive early modern theology can be shown. At the same time a portion of the dense passage from traditional natural philosophy to many specific natural sciences can be charted. Seventeenth-century practice in natural philosophy was a turning point in this passage.

Boyle advanced Bacon's differentiation of natural philosophy by developing what he called, variously, mechanical, corpuscular, and atomic natural philosophy. The epochally novel epistemological dimension of this life-long project can be seen in four features of Boyle's work. He differentiated chemistry and medicine, developed a carefully delimited experimental chemistry, including the distinctive genre of the laboratory report, differentiated a critical reflective philosophy of science, and advocated the distinct integrity of empirical knowledge in a time of considerable longing for the rule of reason alone.

Boyle did not, however, establish chemistry as one of many mature "natural sciences." For neither chemistry nor the concept of "natural sciences" was established until the eighteenth century. But differentiation of the discipline was representative of the general phenomenon of increasing differentiation of knowledge. This has frequently been neglected or short-circuited by reading in later concepts of "natural science," "mechanism," "revolution," and "secularization." Both the passing of the old and the emergence of the new took place under the complex, yet loosening, canopy of natural philosophy.

In seeking to fashion a distinctly critical conception of chemistry, Boyle was deeply unsatisfied with both Spiritualist fusions and scholastic incorporations. Although his *Sceptical Chemist* did not establish the seminal body of chemical theory that was essential to a fuller and later differentiation of chemistry as a natural science, his attack on the "spagyrists" and scholastics did chart the way. Boyle argued that Helmont's very approach as a "philologer" of Scripture, from which a fusion of natural philosophy, medicine, and chemistry (as well as theology) derived, should not bind natural philosophy. He was particularly critical of his grand claims on water as the universal material source and his equally sweeping appeals to the mysterious "alkahest."[62] Elsewhere, he scored the "irreverance" of Helmont's direct argument from Providence to the healing of diseases. Like Bacon, Boyle did not rule out the significance of Jesus as a model for the work of the physician, but he did sever the tie between natural philosophy and a cosmic or spiritual christology of the Great Physician. He was equally critical of the scholastics.[63]

Boyle's critical effort to differentiate chemistry was also clear in his defense of his own theories of the elasticity and weight of air. He sought to undercut the objections of Franciscus Linus by showing the irrelevance of the latter's appeal to the philosophy of essence in Thomas and Suarez. Diverse ontological and voluntaristic theological presuppositions were in conflict here, and for Boyle a beginning of relatively autonomous chemistry vs. its incorporation in Aristotelian natural philosophy was also involved. Boyle questions the intelligibility of Linus' "funicular" hypothesis, which turns upon the strange possibility of substantial rarefaction — strange because this would be an aerial "substance" without place or space. Then Boyle considers Linus' view that such a substance is possible by the miraculous power of God. Insisting that he is "willing to adore" God's omnipotence, Boyle appeals both to the "ordinary course of nature" which can neither create nor annihilate itself, i.e., creation ordered by God's law, and to physical matter, rather than "*divinitus* (as he speaks)" in bodies. For Boyle both the discipline of inquiry and the reality of that which is physical are sharply differentiated.[64]

Although, from one perspective, Helmont *fused* natural philosophy, chemistry, and so on, from another equally valid perspective, he *expanded* chemistry. For his "Christian natural philosophy" was also a grand "chemical philosophy." Chemical inquiry was enlarged to ultimate significance for medical treatment, pyrochemical analysis, and a grand synthesis of the ways of God, man, and the cosmos. For a brief intense time, chemistry was seen as the "key" to both natural philosophy and divinity until Boyle's more representative and many-sided critique. Henceforth, chemistry was not to be confused with theology because God was the Author, not the Spirit of creation. Congruently, the universality of the doctrine of matter as water gave way as chemical processes were seen to be but one part of a new conception of natural philosophy.

Without Boyle's lifelong practice of careful experimentation — a practice which implied that as much significance should be given to the weight of particular experiments as concepts of nature — his critique would have been ineffective. Whereas Helmont's experimentation was intrinsically related to his entire wholistic enterprise, Boyle granted each particular experiment — not excepting those of Helmont — a distinct integrity. There was room to differentiate experiment and theory. His chemistry — indeed his thought in general — was far more discriminating than that of the Spiritualists.[65]

Boyle's epochal contribution here was the advancement of carefully differentiated scientific writing, namely, the laboratory report. Much of his writing can be characterized as careful reporting in chemistry and pneumatics, noteworthy for its exact descriptions.[66] In addition, his reflective piece on scientific literature, *Proemial Essay with some Considerations touching Experimental Essays in general*, differentiated particular "experimental essays" from other genres. He argued that whole systems of natural philosophy which required a complete expression in books suppressed valuable particulars, inflated a few topics into a whole system, and succumbed to rules of method at the price of investigation into "things themselves." Gassendi was exempt from this judgment, but Descartes fell partly under its weight. The systems and writings of Campanella and Aristotle received especially pointed censure. He held that earlier "chemists" padded their inquiries with endless quotations and testimonies. Ultimately, they fell prey to the rhetorical model which substituted "exotic words and terms borrowed from other languages" for sober inquiry. Boyle did not name his opponents, but his derogation of their German and "Hermetical language" indicates criticism of the Spiritualists, perhaps the Paracelsians. In any case, only accuracy of description could justify long sentences and parentheses.[67]

Although Boyle noted that his own inquiries were initially intended to complete Bacon's classificatory natural history, he concluded that Bacon's *Sylva Sylvarum* was simply a good beginning. It was not thoroughly experimental, for while "attention alone might quickly furnish us with one half of the history of nature, . . . industry is requisite, by new experiments, to enrich us with the other." When experimentation was institutionalized in the Royal Society, Boyle's great influence supported experimental inquiry in particular disciplines rather than a mere continuation of Bacon's program, which was supported by the "empiricks" in the Society.[68]

The most sophisticated presentation of Boylean differentiation *within* natural philosophy can be found in his reflective philosophy of science. Although not original, his general caution was epochally different from that of Helmont, who did not differentiate the purpose, method, and subject matter of his vast natural philosophy. Boyle repeatedly examined the various genres of scientific activity and advocated the laboratory report in contrast to natural histories, deductive systems of natural philosophy, and Helmont's divine chemistry based upon Scriptural exegesis. In *A Free Inquiry into the Vulgarly received Notion of Nature*, he analyzed both scholastic and Spiritualist concepts of nature, providing a catalogue of philosophic and linguistic meanings of "nature" from Aristotle to his own time. Deeply critical of traditional ideas of nature as "notions," he presupposed an economical theological concept of nature as creation and re-employed the concept of nature in a limited way.[69]

Boyle also gave much attention to the idea of method, which became a general topic of special interest in early modern philosophy of science. His *Requirements of a Good and Excellent Hypothesis* argued that hypotheses must both comprehend relevant experimental data and be fruitful in suggesting further conclusions. Extending Bacon's criterion of hypotheses limited to the function of comprehension, Boyle's move from "good" to "excellent" hypotheses enlarged the power of method per se. Later Newton's Rules of Reasoning in Philosophy, especially his concern for simplicity in the Third Rule, reinforced this development toward a method that would enable prediction.[70]

In his *Disquisition about the Final Causes of Natural Things: Wherein it is inquired, Whether, and (if at all) with what Cautions, a Naturalist should admit them*, Boyle's approach was guarded so as not to hamper the chief experimental search for efficient causes. His carefully defined acceptance of particular final causes, God's "hidden" ends in creation, not only shows his methodological acuity, but also expresses a somewhat different theological orientation than that of Descartes. Both appeal initially to theological considerations for their respective positive and negative answers on admitting final causes in natural philosophy, but Boyle charges that Descartes' flat prohibition honors only the power of God at the expense of His goodness and wisdom, all of which are known, not per se, but as expressed in His creation. Replying to Descartes' claim that it is presumptuous to argue from God's ends, Boyle says that it is more presumptuous to argue from God's immutability that of necessity man can know no divine ends in nature.[71] It is clear that Boyle wishes to protect both the freedom of God and the radical contingency of creation. God may and does publish Himself in creation, and the mind's relation to God and creation is more contingent and experimental than necessary.

On the basis of a theology keyed to divine will and design, a theology which is open to dialectical relations between God and the world in which the distinct integrity of the creation is affirmed, Boyle advances a series of four general divine ends. These are God's own universal self-expression, the designed creation per se, the fittingness of animals and their environments, and the polarity of the non-human creation made for man's sake while at the same time man is made to have dominion over that creation. These ends are sufficiently general to constitute no serious impediment to experimental mechanical philosophy, the search for efficient causes.[72]

However, Boyle also speaks of some particular final causes in nature that are not hidden. His arguments here are neither restrained nor abstract. In analyzing his chief example, the eye, he dwells not on its general function in vision, but, rather, upon the concrete variety of creation it illumines.[73] He has so clearly differentiated between piety and science that he can affirm a pious or religious "use" of natural phenomena, much as he can reverse his field and accept a scientific or experimental "use" of the world as God's creation. This comports with the self-consciousness of his religious apology for the *Usefulness of Natural Philosophy*, and his scientific apology for the *Excellency of Theology*. In short, *Final Causes* may be read both as a kind of religious Reflection setting forth the heart of a teleological argument of great power given the presupposition of a Creator-Author of an indirectly revelatory creation, and as a careful exercise in methodological discrimination which shows the highest respect for experimentally searching out efficient causes. Boyle's achievement of a sustained differentiation of consciousness was considerable.

Boyle's emphasis on the concrete objects and process of empirical knowledge and on a balance of reason and experiment was not original. More prone to rational reconstruction than Bacon, he was less committed than Newton to mathematics, although he affirmed its validity and use. Nor did he take up the highly reflexive epistemological task of justifying empirical knowledge according to the primacy of clear and distinct ideas (Descartes) or simple ideas (Locke). Boyle's thought was more plainly representative of the growing empirical tradition than such extended ventures.[74] In general he was content with an affirmation of the validity of reason, experiment, hypothesis, and, most strongly, knowledge of particular phenomena. Yet this view of knowledge was also guided at a distance by a definite theology, primarily voluntaristic, but also aesthetically attuned to creation.

Bacon's moral/religious focus on enabling the will to know creation aright was extended in Newton's notion of a virtual theological duty to experimentally study creation contingent upon God's will but also manifesting His design. For Newton, no "short-cut" through divine Ideas or Spirit, necessary or sufficient reason, was possible in creation ruled by the will of its supreme Author and Lord. Roger Cotes' statement in the Preface to the second edition of the *Principia* puts it well:

> Without all doubt this world, so diversified with that variety of forms and motions we find in it, could arise from nothing but the perfectly free will of God directing and presiding over all.
>
> From this fountain it is that those laws, which we call the laws of Nature, have flowed, in which there appear many traces indeed of the most wise contrivance, but not the least shadow of necessity. These therefore we must not seek from uncertain conjectures, but learn them from observations and experiments. He who is presumptuous enough to think that he can find the true principles of physics and the laws of natural things by the force alone of his own mind, and the internal light of his reason, must either suppose that the world exists by necessity, and by the same necessity follows the laws proposed; or if the order of Nature was established by the will of God, that himself, a miserable reptile, can tell what was fittest to be done. All sound and true philosophy is founded on

the appearances of things; and if these phenomena inevitably draw us, against our wills, to such principles as most clearly manifest to us the most excellent counsel and supreme dominion of the All-wise and Almighty Being, they are not therefore to be laid aside because some men may perhaps dislike them.[75]

Besides his own interest in natural theology, Cotes was opposing experimental or empirical inquiry into the laws of nature imposed by divine will to the presumptuousness of rationalistic exercises of reason. It is likely that Newton would have agreed.

However, more than a moral point was involved. As Koyré has shown, Newton's representative, Samuel Clarke, would not grant Leibnitz's "principle of sufficient reason" in explaining God's relations to creation. The Newtonian presupposition of God's freedom and the contingency of creation ruled out a rational necessity of creation. For Newton this meant less confidence in speculative reason, despite the demands of strict consistency. Leibnitz, on the other hand, presupposed that man rationally participates in divine ideas. Accordingly, he did not resist the weight of "sufficient reason" in inquiring into both the ways of God and man with respect to creation.[76]

Equally significant, Newton did *not* follow More in affirming the "divinity of reason," despite their lifelong common concern for God's presence in nature. Like Boyle, he insisted upon an essentially experimental and hypothetical exercise of reason in natural philosophy. Attention to the appearances of particular phenomena was emphasized, and the exercise of necessary reason, presupposing participation in the divine Mind, was denied. Both the "divine reason" of More and the "sufficient reason" of Leibnitz represented a fundamentally different orientation to creation than the voluntarism of Newton and Boyle.

Thus, the turn to extended experimental study of concrete processes (and laws) was not a sheer conversion from the darkness of theological knowledge to the light of man's knowledge of the world. Contrary to the secularization thesis, it was a shift from knowing the world in its (hierarchical) place to knowing the creation more simply yet reliably dependent upon the will of God. Most dramatically, it was a turn from knowing the world in God and God in the world (Spiritualism) to a transcendent human knowing of the same creation transcended by the

Creator. Rather than a world formed by the logos and moved by the Spirit, it was a world ruled by law.

Boyle's understanding of this point is evident in a remarkable passage from his *Excellency of Theology*. Both the basic doctrines of Christianity and the entire budding edifice of the new science are located within a framework that is both unmistakably theological and a kind of "universal hypothesis":

> Neither the fundamental doctrine of Christianity, nor that of the powers and effects of matter and motion, seems to be more than an epicycle (if I may so call it) of the great and universal system of God's contrivances, and makes but a part of the more general theory of things, knowable by the light of nature, improved by the information of the Scriptures: so that both these doctrines, though very general, in respect of the subordinate parts of theology and philosophy, seem to be but members of the universal hypothesis, whose objects I conceive to be the nature, counsels, and works of God, as far as they are discoverable by us (for I say not to us) in this life.[77]

Boyle's theology was on the whole keyed to will rather than reason or spirit. In turn, a theology that took little for granted even in man's knowledge of God apart from His work was manifest throughout his understanding of empirical knowledge. For in this theological context more than hypotheses were enhanced. The act of "attention," an empirical waiting upon concrete processes, was stressed. The duty of dealing with particular phenomena entailed discipline which never strayed from the experimental tests they afforded. Finally, the search for positive laws was based on the presupposition that God's will was published in creation as a lawful order. This assumption was also paramount in Boylean empirical knowledge. In short, hypotheses, attention, the search for particulars, and laws of nature were all part and parcel of a new empirical way of knowing indebted to a critical (and carefully constructive) voluntarist theology of creation.

A basic contrast may be helpful here. For the venerable Augustinian tradition knowing consisted of *participation* in the known, an activity reinforced by the primacy of *sapientia* (wisdom). This tradition was altered in the Thomistic emphasis upon *scientia*, in which the activity of knowing consisted of *abstracting* the forms of things. Both these traditions presupposed the logos of being, a knowledge of implicit rational structures of being. This ontological orientation of knowledge was reinforced by the high value of contemplative knowledge, which genuinely symbolized the theology of Being in all things. The presupposition that the order of knowing followed that of being was basic.[78]

When Boyle and Bacon, like Descartes, reversed this traditional order, a venture of knowing itself emerged. As practical and experimental knowledge gained primacy in use and value over contemplative knowledge, the very activity of knowing acquired an integrity of its own. Henceforth, this activity closely approximated making or reconstruction rather than participation or abstraction.[79] In this epochally new order the directing if not spontaneous significance of will, which presupposed the often distant yet all-powerful will of God, disregarded the old maxim that the will moves according to the last dictate of understanding. Sharp distinctions between Creator and creation and man and world were also manifest between knower and known. A new field for individual will emerged.

The problem of skepticism attended this modern view of knowledge. In emphasizing the gap between knower and known, the transcendence of the external world in the modern activity of knowing, the practical question of a genuine relation of knowing was acute.[80] This issue was prominent in the conversion accounts of major figures in natural philosophy, and the divergent paths chosen by Descartes, Helmont, and Bacon were deeply instructive.

Descartes gave a truly radical answer to skepticism through highly mathematical reason, and Helmont gave a quite different yet equally radical answer by calling man to be immersed in the senses and the understanding. Not surprisingly, Descartes presupposed a certain relation between mind and extended reality, to wit, the God who would not deceive man, while Helmont presupposed an equally reliable although very different kind of total intimacy between "Spiritual understanding," the seeds of creation, and the Creator-Spirit. For Bacon, however, the sensible answer to skepticism was control over, rather than resting in, things. Thus a limited reliance on reason was necessary. Both sense and reason were relativized; they were rendered probable both in their mutual relations and their external relations to matter and ideas. In effect, Bacon outflanked skepticism with a complex realm of knowledge in which most of its constituent elements had some voice. This partly politicizing conceptual response led to a considerable difference between the Helmontian passion for truth in natural philosophy and the modern English preference for hypotheses.[81]

Although Bacon, like Helmont, insists on the necessity of charity and humility for natural philosophy, he sees these only as religious/moral preconditions, initial "cleansings" of the mind, so that the power of knowledge may be released. Thus the simultaneity of piety and science in Helmont differs profoundly from their differentiation and ordered succession in Bacon.

In general Boyle followed Bacon's response to skepticism. For he sought to balance the claims of sense and reason, theory and experiment, law and hypothesis, even though his thought on these specific topics was considerably more sophisticated than that of Bacon. Boyle's typical witness to differentiated empirical knowledge stood in sharp contrast to Helmont, and in a mild contrast to Descartes.

Boyle shared with Helmont a belief in the divine and humane purposes of knowledge. He also respected Helmont's focus on concrete objects of knowledge and experimental production.[82] However, Boyle showed none of Helmont's rejection of reason, and very little of his passion for empirical immediacy, and inner certainty — all of which ultimately presupposed a sweeping identification of knower and known. It was precisely these distinctive features of Helmont's empiricism, which, in turn, were most intimately related to his Spiritualist theology, that Boyle left behind. For Boyle, objects of knowledge were discrete as well as concrete. Atoms could not be "understood" (like seeds), but in basic lawful combinations they admitted knowledge subject to testability. Although he stressed "attention" to the "instruction" of concrete things, it was precisely his presupposition of distance between knower and known that led him (unlike Helmont) to praise the surprising knowledge that could come from particular phenomena. The appearance (appearing) of empirical reality for Boyle was far more important than an immediate awareness of hidden truths or an abstraction of formal causes. Furthermore, the task of fashioning positive laws, as well as hypotheses, was a distinct part of this venture. In short, Boyle's approach broke up the coherent wholism of Spiritualism, advocating instead a relative tolerance of hypotheses, a constant balancing of fact and theory, experiment and reason.

The orientation toward balance, Boyle's working reply to the passion for completeness in Spiritualism, was also manifest in a relative but important difference between Boyle and Descartes. Less inclined to *oppose* the self as thinking substance to extended external reality, Boyle's attention to the design and particular variety of creation softened the dualistic tendencies of Cartesianism. Creation was the work of the divine Author; it was not solely a work of sheer will. Hence, Descartes' dichotomy of spectator-like observation and ideal mathematical reconstruction was modulated to express greater respect for the variety of phenomena; the "texture" of appearances was respected. Boyle favored a variety of mechanical, legal, and chemical constructs rather than the single ideal of mathematical purity. Descartes tended to exploit differentiation, whereas Boyle tended to extend it. In this respect, he was typical of the seventeeth-century English appreciation of Descartes at a distance.[83]

In sum, an alternative interpretation to success stories of the sciences and fall stories of religion has been sketched. Rather than outright revolution or sheer secularization, the modern reformations of natural philosophy that led to the natural sciences were part of a manifold process of development in many disciplines that exhibited a structure of increasing differentiation and individuation. The novel systematic feature of this development, apparent in the idea of nature, will be discussed in Chapter 6.

CHAPTER FIVE:

Boyle's Theology of Creation

In the rise of modern natural science, a lively sense of re-form clearly presupposed early modern theology. Indeed, the very structure and process of modernity, at least in its initial stages, was also indebted to a theology which featured tran-scendence, differentiation, and individuality. All of this is evi-dent not only in the analytically distinguishable component of modernity, but also in that of knowledge. The modern reversal of the conviction that knowing must follow being presupposed transcendent otherness between God and man, knower and known. Henceforth the integrity of knowing was no longer cen-tered in participation or identification; knowing itself became a temporal project, a search for the known in many different ways. Many carefully differentiated and systematic epis-temological pursuits were henceforth underwritten by the sovereign Will, rather than by the eternal Being, of God. In-deed, a third component, the idea of nature expressed in this new orientation, also presupposed a modern theology of creation.

So far I have concentrated on showing the critical significance of this theological orientation, which was most ob-vious in voluntarist currents of thought. Systematically, the critical edge of such theology was most prominent in the convic-tion of transcendent otherness expressed in both divine and human relations to the world. However, the formal critical significance of this modern orientation also included a definite positive guidance. Belief in the transcendent Creator was a directing as well as a critical principle for understanding nature in the new science, even though its positive significance tended to be more regulative than sheerly executive. In largely voluntarist modern thought belief in the Creator was indirectly efficacious in an epochally new view of nature. This development was opposed to Spiritualist appeals to the immediate significance of the divine creative Spirit in nature itself.

However, the predominant modern orientation did involve mediating principles functionally similar to those which were effective in other Western times of intensified belief in the critical significance of divine transcendence. For example, although ancient Israel affirmed the transcendence of Yahweh, before whom no other gods had power and who was not to be set forth in images, the Law of Yahweh was definitive in the formation of ancient Hebrew culture and its opposition to Caananite culture. The heightened sense of God's transcendence in sixteenth-century Protestantism also called for a new affirmation of God's Word in preaching and Scripture. This implied a definite new shape for Christianity — Protestantism in opposition to Roman Catholicism. Again, centuries earlier Augustine's affirmation of God's Eternal Being was, in turn, conveyed by the powerful early medieval institutions of church orders and a sacramental system. In at least the first two of these examples, the affirmations of divine Law and Word did not compromise God's transcendence but bespoke a relationship between God and man, and among men, that deepened respect for the distance between things finite and infinite.

This general feature of mediating divine transcendence was evident in seventeenth-century theology and culture. This is apparent, for example, in Boyle's carefully controlled modern methodological skepticism. The very discipline of method, a systematic reinforcement of the integrity of knowing, mediated between knower and known. The generation of a new kind of constructive empirical knowledge served to overcome and not merely check common waves of skepticism. Similarly, there was a concomitant mediation of divine transcendence in new ideas of natural order which featured law, design, and mechanical arrangements. However, to grasp the basic positions, questions, and problems in this modern idea of nature, a more detailed accounting of the content of its theological presuppositions is in order. I shall return to the early modern idea of nature in the next chapter.

Boyle's theological (and philosophical) writings — seen in

relation to those of Helmont, Bacon, Newton, and Descartes — show the advent of the modern idea of nature and its basic presuppositions. Although he was an amateur in this area, his lifelong theological labors were fairly representative of the works of such prominent Puritan and Anglican divines as Wilkins and Glanvill, who were closely associated with the Royal Society. Just as Boyle's thought in natural philosophy was highly representative of an emerging early modern scientific consciousness, so too his underlying religious thought was highly representative of powerful common motifs in mid-seventeenth-century English theology.[1]

The Celebratory Mood

Some have seen Boyle primarily as an irenic, even eclectic, thinker, while others have noted his anti-metaphysical, if not skeptical, propensities, and still others have found him exceedingly pious yet drawn into a natural theology which worked against his religious interests.[2] These interpretations are plausible, but they do not get to the fundamental mood which characterized his lifelong work in theology. For Boyle was a vigorously doxological theologian. His delight in the praise of God, especially as Creator, lent shape to his irenicism, rendered his skepticism critical of all that fell short of the "excellency" of God, and characterized even the apologetic defensiveness that did appear in his writings.

The solid authenticity of Boyle's piety, manifest in his entire career, is obvious in Birch's account, notwithstanding its partly legendary flavor:

> He had so profound a veneration for the Deity, that the very name of God was never mentioned by him without a pause and visible stop in his discourse; in which *Sir Peter Pett* who knew him for almost forty years, affirms, that he was so exact, that he did not remember to have observed him once to fail in it.[3]

His doxological religion stressed personal perfection, sanctification, and achievement, as well as cultural reform. Not as optimistic as Bacon, who cited many signs of a new time, Boyle came closer to Newton's veneration of God's greatness as in

ancient Israel. He shared a particular appreciation for David's
exemplary praise of the Creator in the Psalms.

Boyle frequently broke into praise of the mighty Author of
all things. A passage from his early plea for the *Usefulness of
Natural Philosophy* is typical:

> And first, how boundless a power, or rather what an almighti-
> ness is eminently displayed in God's making out of nothing all
> things, and without materials or instruments constructing this
> immense fabrick of the world, whose vastness is such, that
> even what may be proved of it, can scarcely be conceived. . . .
>
> *How manifold are thy works, O Lord; in wisdom hast thou
> made them all.* And therefore I shall content myself to observe in
> general, that, as highly as some naturalists are pleased to value
> their own knowledge, it can at best attain but to understand
> and applaud, not emulate the productions of God.[4]

In his *Style of Scriptures*, which aimed "to celebrate rather than
vindicate the scripture," Boyle's praise of the richness of Scriptural law was epochally different from Enlightenment oppositions of human autonomy and external law and, in particular,
from the great affirmation of the self-legislating power of human
reason which Kant presupposed. Boyle, like the psalmists, took
great delight in God's law:

> This inexhausted fulness occasioned that panegyrical precept
> of the Rabbies concerning the law; הפיך ארי כולי בה *Turn it
> over, and again turn it over, for all is in it.*

He further recommended the practical "experiment" of the
Psalmist, whose *Chaphatz* was the law of the Lord. On translating חפץ, "delight," he noted its Latin rendering both as
voluntas and *studium* and claimed that the Hebrew signified all
these senses, and also

> seems . . . emphatically to signify a study replenished with so
> much delight to the devout and intelligent prosecutors of it,
> that, like the hallelujahs of the blessed, it is at once a duty and
> a pleasure, an exercise and a recompence of piety.[5]

Celebrating God's entire work of creation as well as its law,
Boyle epitomized the mood of many seventeenth-century natural philosophers, especially those who called themselves Christian *virtuosi:*

> If it were seasonable, *Lindamor,* to entertain ourselves but
> with those attributes of God, which are legible or conspicuous

in the creation; we might there discern the admirable traces of such immense power, such unsearchable wisdom, and such exuberant goodness, as may justly ravish us to an amazement at them, rather than a bare admiration of them. And I must needs acknowledge *Lindamor*, that when with bold telescopes I survey the old and newly discovered stars and planets, that adorn the upper region of the world; and when with excellent microscopes I discern, in otherwise invisible objects, the unimitable subtility of nature's curious workmanship; and when, in a word, by the help of anatomical knives, and the light of chymical furnaces, I study the book of nature, and consult the glosses of *Aristotle*, *Epicurus*, *Paracelsus*, *Harvey*, *Helmont*, and other learned expositors of that instructive volume: I find myself oftentimes reduced to exclaim with the *Psalmist*, *How manifold are Thy works, O Lord! in wisdom hast Thou made them all!* (Ps. 104:24)[6]

Although Boyle never relinquished his praise for God's works, his later thought did manifest an apologetic consciousness which, however, fell short of deism.[7] In 1665, in an inserted section of the *Usefulness of Natural Philosophy* entitled "Containing a requisite digression concerning those, that would exclude the Deity from intermeddling with matter," he considered the possibility of the existence of atheists but found the order, design, and variety in creation too obvious to give credence to ancient Epicurean views of chance and chaos in the beginning.

And really it is much more unlikely, that so many admirable creatures, that constitute this one exquisite and stupendous fabrick of the world, should be made by the casual confluence of falling atoms, jostling or knocking one another in the vacuity, than that in a printer's workinghouse a multitude of small letters, being thrown upon the ground, should fall disposed into such an order, as clearly to exhibit the history of the creation of the world, described in the 3 or 4 first chapters of *Genesis;* of which history, it may be doubted, whether chance may ever be able to dispose of the fallen letters into the words of one line.[8]

By 1675 he still regarded theology as that from which, rather than toward which, one argues. He wrote the following counsel to a friend troubled by another's hesitations:

For your friend does not oppose, but only undervalues theology; and professing to believe the scriptures, (which I so far credit, as to think he believes himself when he says so) we agree upon the principles: so that I am not to dispute with him, as against an atheist, that denies the author of nature, but only against a naturalist, that over-values the study of it. And the truths of theology are things, which I need not bring arguments for, but am allowed to draw arguments from them.[9]

Nevertheless, Boyle felt the weight of those who charged that the new philosophy threatened religion. In *A Discourse of Things above Reason*, he distinguished a class of "privileged subjects" defined by the sublimity and infinity of God, yet one can sense defensiveness in his placement of mysteries of the faith in a realm where they may remain unscathed because untouched.[10] Similarly, the claim of "reconcileableness" in *Reason and Religion* (1675) was apologetic. *Some Physico-Theological Considerations about the Possibility of the Resurrection* (1675) argued that "corpuscularian principles may not only be admitted without Epicurean errors, but be employed against them."[11] Not content to differentiate or draw analogies between disciplines, Boyle sought to make the resurrection more plausible partly by appeal to processes of chemical transmutation.

This argument, which shows how an essentially critical theology could be employed apologetically, is of added interest because it manifests the most visible marks of a voluntarist orientation to creation. Boyle begins by ascribing the resurrection to the order of God's activities, however miraculous. He strengthens this line of argument by setting aside the suggestion of a mediating "plastic power" and affirming that "an external and omnipotent agent can, without it, perform all that I need contend for." He also affirms the supremely free power of God in a typical voluntarist way, including the stock example of God's dealing with Daniel.

> Thus the operation of the activest body in nature, flame, was suspended in *Nebuchadnezzar's* fiery furnace, whilst *Daniel's* three companions walked unharmed in those flames, that in a thrice, consumed the kindlers of them.

In spite of all this, Boyle's appeal for the plausibility of the resurrection concludes by noting that the proximity of a new flame to a recently extinguished candle suddenly reveals a glorious shiny body.[12]

However, the defense of the mysteries of faith with natural philosophy did not erase the more basic doxological mood of Boyle's later theological writings. At the most sophisticated rational level, his teleological arguments remained a loosely stated body of perceptions presupposing design and revelation in creation. He consistently reasoned from, not to, design. (Hume's thoroughly radical presupposition of material *and mental* atomism, which exchanged the reality of relations for associations, was not yet operative.) Moreover, the law he praised was deeply formative. This will be apparent in the structure of both created law and design that Boyle celebrated.

A Representative View of God

Boyle's theology per se, centered in the elements of God's greatness, free power, and love, was neither an articulation of the Reformation experience of redemption nor a defense of medieval confidence in Being; rather, it was a definite expression of the relatively optimistic seventeenth-century religious interest in creation.[13] Thus, an elucidation of the central elements in Boyle's theology will show the centrality of voluntarism and the reality of law in early modern theology of creation.

In one of his earliest treatises, *Seraphick Love,* Boyle asserted his confidence in the greatness and freedom of divine love in the midst of one of the most heated theological debates of his time. Cutting through the endless controversies between strict Calvinists and Arminians on predestination, he charged both with focussing so narrowly upon the "manner" of God's grace that they not only obscured His freedom but, more seriously, failed to appreciate His immensity. Boyle's emphasis on greatness and freedom, and his notion of a law compatible with love also marked one of his last published works, *Greatness of Mind Promoted by Christianity.*[14]

The littleness of man in contrast to the greatness of God is frequently emphasized throughout Boyle's work:

> Few men are (methinks) more likely to be mistaken in the nature of what is infinite, (and consequently of God's attributes) than those that think descriptions can comprize it. Nor will an assiduity and constancy of our speculations herein relieve us; for too fixed a contemplation of God's essence does but the more confound us.[15]

He frequently described divine greatness as the "transcendent excellency" of a great sovereign.

> The genuine effect of a nearer or more attentive view of infinite excellency is a deep sense of our own great inferiority to it and of the great veneration and fear we owe (to speak in such scriptural phrase) to this glorious and fearful name, (that is, object) *The Lord our God.*

Such deep respect for divine greatness necessitated criticism both of the Scholastics who closely related divine ideas and human thinking and of Descartes and others who seemed to place God in a class with other things.[16]

Boyle stressed God's "great fecundity" and, pointing beyond the infinite quantity of His attributes, His sublimity. Indeed, ". . . there are effects and properties, whose sublimity or abstruseness surpassing our comprehension, makes the divine cause, or author of them, deserve our highest wonder and veneration."[17] He presented these divine attributes not as mere logical possibilities, but as proof of the positive freedom or self-determination of God. For God's immensity and infinity were not "negative attributes," but positive expressions of His greatness. "Such is His immensity, and, if I may so speak, fecundity, that he is unspeakably various in the capacity of an object."[18] The principal meaning of divine fecundity is the personalization of what might otherwise be taken as a set of impersonal possibilities.

Such terms as "excellency," "greatness," and "sublimity" point to Boyle's intense concentration on the reality of God. The conception of the Deity in less differentiated theologies gave way to the sharply focused authority of a great sovereign, the rule of the mighty Jehovah. This shift is obvious in Boyle's favored name for God, "Author." This title proclaims the supreme individuality of God;[19] it makes His reality personal in a majestic way, and highlights His activity.

Commenting on the validity of the comparisons of theology and "physicks," Boyle held that they were not like comparisons of "theology and necromancy or some other part of *unlawful magick,* whereof the former could not be well relished without an abhorrence of the latter." He precluded the practice of natural magic, affirmed by many Spiritualists, because it violated the legal order of things. Moreover, "as the two great books, of nature and of Scripture, have the same author; so the study of the latter does not at all hinder an inquisitive man's delight in the study of the former." In short, the title "Author" indicates a basic theological presupposition which links all the works of God. God is a sovereign legislator of all the ways of man and creation at large.

Praising both natural philosophy and careful biblical exegesis in the *Excellency of Theology*, Boyle honored "the author both of nature and of man."[20] In the *Veneration Man Owes to God*, he extended the scope of the Creator as Author even further:

> Whatever excellencies there be, that are simply and absolutely such, and so may, without disparagement to his matchless nature, be ascribed to God, such as are eternity, independency, life, understanding, will, etc. we may be sure, that he possesses them; since he is the original author of all the degrees or resemblances we men have of any of them. . . .

At great length and with considerable enthusiasm, Boyle gave a rational celebration of the magnificent Author.

> And, indeed, what can be more suitable to a rational creature, than to employ reason to contemplate that divine being, which is both the author of its reason, and the noblest object, about which it can possibly be employed.[21]

For Boyle, the vast extent of divine authorship could not be doubted. God was presupposed and named as the Author of nature, Scripture, and man himself.

In *Reason and Religion*, Boyle's witness to the voluntarist tradition was apparent in his affirmations that God is limited solely by the law of noncontradiction and that a Deity of such transcendent power bends to tell us what we are to know of Him. In a classic statement of God's ordained and absolute power in relation to creation, he wrote that

> indeed, if we consider God as the author of the universe, and the free establisher of the laws of motion, whose general concourse is necessary to the conservation and efficacy of every particular physical agent, we cannot but acknowledge, that, by withholding his concourse, or changing these laws of motion, which depend perfectly upon his will, he may invalidate most, if not all the axioms and theorems of natural philosophy: these supposing the course of nature, and especially the established laws of motion, among the parts of the universal matter, as those upon which all the phaenomena depend.

His own estimate of the widespread importance of voluntarist theology is manifest in his citation of Descartes' roughly similar convictions:

> Though he were urged by a learned adversary with an argument, as likely as any to give him a strong temptation to limit the omnipotence of God; yet even on this occasion he scruples not to make this ingenious and wary acknowledgement, and that in a private letter (Vol. II Lettre 6); "For my part, says he, I think we ought never to say of any thing, that it is impossible to God. For all, that is true and good, being dependent on his all-mightiness, I dare not so much as say, that God cannot make a mountain without a valley, or cannot make it true, that one and two shall not make three; . . . but I cannot conceive a mountain without a valley, nor that the aggregate of one and of two shall not make three, etc. and I say only, that such things imply a contradiction in my conception."

Boyle also found an example of the two-fold dialectic of God's power in the protection and rescue of Daniel's friends:

> It is a rule in natural philosophy, that *causae necessariae semper agunt quantum possunt;* but it will not follow from thence, that the fire must necessarily burn Daniel's three companions, or their clothes, that were cast by the Babylonian king's command into the midst of a burning fiery furnace, when the author of nature was pleased to withdraw his concourse to the operation of the flames, or supernaturally to defend against them the bodies, that were exposed to them.[22]

Here the clear affirmation of God's ordinary and extraordinary power is moderated partly by Boyle's conviction that the divine Author of all things operates as a single agency.

One of the best examples of Boyle's exaltation of God's power is his discussion of Adam and Eve, which comprehended annihilation and covenant under the dominion of God.

> I will not here enter upon the controversy *de jure Dei in creaturas*, upon what it is founded, and how far it reaches. For, without making myself a party in that quarrel I think, I may safely say, that God by his right of dominion, might, without any violation of the laws of justice, have destroyed, and even annihilated *Adam* and *Eve*, before they had eaten of the forbidden fruit, or had been commanded to abstain from it. For man being as much and as entirely God's workmanship as any of the other creatures, unless God had obliged himself by some promise or pact, to limit the exercise of his absolute dominion over

> him, God was no more bound to preserve *Adam* and *Eve* long
> alive, than he was to preserve a lamb, or a pidgeon;[23]

This rivals the strongest statements of the voluntarist tradition
yet, at the same time, shows its constructive bent. The idea of a
pact or covenant which was already central to the voluntarist
theology of protest in late medieval thought had become a formative presupposition in the seventeenth century. Indeed, the
proliferation of covenants which mediated God's will and regulated human life were building blocks in much seventeenth-
century theology and culture.[24]

Although Newton also spoke clearly about the will of the
Lord and Author of creation, his resistance to Leibnitz's
principle of sufficient reason, and his determined affirmation of
a theology of history in contrast to Descartes, may indicate that
his voluntarism was more sophisticated than Boyle's. However,
he was also indebted to Cambridge Platonism and the
Spiritualist search for origins. The complexity of the theological
issue here is intensified by, on the one hand, Newton's clear
differentiation of religion and natural philosophy, and on the
other hand, his articulation of a theology of space. Until the
problem of theological sources has been resolved, any estimate
of his view of God remains provisional.[25] Yet, notwithstanding
his indebtedness to Spiritualist resources, Newton's broadly
voluntarist orientation, his keen sense that God was, as Koyré
puts it, the mighty Jehovah, cannot be doubted.

The first paragraph of Newton's "Religion. Three Para-
graphs," is pervaded by an understanding of God as Law-giver
and by an awareness of the weight of His commands.

> Our Religion to God: God made the world and governs it in-
> visibly, and hath commanded us to love, honour and worship
> him and no other God but him and to do it without making any
> image of him, and not to name him idly and without reverence,
> and to honour our parents, masters and governors, and love our
> neighbors as ourselves, and to be temperate, modest, just and
> peaceable, and to be merciful even to brute beasts.[26]

His classic statement in the General Scholium distinguishes
God from creation, most likely in opposition to the Scholastics,
Descartes, and, perhaps, Henry More:

> The Supreme God is a Being eternal, infinite, absolutely per-
> fect; but a being, however perfect, without dominion, cannot

be said to be Lord God: for we say, my God, your God, The God of *Israel*, the God of Gods, and Lord of Lords; but we do not say, my Eternal, your Eternal, the Eternal of *Israel*, the Eternal of Gods; we do not say, my Infinite, or my Perfect: These are titles which have no respect to servants. The word God usually signifies *Lord;* but every lord is not a God. It is the dominion of a spiritual being which constitutes a God: a true, supreme, or imaginary dominion makes a true, supreme, or imaginary God.[27]

It is important to note that the first two sentences here identify God as Lord. The *dominion* — the power, will, and law of God — is basic. At the same time the last sentence underlines God's spiritual dominion. While these crucial texts do not settle the issue of the nature of God's spiritual dominion for Newton, they do warrant the judgment that his view of God was basically similar to Boyle's in its stress upon will and law.

Boyle critically appropriated for his own theology the idea of divine love which was central for the Cambridge Platonists. In effect, he subordinated love to a voluntarist orientation. In his early *Seraphick Love,* which held that love was the "first attribute" of God because its "greatness" and freedom are evident in all of His attributes, Boyle argued that God's love was exercised before human existence through the work of Christ, and against nature.

> God loved you numerous ages before you were; and his goodness is so entirely its own motive, that even your creation . . . is the effect of it. . . . [Moreover, Christ] to teach man, how much he valued him above those creatures, that man makes his idols . . . often altered and suspended the course of nature for man's instruction, or his relief, and reversed the laws established in the universe, to engage men to obey those of God, by doing miracles so numerous and great, that the Jews unbelief may be almost counted on.

This statement is reminiscent of the possibilities open to God according to His *potentia absoluta.* His free love is exercised arbitrarily, without obligation on His part.

> God . . . for being necessarily kind, is not less freely or obligingly so, to you, or me. For though some kind of communicativeness be essential to his goodness, yet his extension of it without himself, and his vouchsafing it to this or that particular person, are purely arbitrary.[28]

A voluntarist conception of divine love is also evident in Boyle's discussion of its "disinterestedness," which he elucidated by stressing the holiness of divine laws, and "constancy."[29]

> Nor is he only constant in making us the objects of his love, but also in bending and inclining us to make him the object of our strongest affections; so that he not only persists in continuing to [give] us both the offer of a value of his love, but perseveres to give us a receptive disposition to welcome it to us, and reflect it up to him.

Finally, Boyle specified God as the object of devotion in the whole of human life. This last "property" of divine love is the

> advantageousness of his love to us, both in the present and the future life. And first, even in this world we owe God no less than all the goods we possess. We owe him both what we have and what we are: for we may say truly of God with the Psalmist, *It is he that hath made us, and not we ourselves* (110:3). . . . His love is the first original and fountain blessing; all the rest are but as pipes (and instruments) to convey, and serve but to hand it to us.[30]

In his *Veneration Man Owes to God,* Boyle more explicitly countered the participatory relation between God and the world which the Spiritualists, most likely the Cambridge Platonists, affirmed:

> And indeed, speaking in general, the creatures are but umbratile (if I may so speak) and arbitrary pictures of the great creator, of divers of whose perfections though they have some signatures, yet they are but such, as rather give the intellect rises and occasions to take notice of and contemplate the divine originals, than they afford true images of them: as a picture of a watch or man, or the name of either of them written with pen and ink, does not exhibit a true and perfect idea of a thing (whose internal constitution a surface cannot fully represent) but only gives occasion to the mind to think of it, and to frame one.

He went on to underline the great distance between the transcendent Creator and His creatures:

> The distance betwixt the infinite creator and the creatures, which are but the limited and arbitrary productions of his power and will, is so vast, that all the divine attributes or perfections do by unmeasurable intervals transcend those faint resemblances of them, that he has been pleased to impress either upon other creatures, or upon us men.[31]

These texts presuppose great distance between the Creator and creation. Boyle's use of the category of occasion marked a decisive turn away from the Spiritualist conception of the creatures as virtual signatures of God's power. Indeed, it is apparent that Boyle's epistemological or linguistic nominalism functioned largely within the context of a voluntarist theology.

Boyle's view of God was thoroughly representative of voluntarism, for the will of the majestic Author and Creator of all things stood forth like the will of the mighty biblical Jehovah. Indeed, Boyle was a serious and competent theologian. Notwithstanding the amateur status for which he often apologized, Robert Boyle's achievements clearly enriched the vigorous early modern theology of creation that thrived in seventeenth-century England.

The Lawful Order of Creation

Boyle's commitment to order is as apparent in his theological reflections on such topics as ethics and Christianity as it is in his natural philosophy. The order he presupposed in creation was not the same as, although it was very closely allied with, the mechanical order in his natural philosophy. He protested against conceiving of God as a "mere Mechanician," and his view of God as the Author of law and design was far from the deists' view of the divine clockmaker. Yet, in historical perspective, his presupposition of order in creation was an epochal departure from classical medieval theology. When God's law was given the priority traditionally ascribed to the divine logos both *in re* and in the mind, creation ordered by the logos of being gave way to a rule of law which presupposed the transcendent and sovereign will of God.

One of the better analogies to the seventeenth-century confidence (even delight) in God's law is Old Testament Judaism. Much as the ancient Hebrews learned to live with the transcendent Yahweh by obeying His law, so too the early modern divines and natural philosophers honored God's law.[32] In fact, the scholarly recovery of the Old Testament in Hebrew may have contributed to the general confidence in divine law. Newton held that the moral law of all nations, even the most ancient, was rooted in divine law as in Noah's generation.[33]

Two major characteristics of such order appear in Boyle's account. First, law was neither simply the way man conceives of the universe nor the iron necessity of a fateful cosmos. Instead, it was as real as God and His creation. Secondly, this law was imposed. It was promulgated as the real command of a transcendent sovereign rather than simply given in the nature of things as the inherent rationality of the cosmos itself. Law of this sort was akin to the spoken word.

> And accordingly we find in Scripture that, whereas about the production of the material world, and the setting of the frame of nature, God employed only a few commanding words, which speedily had their full effects.[34]

Boyle's ethics championed the command of God, His supreme authority, and the obligations which befall man upon receiving His injunctions.

> It needs not, I suppose, be solicitiously proved, that it is the will and command of God that men should learn those truths, that he has been pleased to teach, whether concerning his nature or attributes, or the way, wherein he will be served and worshipped by man . . . and if it appear to be his will, that a person so qualified should search after the most important truths, that he hath revealed, it cannot but be their duty to do so. For though the nature of the thing itself did not lay any obligation on us, yet the authority of him, that commands it, would; since, being the supreme and absolute Lord of all his creatures, he has as well a full right to make what laws he thinks fit, and enjoin what service he thinks fit, and a power to punish those, that either violate the one, or deny the other; and accordingly it is very observable, that before *Adam* fell, and had forfeited his happy state, by his own transgression, he not only had a law imposed upon him but such a law, as, being about a matter itself indifferent, (for so it was to eat, or not to eat, of the tree of life, as well as of any other,) derived its whole power of obliging from the mere will and pleasure of the lawgiver. Whence we may learn, that man is subject to the laws of God, not as he is obnoxious to him, but as he is a rational creature, and that the thing, that is not a duty in its own nature, may become an indispensable one, barely by its being commanded.[35]

The sheer authority of God is sufficient for ethical order, for that authority is expressed in the created order as a law which is binding irrespective of the nature or substance of the creature subject to it. Ultimately, the law is fundamental to man as creature; it is his proper backbone.

Clearly, a dutiful life was an appropriate response to God's law in this rather stern ethic. But Boyle's view of morality depended on far more than extrinsic duty. Within the framework of law, command, and duty, he developed the concept of virtue. Neither autonomous nor simply given, virtue belongs to man *qua* creature and is strengthened by the same law which limits him. This viewpoint is put most succinctly in his *Tract Against Swearing:*

> The commands of God, differ from those of men, in that the latter but lay on us an obligation; the former invest us with a power to obey them . . . and in the first creation, that powerful command, "Let there be light," gave that bright creature an existence, to make it capable of paying him an obedience.

Moreover, God does not command more than we are able to perform, for He "promises to do in us what he commands."[36]

Consistent with the prominent place of divine law in his ethics of duty and created moral virtue, Boyle articulated the distinctiveness of Christianity in legal terms:

> And first, the prime author of the doctrine of the gospel being God himself, who both knows man perfectly, is mentioned in scripture as a φιλάνθρωπος, or lover of mankind, . . . it is but reasonable to suppose that the doctrines and laws he caused to be solemnly delivered to mankind, and confirmed by miracles . . . should be fitted to beget and advance solid and sublime virtue, and be, more than any other institution, perfective of human nature. . . . Next, the rules, and (if there be any such) the counsels of the Christian religion require, and tend to, extraordinary degrees of virtue. The divine legislator, being able to look into the hearts of men, makes his laws reach those, and those principally too.

Positively summarizing moral law as love of God and neighbor, Boyle recommended the example of Christ: "And his sinless life, *which was a living law,* did not only surpass the examples, but even precepts and the ideas too, of the heathen moralists and philosophers and may be elsewhere shewn."[37] Thus, the legal cast of Boyle's thought includes rather than excludes human integrity in the spheres of ethics and the gospel. A creation subject to law is open, in the deepest sense, to God the Supreme Lawgiver.

Boyle further argued that Christianity should be promulgated practically, not "only as a system of speculative doctrines, but also as a body of laws." For the Christian religion "teaches us, that God commands us to worship him, and regulates our lives." Insisting that such religion is put before man as a matter of choice, he held that

> the Christian religion is not proposed barely as a proffer of heaven in case men embrace it, *but as a law*, that men should embrace it upon the greatest penalty, and as the only expedient and remedy to attain eternal happiness, and escape endless misery.[38]

Given this legal specification of the fundamental religious choice, it is hardly surprising that Boyle regarded Scripture as a body of positive laws which uniquely clarified the revelation of God's will. In the *Style of Scriptures*, for example, he wrote:

> When I find anything enjoined in Scripture, my consciousness to its being imposed by that *father of spirits* (Heb. 12:9), (who has . . . [the] . . . right to enact laws, which must be therefore just, because he enacts them . . .) I think it my part without disputing them to obey his orders, and acquiesce more in that imperious ἀληθῶς, *thus saith the Lord*, than in a whole dialogue of *Plato*, or an epistle of *Seneca*. I therefore love to build my ethicks (as well as my creed) upon the rock, and esteeming nothing but the true, proper, and strict sense of the scripture, (and what is convincingly deducible from it) to be indispensably obligatory, either as (in matters of mere revelation) to faith or practice.[39]

Surely, Boyle did not deny that one may find ethical truths in heathen moralists. Indeed, one should expect to find them there, because God is "both an omniscient spirit and the supreme law-giver to the whole creation." Furthermore, the laws of princes and wise men are most "curious" if they do not originate in the law of Moses. Nevertheless, it remains true that the positive law of Scripture is "better" because it is clear and powerful. As Boyle puts it, "books of morality . . . have a power but to persuade, not to command."[40] Here again, the authoring power and the guidance of law derive from God.

In general, Boyle held that the course of the Christian life, most clearly revealed by Christ, should accord with the psalmist's fidelity to God's law. The glory of David, Boyle's favorite biblical figure, was that his eyes were opened to the "wondrous things of God's law."[41] Newton found the morality of Old Testament law similarly constitutive of Christian life:

> We are to have recourse to the Old Testament, and to beware of vain Philosophy, for Christ sent his apostles not to teach Philosophy to the common people . . . but to teach what he had taken out of Moses and the Prophets and Psalms concerning Christ.[42]

One of Boyle's rare theological claims about politics was made in the *Martyrdom*, where Didymus' civil disobedience in rescuing Theodora evinced his loyalty to the higher law of God.

> For God being, as the only Creator, so the supreme governor of man, his laws are those of the truest supreme authority: and princes themselves being his subjects, and but his lieutenants upon earth; to decline their commands, whenever they prove repugnant unto his, is not so much an act of disobedience to the subordinate power, as of loyalty to the supreme and universal sovereign.[43]

The presupposition of divine lawful order evident in the thought of Bacon was not as fully elaborated as it was by Boyle and Newton. But a striking passage in Bacon's early *Confession of Faith* (1597) clearly indicated that God's creation, ordinarily denominated as Nature, was virtually identical with God's Law. In a characteristically strong affirmation of divine transcendence, Bacon stated that God

> created heaven and earth, and all their armies and generations, and gave unto them constant and everlasting laws, which we call Nature, which is nothing but the laws of the creation; which laws nevertheless have had three changes or times, and are to have a fourth and last. The first, when the matter of heaven and earth was created without forms; the second, the *interim* of every day's work: the third, by the curse, which notwithstanding was no new creation, but a privation of part of the virtue of the first creation: and the last, at the end of the world, the manner whereof is not yet revealed. So as the laws of Nature, which now remain and govern inviolably till the end of the world, began to be in force when God first rested from his works and ceased to create; but received a revocation in part by the curse, since which time they change not. . . .
> God doth accomplish and fulfil his divine will in all things great and small, singular and general, as fully and exactly by providence, as he could by miracle and new creation, though his working be not immediate and direct, but by compass; not violating Nature, which is his own law upon the creature.[44]

Boyle extended this point of view by presupposing that all creation manifested God's order of design. Yet his appreciation of God's beauty and scope of design was not as extensive as his testimony to God's law. Whereas the order of law was fundamental to Boyle's ethics, Scriptural exegesis, general conception of Christianity, politics, and natural philosophy, the order of divine design was manifest almost solely in his natural philosophy. Nevertheless, he did make clear the teleological design of Scriptural prescriptions, for ". . . the laws of order in the scripture being rarely declined, but, as the laws of nature are in the world, for man's instruction" and God's glory.[45]

This teleology had a vast scope. The beautiful design of creation had benefits for man and bespoke the glory of God. In his affirmation of such ends of creation, Boyle not only clearly represented seventeenth-century thought in general, but also shared and was perhaps indebted to Helmontian and other forms of Spiritualism which insisted that those ends be taken seriously.[46] However, his additional insistence that the divine order was to be found in the beautiful design of creation per se accorded it an integrity that was absent in Spiritualism and tightly controlled if not suppressed in much rigorously Calvinistic theology.

Boyle's frequent praise of God's glory and man's delight in creation never threatened the distinct value of creation in and of itself. He compared creation to an open book, a "vast fabrick," and a "well-contrived romance." In one of many passages on this subject he held that creation provides man

> not only necessaries and delights, but instructions too. For each page in the great volume of nature is full of real hieroglyphicks, where (by an inverted way of expression) things stand for words, and their qualities for letters. The Psalmist observes, *That the heavens declare the glory of God:* and, indeed, they celebrate his praises, though with a soundless voice, yet with so loud a one (and which gives us the moral of *Plato's* exploded notion of the musick of the spheres) to our intellectual ears, that he scruples not to affirm, that *there is no speech nor language, where their voice is not heard* . . . their language having so escaped the confusion of tongues that these natural immortal preachers give all nations occasion to say of them, as the assembly at pentecost did of the inspired Apostles, *we do hear them speak in tongues the wonderful works of God.*[47]

Boyle elaborated this comparison by contrasting the "great volume" with fables:

> For it fares not with an inquisitive mind in studying the book of nature, as in reading *Aesop's* fables, or some other collection of apologues of differing sorts, and independent one upon another. . . . But in the book of nature, as in a well-contrived romance, the parts have such a connection and relation to one another, and the things we would discover are so darkly or incompleatly knowable by those, that precede them, that the mind is never satisfied till it comes to the end of the book.[48]

Repeatedly he spoke of the "fabrick" of creation in terms of the three divine attributes of wisdom, power and goodness:

> He created this vast fabrick of the world to manifest his wisdom, power, and goodness; and in it created man, that it may have an intelligent spectator, and a resident, whose rational admiration of so divine a structure may accrue to the glory of the omniscient and almighty architect.[49]

This threefold schema was a commonplace in Western theology from Augustine to Calvin, but in seventeenth-century theology the attributes were seen as publications of God *qua* Author or as the edifice of the divine Architect. The open display of God's power and the revelation of His wisdom were more crucial than its hidden meaning. Deeply committed to the final glory of God, Boyle was constantly impressed by His magnificent design in creation.[50]

In sum it is clear that Boyle's representative early modern theology of creation celebrated the greatness, free power, and, above all, the mighty will of God the Creator. In this lively theological context he gave a voluntarist shape to the meaning of love, duty, and virtue in ethics, and the promulgation of Christianity. This theology, one of the richer harvests of the late medieval voluntarist beginnings, showed the marks of that earlier tradition and yet made its own vigorous statement of the Creator and Author whose law was the chief order of the entirety of creation. Such theology had profound effects for the idea of nature, which is the subject of the next chapter.

CHAPTER SIX:

Theology and the Idea of Nature

In his *Notion of Nature*, Boyle explicitly stated that the idea of nature, "the fruitful parent of other notions," is of "great moment" for the "speculative and practical part of physiology" and of "vast importance" to philosophy and physics.[1] Virtually all the major figures in the new science understood themselves to be engaged in natural philosophy as they wrestled with new sets of problems. The new questions they raised clustered around their conceptions of the totality of the natural world, its structural order and relations, and the issue of particulars (bodies, atoms, etc.) in nature. At the same time, they were grappling with similar matters in religion and culture at large. These problems can be traced back to their origins in basic presuppositions, which can then be used as the basis for an analysis of the chief conceptions and questions of the early modern thinkers. The effectiveness of their basic theological presuppositions can be seen more clearly from our later perspective, yet to see this does require disciplined, empathetic imagination.

This is not to say that Boyle's chemistry, for example, was derived from his theology. Indeed, the very point of Boyle's modernity was the rejection of such an "Helmontian" confusion. But the theology of creation he represented was presupposed in the highly signficant idea of nature. The relatively direct significance of theology, both constructively and critically, for Boyle was very different from Helmont's view that both nature and knowledge are immediately related to God.

Given his presupposition of the natural world as God's creation and the definite view of God which he held, Boyle was opposed to virtually all organic and spiritual images and

147

categories. In affirming a legal-mechanical view of nature as creation, he battled the Aristotelian tradition at great length. (However, some of this wrestling was little more than ritual because he shared so much with others who made this break.) Boyle also struggled against the Spiritualist view of nature of the Helmontians and Cambridge Platonists. His differences with Epicurean and Cartesian thought were less severe, but not insignificant.

The point that the idea of nature was the "fruitful parent of other notions" has not been sufficiently recognized by Boyle scholars, who too often focus upon his "atomism," "mechanism," or apologies for theism at the expense of his total if not global project in natural philosophy. His relatively neglected presupposition of the natural world as creation is the theme of this present inquiry.[2] The major texts for my inquiry are those he wrote in the 1660's. In such crucial statements as the *Origin of Forms and Qualities* and especially the *Notion of Nature* (and to a lesser extent, the *Skeptical Chemist* and *Certain Physiological Essays*), Boyle paused in his incessant laboratory work to examine the meaning of "nature" among both ancients and contemporaries. He countered what he believed to be erroneous natural philosophies and advanced his own legal-mechanical view of nature as creation.[3]

The chief purpose of the *Notion of Nature* was the improvement of natural philosophy by specifying the nature of the nonhuman world and by providing proper explanations thereof, but it also set out to defend and improve true religion. Boyle's concerns were related but seldom confused, however, and his critical stance toward nature in the *Notion of Nature* was that of "free" rather than "dogmatic" inquiry. Thus he held that his critique had integrity apart from religion. His disavowal of dogmatic inquiry meant that he would not engage in "positive doctrine" based solely upon Scripture. Nevertheless, a concluding statement in his Preface indicated his deeper theological "intentions."

> I may make bold to say, they were to keep the glory of the divine author of things from being usurped or intrenched upon by his creatures, and to make his works more thoroughly and solidly understood by the philosophical studiers of them.[4]

In light of this purpose and the grand scope of the *Notion of*

Nature, it is not adequate to interpret Boyle's work exclusively or narrowly as a religious, or a scientific, or a philosophical statement. Marked by grand designs and careful differentiation, his thought is best interpreted historically and systematically. This will be apparent by following an order of tracing the effectiveness of basic presuppositions in his efforts to understand nature as a totality, its general structure, and its particular units such as atoms.

Theological Presuppositions in the Rejection of Nature as Divine

A person's questions, particularly those addressed to opposing parties, frequently disclose his basic presuppositions. Thus when, in opposing traditional Aristotelian and Spiritualist ideas about nature in his *Notion of Nature,* Boyle posed the question whether nature should be understood in the traditional (and "vulgar") way as "almost divine" or as a merely human notion, he made clear his own theistic presuppositions:

> I have sometimes seriously doubted, whether the vulgar notion of nature has not been both injurious to the glory of God, and a great impediment to the solid and useful discovery of his works. . . . [Moreover] it seems to detract from the honour of the great author and governor of the world, that men should ascribe most of the admirable things, that are to be met with in it, not to him, but to a certain nature, which themselves do not know well what to make of.

Questions of this sort arise throughout the *Notion of Nature.* If nature is divine, how then does one explain all the anomalies? If there really is a divine nature she must be blind, impotent, or foolish.[5] Such arguments, much like Elijah's testing of Baal in the name of Yahweh, give the impression of a cat playing with a mouse. Indeed, Boyle took the divine Author of creation so much for granted that he regarded nature as an intrusion and never raised similar critical questions about his own position.

In arguing against the simple deification of nature, Boyle's final ground was the radical distinction between Creator and creation. This called for a twin emphasis upon divine transcendence and the radical contingency of creation. Noting that the vulgar notion of nature mistakes nature for God, Boyle argued in the *Notion of Nature* that, among other things, the glory and majesty of the one jealous God simply forbids such a substitute.[6] Section II catalogued various meanings of the term "nature," particularly those used by "naturists" rather than "naturalists," and proposed that the sense of nature as a "goddess" be simply dropped, without any substitute.[7] Also, referring to the (perhaps Spinozistic) sense of nature as *natura naturans*, Boyle argued that such a confusion of Creator and creature should be given up, and the proper name "God" should be used for the primary reality; the questionable *naturans* formulation made God differ very little from a "created or even imaginary being."[8]

Moreover, for Boyle, nature as divine was "prejudicial to the discovery of his works." Any equation of God and nature would impede the discernment of particular causes and detract from man's divinely appointed empire over creatures.

> The veneration, wherewith men are imbued for what they call nature, has been a discouraging impediment to the empire of man over the inferior creatures of God: for many have not only looked upon it, as an impossible thing to compass, but as something impious to attempt, the removing of those boundaries which nature seems to have put and settled among her productions; and whilst they look upon her as such a venerable thing, some make a kind of scruple of conscience to endeavour so to emulate any of her works, as to excel them.

Boyle's own contrasting presupposition of creation was clear: ". . . I call the creatures I admire in the visible world, the works of God, (not of nature) and praise rather him than her, for the wisdom and goodness displayed in them."[9]

Boyle also argued against nature as a kind of secondary Deity, a divine agent or vicegerent. In Section III of the *Notion of Nature*, he began in typical linguistic fashion by noting the ambiguity of Aristotle's definition of nature. He further declared that Aristotle apparently meant that nature is an incorporeal substance. Not content to rest his critique on a linguistic point, Boyle discerned the similarity between this view of nature and the "plastic power" affirmed by some of his contemporaries. Contesting this view, Boyle could not refrain from noting that the Scriptures agree in their silence, for they do not mention the term "nature" at all. "Nature" has no function in creation. Indeed,

> whereas philosophers presume, that she [nature], by her plastic power and skill, forms plants and animals out of the universal matter, the divine historian ascribes the formation of them to God's immediate *fiat, Gen.* 1:11.[10]

Boyle also criticized the anthropomorphic "epithets" attributed to the quasi-divine "reality" of nature. Given God's "architectonic, provident, and governing power," he rejected any "panegyric" which held that nature is a most wise being always seeking her proper ends in either the macrocosm or microcosm. Similarly, he launched into an "excursion identifying ancient and current confusions of the Creator and His creation," and found that

> the ascribing to nature, and some other being, (whether real or imaginary) things, that belong but to God, have been some, (if not the chief) of the grand causes of the polytheism and idolatry of the gentiles.[11]

Boyle found this "Gentile" error in the "Chaldeans and Stoicks." Hippocrates' *De principiis aut carnibus* was singled out as the occasion for his claim that only by knowing the true God can one be free from ancient pantheistic errors.

> I cannot but look on this book, as a remarkable instance of this truth, that, without having recourse to the true God, a satisfactory account cannot be given of the original or primitive production of the greater and lesser world, since so great a naturalist as *Hippocrates*, by the help of his idolized θερμόν was unable to perform this task, with any satisfaction to an attentive, and intelligent inquirer.[12]

He took special note of a "new sect" (the Spiritualists) which mixed natural philosophy and true religion:

> Even in these times there is lately sprung up a sect of men, as well professing Christianity, as pretending to philosophy who (if I be not mis-in-formed of their doctrine) do very much symbolize with the ancient Heathens, and talk much indeed of God, but mean such a one, as is not really distinct from the animated and intelligent universe; but is, on that account, very differing from the true God, that we Christians believe and worship.[13]

Boyle's main critique concluded by attacking those who make God the "soul of the world." Against Aristotle and the "Stoicks," he held that the *anima mundi* doctrine replaced the final and simple distinction of Creator and creature with that of form and nature in a kind of unsteady mutuality. This was analogous to "two co-ordinate governors like two Roman consuls."[14]

Newton also resisted such accounts of divine presence in nature as a totality. This is important because, either by virtue of his consideration of a greater range of realities in natural philosophy or because he was more indebted to the Spiritualism of the Cambridge Platonists, Newton was less committed to the "mechanizing" of natural philosophy in general than was Boyle. Nevertheless, in his early *De Gravitatione et aequipondio fluidorum*, he carefully set aside an account of sources of activity in the physical world through intermediaries. "But I do not see why God himself does not directly inform space with bodies; so long as we distinguish between the formal reason of bodies and the act of divine will."[15] Moreover, in the General Scholium of the *Principia*, he wrote:

> This Being governs all things, not as the soul of the world, but as Lord over all; and on account of this dominion he is wont to be called *Lord God* παντοκράτωρ, or *Universal Ruler*; for *God* is a relative word, and has a respect to servants; and *Deity* is the dominion of God not over his own body, as those imagine who fancy God to be the soul of the world, but over servants.[16]

In short, Newton, like Boyle, affirmed the direct rule of God, but steered clear of the immediacy of mind or Spirit.

In the final Section of his *Notion of Nature* Boyle criticized the attribution of life and mind to the natural world at large:

> But if nature be affirmed (as she is, at least by all Christian philosophers) to be a created being, I then demand, whether or not she be endowed with understanding, so as to know what she does, and for what ends, and by what laws she ought to act?

He stressed that this conception of nature will not explain many phenomena which can be produced mechanically and, against the Spiritualists in particular, questioned the conceivability of a created immaterial being moving physical things. Moreover, on the supposition that a deified nature was corporeal, how could one conceive her as thinking and provident? How could such nature interpenetrate everything? Indeed, Boyle asked, how could any natural principle of motion originate short of God, and how could such an entity observe the laws of motion?[17]

This entire line of questioning shows that for Boyle nature as any significant entity was itself in need of explanation. It was precisely when one considered the totality of the natural world that his questions exploited Spiritualist "confusions" and disclosed his own presuppositions. Accordingly, the reality of the world turns on making sense of "creation," "motion," "mechanism," "law," etc., but not "nature." In other words, Boyle did not grant nature an a priori or ontological status apart from creation. The physical world in general was not constricted to a definite necessity of place in the classical hierarchy of being, for it was simply a work of divine creation.

Moreover, Boyle did not see God chiefly as the principle of Being. Rather, He was the powerful Author who both transcends and is expressed in His well-designed works. Although those works remain open to, dependent upon, and contingent vis-a-vis God, they are far removed from any ontological "nature," whether divine, semi-divine, or a principle of the world per se. It is fair to say that in Boyle's view of nature as a totality ontology is subordinated to theology. This orientation radicalizes the significance of creation just as it intensifies the importance of the Creator.

Shifting Basic Images of the Creation

Boyle's rejection of the deification of nature raises the question of his own presuppositions in understanding the natural world in its totality. They are partly reflected in the basic images of creation in his natural philosophy. Frequently interpreted as a simple mechanist,[18] Boyle's thought was characterized by at least three basic images. These may be loosely comprehended as artistic, legal-mechanical, and ecclesiastical, and their constant theological and physical references indicate that they were more than just metaphors for Boyle and his contemporaries. Actually, they were highly significant in shaping the course of natural philosophy. Although Boyle's basic images of creation overlapped — a normal occurrence for total images of the world — the standard reading of scientific progress as a direct passage from an organic to a mechanistic view of nature is simplistic if not erroneous. Rather, traditional organic images and renewed Spiritualist images were mediated and redirected by new legal-mechanical images.

Boyle's basic artistic image of the physical universe was evident in his conception in the *Notion of Nature* of a well-designed edifice. He rejected deified nature not only to explain origins, but also in order to maintain the "overall designs" of the physical world. Insisting on the image of a well-designed world, he firmly opposed images of chance, chaos, and, in the case of the Epicurean view, of a confused world order; he held that the "curious contrivances" of the universe were "matters of fact" clearly open to direct "inspection." Hence there was no need for any "hypothesis" of nature.[19] Confidence in the vast design of the universe was a kind of given, a witness to its divine Architect.

Boyle's confidence in the designed world was evident in a number of concrete analogies. For example, he considered the eye a window to larger design. Yet he explicitly argued in the *Notion of Nature* that the natural philosopher should study the "texture" or "fabric" of the world as a totality rather than assume an aggregate of powers.[20] Elsewhere, he made it clear that the "fabrick" of the great "engine" of the universe exceeds that of the most exquisite watch or clock. For each fabricated engine in creation is made up of many lesser engines, "each subordinate engine excellently fitted for this or that particular use. . . . Which manifests, that this great artist had the whole fabrick under his eye at once, and did at one view behold all, that was best to be done. . . ." In discussing creation as a whole as well as its constitution on the level slightly more coarse than that of primary mechanical affections, Boyle manifested a basic artistic image. Speaking of the divine Wisdom and its material visibility, he drew attention to the "fabrick" of particulars — their contrivances, the variety of things, and the symmetry of dependence and relatedness among all engines.[21] This summary statement clearly shows the extensiveness of divine design in creation.

The basic artistic image in Boyle's natural philosophy

clearly characterizes the same physical world which depends upon the Author of creation. Moreover, it does not conflict with the more mechanical notion of "engines." Indeed, at one point, Boyle comprehends "all inanimate and animate parts" within the scope of the artistic image. Thus, he should not be interpreted as a consistent mechanist along eighteenth-century, or perhaps Cartesian, lines.

This point is reinforced by Boyle's most prominent and representative basic image, that of a legal-mechanical world. Creation was both thoroughly law-like and mechanical. With this image Boyle intended neither a narrowly legal nor a rigidly mechanistic view of things. Among the many expressions of this image his well-known comparison of the creation to the Strasbourg clock is of central importance, for it shows that the mechanical view of the world was a great discovery.[22] To understand the creation in such terms was to experience a liberation from traditional organic views of nature. Creation was experienced as simultaneously novel, beautiful, useful, and a good publication of God's own Providence. Boyle wrote that the world

> is like a rare clock, such as may be that at *Strasbourg*, where all things are so skillfully contrived, that the engine being once set a moving, all things proceed, according to the artificer's first design, and the motions of the little statues, that at such hours perform these or those things, do not require, like those of puppets, the peculiar interposing of the artificer, or any intelligent agent employed by him, but perform their functions upon particular occasions, by virtue of the general and primitive contrivance of the whole engine.[23]

Since the mechanical world is so well formed from the beginning, there is no need for interruption.

However, Boyle spoke with equal force in a basically legal image, according to which all nature was at the direct command of God:

> These things are mentioned [the many discoveries in astronomy, etc.], that we may have the more enlarged conceptions of the power as well as wisdom of the great Creator, who has both put so wonderful a quantity of motion into the universal matter and maintains it therein, and is able, not only to set bounds to the raging sea, and effectively say to it, hitherto shalt thou come, and no farther, and here shalt thy proud waves be

stay'd, but (what is far more) so to curb and moderate those stupendously rapid motions of the mundane globes and inter-current fluids, that neither the unwieldiness of their bulk nor celerity of their motions, have made them exorbitant or fly out, and this for many ages; during which no watch for a few hours has gone so regularly.[24]

The two images came together in the single statement of creation as a "pregnant automaton," which follows one of the most programmatic accounts of the law-like view of the world in the *Notion of Nature.*

> According to the foregoing hypothesis, I consider the frame of the world already made, as a great, and, if I may so speak, pregnant automaton, that, like a woman with twins in her womb, or a ship furnished with pumps, ordnance, *etc.* is such an engine, as comprises, or consists of several lesser engines; and this compounded machine, in conjunction with the laws of motion, freely established and still maintained by God, among its parts, I look upon as a complex principle, whence results the settled order or course of things corporeal.[25]

Despite its complexity, joining politics and the machine, this image of the world as a "complex principle" of engines within engines under God's law had rigorous yet liberating reality for Boyle. It was another articulation of his presupposition of God as the actual Creator and Author. Therefore, it should not be confused with more explicitly mechanistic eighteenth-century views, which in turn presupposed a more domesticated and deistic theology of a removed divine Maker.

A third basic image in Boyle's natural philosophy was, in turn, a staple among Spiritualists. In his early *Usefulness of Natural Philosophy*, written while he was still somewhat under the influence of Helmont although in the process of converting to the newer outlook, he articulated his ecclesiastical image of the world as a temple. In an attempt to draw his nephew into natural philosophy Boyle wrote as follows:

> Upon what account *Pyrophilus*, I esteem the world a temple, I may elsewhere have occasion to declare; but this for the present; it would not be rash to infer, that if the world be a temple, man sure must be the priest, ordained (by being quali-fied) to celebrate the divine service not only in it, but for it.[26]

This image speaks not only of the natural world as a temple but also of the role of a priestly natural philosopher. Those who stress Boyle's more frequent mechanical images tend to over-look it, while others have argued that the temple-priest image is a central witness to his break with the utilitarian Baconian tradition.[27] These one-sided judgments miss the critical complexity of the image and, more significantly, Boyle's stance toward it.

The key to a reassessment may be found in the way Boyle introduced the authorities who spoke of the world as God's temple.[28] After quoting "the great *Mercurius Trismegistus*" on the general value of natural philosophy for piety, he argues that

> it was perhaps, *Pyrophilus*, to engage us to an industrious indagation of the creatures, that God made man so indigent, and furnished him with such a multiplicity of desires; so that . . . to relieve his numerous wants, or satisfy his more numerous desires, he might be obliged with an inquisitive industry to range, anatomize, and ransack nature, and by that concerned survey come to a more exquisite admiration of the omniscient Author.[29]

This introduction of the temple-priest image in the context of the gifts and demands which come to man living in the creation of the great Author indicates that it should be understood in terms of the artistic and legal-mechanical images. A Spiritualist reading of Boyle is no more adequate than a purely mechanistic one.

In fact, Boyle reformed the temple-priest image by expanding the sacred center of the alchemist's *Sanctum Sanctorum*. No laboratory or any other place constituted a special locus of the divine. Instead of being focused in an inner holy of holies, the temple became coincident with the entirety of creation. Accordingly, Boyle perceived its "letters" not as mysterious "hieroglyphicks," but as a revelation of an order which the great Author-Creator has published. Creation was revelation, but not in an immediate Spiritualist sense nor in a mysterious inner sense known only to the few. The great Architect and Lawgiver has laid down an order which binds and attracts all men.[30]

This image of the temple in the context of God's order of design and law was shared by Newton. Noting that Newton was criticized for his perhaps misleading account of space as the divine *sensorium*, J. E. McGuire has drawn attention to his unpublished use of the Hebrew conception of Makom, place.

For "when the Hebrews called God Makom, place, the place in which we live and move and have our being, they did not mean that space is God in a literal sense."[31] This position was congruent with Newton's repeated denials of any "soul of the world" or plastic principle. Furthermore, an unpublished *scholium* intended for the 1690 *Principia* reads, "This one God they [the ancients] would have it dwelt in all bodies whatsoever as in his own temple, and thence they shaped ancient temples in the manner of the heavens." Thus, in McGuire's fortunate Johannine phrase, God was "in the world but not of it," for, as Newton said, "the entire universe was rightly designated a Temple of God."[32]

In short, Newton, like Boyle, presupposed that the creation was an ordered and attractive revelation. In line with this orientation, he too was disposed to respectful yet deeply questioning experimental inquiry. Roger Cotes' statement in the Preface to the second edition of the *Principia* puts it well:

> Without all doubt this world, so diversified with that variety of forms and motions we find in it, could arise from nothing but the perfectly free will of God directing and presiding over all.
>
> From this fountain it is that those laws, which we call the laws of Nature, have flowed, in which there appear many traces indeed of the most wise contrivance, but not the least shadow of necessity. These therefore we must not seek from uncertain conjectures, but learn them from observations and experiments.[33]

Boyle reformed the temple-priest image even further by universalizing the elite priesthood of the alchemists.

> It is an act of piety to offer up for the creatures the sacrifice of praise to the creator; for, as anciently among the Jews, by virtue of an Aaronical extraction, men were born with a right to priesthood; *so reason is a natural dignity, and knowledge a prerogative, that can confer a priesthood without unction or imposition of hands.*

It is precisely this universal priesthood that Boyle means when he speaks of the scientist as a "priest, ordained *(by being qualified)* to celebrate the divine service not only in it [the world], but for it."[34] Indeed, just as God's ends of glorifying Himself and benefiting man are unified in the vast design of creation, so too the new natural philosopher reconciles these ends in his own work, which is both in and for the creation.

The fact that Boyle and others like him characterized the natural philosopher as a reformed priest shows that their fundamental view of the relation of the "scientist" to nature had two dimensions. On the one hand, he was the "industrious" overlord, a utilitarian master of natural creation. But his stewardship and respect for that creation were equally important.[35] Industry and appreciation were yoked together. While empiricism cannot be strictly deduced from such moving presuppositions, its twin moments of manipulative experiment and disciplined attention were expressions of such basic relations to nature. Mastery and stewardly respect for creation fostered empirical objectivity.

Change in Basic Categories: Matter, Form, and Motion

In the *Notion of Nature* Boyle rejected the Aristotelian doctrine of the eternity of the material world. In it he found a view of nature which not only suggested a mere "guardian" of things, but also failed to acknowledge the "ruler" and "architect" of matter. Thus his presupposition of *creatio ex nihilo* and the continual dependence of creation upon God was clear. Aristotle's doctrine denied God the "production" and "government" of the world and ignored the One Creator and Lawgiver. Yet, in the same treatise, Boyle defended the difference between God and the material world against Spiritualist "naturists," arguing that all good Christians and Jews recognize that the perfection and excellence of God prevent Him from entering into union with matter.[36] This position was common to Western theology, but the extent to which Boyle insisted upon divine creation of matter over against Scholastics, Spiritualists, Descartes, and Epicurean thought, suggests more than defense of conventional views.

The voluntarist theology of creation involved a radicalizing of the contingency of creation such that the traditional place of matter and hierarchy of formal entities were replaced by an egalitarian matter capable of entering into various new legal-mechanical combinations and scientific constructions (or explanations). This was a reformation of the persistent form-matter motif of scholastic natural philosophy.[37] Put most sharply, Boyle's point was that before the mighty will of Jehovah all things are leveled out in a kind of general creaturely equity. God could, if He chose, recreate the world and its laws. His perfection is not impaired by the establishment of new and different creatures. Indeed, God could even annihilate the very material substance which hangs totally upon Him.[38]

Boyle's presupposition of material creation amounted to an attack upon the hiddenness of matter. Matter was no longer an eternal given, a kind of ever-receding intractable stuff from which things are made and according to which they may receive a relative explanation. Since God creates matter, it was folly to claim that a second-rate god like nature had difficult material with which to work.[39]

Once Boyle had raised matter to a level of reality equal with everything else in creation — indeed, the *Origin of Forms and Qualities* has it that matter and its modifications make up all that there is — he found no need to retain the scholastic "substantial forms."[40] Created matter, now a full-fledged building block in the world, could be used for precise explanations. The conditions were met for characterizing matter universally with such mechanical affections as size, shape, and local motion.

Boyle argued that the variety of material bodies should not be conceived in terms of the "nature" of matter. Within "one uniform conception," created matter was not possessed of hidden powers and potentialities. The true notions of extended, impenetrable, and given material bodies could be known by qualities (e.g., the primary mechanical affections) that were readily available to the natural philosopher.[41] Indeed, Boyle was so insistent on what may be termed the uniform "at-handness" of created matter that he disagreed with Descartes' more complex (and speculative) theory that material bodies are by nature so extended as to be "indefinite," if not infinite. Showing his own theological presuppositions, he wrote that Descartes' view suffers the

> inconvenience, that God cannot, within the compass of this world, wherein if any body vanish into nothing, the place or space left behind it, must have the three dimensions, and so be a true body, annihilate the least particle of matter, at least without, at the same instant and place, creating as much (which agrees very ill with that necessary and continual depen-

dence, which he asserts matter itself to have on God for its very being).[42]

At stake in this critique were not only differences about matter and speculation, but also the distinct integrity of (material) creation for Boyle in contrast to the closer relation of creation to God's will for Descartes.

The other side of Boyle's modern restitution of matter to its created integrity was his attack on the traditionally favored status of form. This exposé was indirectly implied in Boyle's affirmation of created matter and directly implied in his affirmation of the entirety of creation. Not only was the scholastic doctrine of real and distinct "substantial forms" undercut, but the explanation of physical phenomena by means of proliferating *forms* (and their unseen but necessarily posited "arguments" and "conventions") was undermined.[43] This was congruent with the voluntarist excision of ideas and forms from the mind of God. Boyle removed eternal forms as well as eternal matter; neither could claim a favored or uncreated status.

In a special section of the *Origin of Forms and Qualities* devoted to a critique of "substantial forms," Boyle announced that the sum of the controversy concerned the origin and separate reality of forms. Against the claim that such forms are generated or educed from matter, he argued that this seems to allow a power of creating substances which simply does not belong to finite creatures. Pressing his attack, he noted that some Scholastics made the forms depend immediately upon God. This desertion of Aristotelianism implied that God is constantly working "I know not how many thousand miracles every hour to perform that . . . in a supernatural way, which seems the most familiar effect of nature in her ordinary course." He argued further that the very idea of substantial forms was contradictory in that they were held to be both "substantial" and yet dependent upon matter *in fieri* and *in esse*. Yet Boyle would not tolerate substantial, i.e. self-subsisting, powers in a world of "created being."

> For not to ask, how (among physical things) one substance can be said to depend upon another *in fieri*, that is not made of any part of it, the very notion of a substance is to be a self-subsisting entity, or that, which needs no other created being to support it, or to make it exist.[44]

In discussing the argument that substantial forms are necessary to account for the design and texture of things, Boyle expressed his inclination for categories of order. According to the general laws of nature or motion, matter ordinarily remained in one state until modified by other agents also subject to the laws of motion. Thus, variety was best accounted for by the "peculiar texture" of bodies "and the action of outward agents." Boyle added, "I consider further, that various operations of a body may be derived from the peculiar texture of the whole." An appeal to a host of substantial forms, he wrote, is like being told the Devil is responsible for evil when one needs to search for a particular witch or examine the concrete operations of witchcraft. The economy and comprehension found in the laws of motion testify to God's ordered and careful design of creation.[45]

In opposition to "formal causes," Boyle not only rejected the scholastic affirmation but was equally critical of the Spiritualist attribution of mysterious and occult powers to forms.[46] (This conception was common among alchemists, and Helmont wrote interchangeably of "forms" and "seeds.") Once again, the thoroughness and scope of his critique represented a general demystification of form matched by a general restitution of matter, in brief, a profound revision of traditional presuppositions of form and matter. This was but one component in the epochal shift from the medieval hierarchical world of nature, a sophisticated organic world knit together by the "conventions" and "agreements" of substantial forms and real qualities, to the egalitarian material world of the moderns. The latter can be broken into many pieces and analyzed into many parts and then put back together again — both *in re* and in thought — in many different ways.

But what, if anything, took the place of the older form-matter rubric? First of all, Boyle critically differentiated motion from matter. Indeed, "motion is no way necessary to the essence of matter, which seems to consist principally in extension. For matter is no less matter when it rests."[47] (This distinction was as fundamental to Boyle's corpuscular chemistry as it was to Descartes' collision mechanics.)

This basic distinction presupposed Boyle's theology of creation. Against any appeal to "chance," i.e., the idea that the world originated through "fortunate" coincidences of atoms, he held that chance is merely "notional."[48] To ground motion in chance simply did not fit into the view of creation originated and ruled by the great and free Creator-Author of all things.

Boyle was equally critical of the "atheistical" Epicurean position which attributed properly divine power to self-originating atoms. An essential attribution of motion to such atoms, as well as appeals to their fortunate "conventions," betrayed a real (and not merely "notional") confusion between created matter and the basic and regulated laws of motion or nature, which were divinely established.[49] Thus, it ran counter to the legal-mechanical view and its presupposed theology of a distinct and lawful Creator. The sophisticated animism of ancient Epicurean atomism was ruled out.

In more positive terms, Boyle conceived of motion in terms of laws that closely resembled the laws of nature. While he did not develop a general theory of local motion in relation to primary qualities or affections and those laws, he did liken it to efficient causality. Compared to other primary mechanical affections, local motion was the "chief of second causes."[50]

It is important to understand, however, that causality appeared as less than a basic working category in Boyle's view of nature as a totality. Causality appeared relative to his frequently articulated grand principles of matter and motion, as well as that of law. Methodologically, he never allowed final causes to obstruct the search for efficient causes. While he did religiously celebrate both the grand scope and particularity of final causes or ends in creation, his natural philosophy clearly ruled out the reality of formal causes. There is evidence that when he wrote in general of a "scale" of causes, he subordinated them to the more simple and "catholick" principles of laws of nature and particulate matter. Also, it has been shown that, theologically, Boyle diverged from the traditional framework of first and second causes. Yet he was hardly able to avoid the many problems associated with causality. Its exact place and significance in the whole economy of his thought warrants further examination.[51]

Finally, just as he repeatedly understood motion, in a universal sense, in terms of law, Boyle repeatedly understood matter in terms of particular atoms (and corpuscles, etc.). In a sense, these conceptions "replaced" the older form-matter rubric. But they were not mere substitutes, as is clear in his representative thought on the laws of nature and atomism.

Theology and Laws of Nature

In wrestling with the problem of understanding the structure (and relations) of nature as well as its totality, Bacon, Boyle, and Newton differed significantly from such continental philosophers as Descartes, Spinoza, and Leibnitz. The latter addressed the problem in the classic manner, articulating a philosophy which strived for completeness. Extended reflection upon such categories as "substance" was typical of their enterprise. The English line, although given to total images and categories, adopted a less complete if no less systematic approach. English thought was more differentiated than that of the continental rational idealists, partly as a result of its critical voluntarism in theology, natural philosophy, and epistemology. Yet it may be assumed that the idea of law fairly represented their answers to the problem of the general structure of nature.

Such highly visible conceptions as Boyle's law in pneumatics and Newton's universal law of gravity call for an account of the basic idea of law in the early modern view of nature. I shall argue that the same theology presupposed in early modern differentiation, legal-mechanical images of nature, the fundamentals of matter (and form), and many other spheres ordered by divine law was at work in the increasingly prominent idea of laws of nature in seventeenth-century natural philosophy. Although the importance of the modern concept of physical laws of nature has been suggested in various quarters, the full historical novelty, context, and extent of this general idea has not yet received its due.[52]

Boyle's thought on laws of nature, like his view of local motion, was not thoroughly elaborated in any one place in his voluminous writings. However, his views were worked out over against traditional and Helmontian positions, and in relation to Descartes. The result was a position which may be highlighted systematically, prior to an examination of the important texts.[53]

In brief, Boyle presupposed that the structure of natural

creation was a system of law established and maintained by the Creator. Simultaneously committed to divine freedom, he thoroughly resisted necessary relations in creation, including those integral to organic and spiritual views of natural processes. Moreover, the real character of law in nature was presupposed to be imposed rather than immanent. This position enhanced the search for and careful formulation of specific physical laws of nature. Although particular scientific theories or results were never deduced from divine laws of nature — there was no direct line from the law of God to Boyle's Law — there was a positive relationship between the presupposition of divinely established laws of nature and the fellow presupposition that the structure of nature was to be understood in terms of law.

Boyle's frequent references to divine laws of nature and motion virtually specified a divine basis for nature and inquiry. Seeking to purge the epithets often attributed to nature, he claimed that "concerning nature's actings, it may not be improper, nor unuseful, to try, if we can clear the way, by considering in what sense nature may, or may not, be said to act at all." Boyle then proposed a major guideline for the reconstruction of nature as a system of divine rules:

> Sometimes, when it is said, that nature does this or that; it is less proper to say, that it is done by nature, than, that it is done according to nature: so that nature is not to be looked on, as a distinct or separate agent, but as a rule, or *rather a system of rules, according to which those agents, and the bodies they work on, are, by the great Author of things, determined to act and suffer.*

While the critical goal of this project was to do away with explanation and inquiry which appealed to the ways of nature, Boyle invoked the reality of divinely established laws of nature, arguing that the vulgar notion of nature was neither proven nor necessary. Upon supposing divinely originated laws of motion, local motion, and God's ordinary concourse, Boyle felt that burdens of proof definitely rested upon options other than those which affirmed God's law.[54]

It should be added that Boyle held that God not only originated law in creation but, in continuation of His original impartation of motion to matter, regulated matter through the laws of nature or motion. He noted "the great force of the local motion that was imparted to it, and is regulated by it."[55] Such regulation was derived not from local motion per se, but rather from divine law. In apparent agreement with Descartes, Boyle wrote:

> For first, according to the Cartesians, all local motion (which is, under God, the grand principle of all actions among things corporeal) is adventitious to matter, and was at first produced in it, and is still every moment continued and preserved immediately by God: whence may be inferred that he concurs to the actions of each particular agent (as they are physical) and consequently, that his providence reaches to all and every one of them.[56]

A remarkable passage in the *Notion of Nature* made the same point by stressing the lawful "general concourse" of divine Providence, from which Boyle concluded that organic and spiritual structures of nature were ruled out.

> I conceive, then, that the most wise Creator of things did at first so frame the world, and settle such laws of motion between the bodies, that, as parts, compose it, that by the assistance of his general concourse, the parts of the universe, especially those, that are the greater and the more noble, are lodged in such places, and furnished with such powers, that by the help of his general providence, they may have their beings continued and maintained, as long and as far forth, as the course he thought fit to establish, among other things corporeal, requires.
>
> Upon this supposition, which is but a reasonable one, there will appear no necessity to have any recourse, for the preservation of particular bodies, to such an internal appetite and inbred knowledge in each of them, as our adversaries presume; since, by virtue of the original frame of things, and established laws of motion, bodies are necessarily determined to act on such occasions, after the manner they would do, if they had really an aim at self-preservation.[57]

Moreover, in his *Excellency and Grounds of the Mechanical Hypothesis*, Boyle argued against the Epicurean affirmation of chance and those who held that God only originated matter in motion. He held

> not only that God gave motion to matter, but that in the beginning he so guided, the various motions of the parts of it, as to contrive them into the world he designed they should compose . . . and established those rules of motion, and that order amongst things corporeal, which we are wont to call the laws of nature.

Given this divine establishment, the phenomena of the world are produced "by the mechanical affections of the parts of matter, and . . . they operate upon one another *according to mechanical laws.*"[58]

Furthermore, the lawful work of God extended throughout matter. Affirming "Catholic laws of motion," Boyle countered the attractive supposition of hidden transactions between particles of matter. For, "the mechanical affections are to be found, *and the laws of motion take place,* not only in the great masses, and the middle-sized lumps, but in the smallest fragments of matter."[59] In the *Notion of Nature*, Boyle made one of his boldest claims. He ventured that if he were to "define" nature he would

> distinguish between the universal and particular nature of things. And, of universal nature, the notion I would offer should be some such as this; that nature is the aggregate of the bodies, that make up the world, framed as it is, considered as a principle, by virtue whereof they act and suffer, according to the laws of motion prescribed by the Author of things, Which description may be thus paraphrased; that nature in general, is the result of the universal matter, or corporeal substance of the universe, considered as it is contrived in the present structure and constitution of the world, whereby all the bodies, that compose it, are enabled to act upon, and fitted to suffer from one another, according to the settled laws of motion.[60]

With respect to universal nature, this passage clearly shows, once again, how basic Boyle's presupposition of law was. Much as atoms were basic to the structure of particulate matter, so law was basic to the structure of motion. Boyle's presupposition of law amounted to a universalization of motion much as his presupposition of atoms amounted to a radical individuation of matter.

Boyle went on to define particulars in terms of primary mechanical affections. He also characterized the two structural aspects of "universal" and "particular" nature, respectively, as the "cosmical" and "individual mechanism" of things.[61] Another crucial passage articulated a distinction, but not separation, of law appropriate to "fundamental" (universal) and "municipal" (particular) things in nature.

> And here it may not be amiss to take notice, that we may sometimes usefully distinguish between the laws of nature,

more properly so called, and the custom of nature, or, if you please, between the fundamental and general constitutions among bodily things, and the municipal laws, (if I may so call them) that belong to this or that particular sort of bodies.[62]

The distinction, although again not a separation, between "laws of nature" and the "custom of nature" was one of Boyle's ways of asserting that creation, while dependent upon the Creator and His law, had an integrity of its own.

Boyle knew that his position on the structure of nature involved problems with respect to both God and nature. In the *Notion of Nature*, he dealt with the apparent anomalies by affirming the generality of God's contrivances:

> The omniscient author of things, who, in his vast and boundless understanding, comprehended at once the whole system of his works, and every part of it, did not mainly intend the welfare of such or such particular creatures, but subordinated his care of their preservation and welfare to his care of maintaining the universal system and primitive scheme or contrivance of his works, and especially those Catholic rules of motion, and other grand laws, which he at first established among the portions of the mundane matter.

Near the end of the same treatise he wrote that the "great rector of the universe foresaw all that would happen as a consequence of his laws."[63] For Boyle, the "catholicity" of God's laws was prejudicial neither to any particulars nor to any apparent contradictions. God was an impartial Lawgiver.

Boyle also addressed the problem of apparent discord between God and the natural world by affirming the free prerogative of God. This argument, however, rested on the presupposition that God's relation to creation was lawful as well as free, in much the same way that creation was contingent upon God yet had its own integrity. Precisely at this point Boyle's disagreements with Descartes, which manifested the subtleties of his own voluntarist theology of creation, revealed another dimension of his view of the laws of nature.[64] (This included the prospect of what may be termed various specific or positive laws of nature in scientific inquiry.) Quite simply, Boyle was ruling out a necessary relation between God and the world when he affirmed the freedom of the former and the contingency of the latter. On the issue of whether the physical world was to be exhaustively defined as *res extensa*, Boyle argued that Descartes could not resist the difficulty of an infinite world, and found his locution of an "indefinite" world a verbal ploy disrespectful of mundane limitations in the face of God.

At the same time, Boyle held open the possibility that God might have created other worlds like our own. Similarly, he considered favorably the possibility of this world ordered either by different laws of motion or by a whole new set of laws which would give priority to quiescence rather than motion. He also noted that the Epicurean position of identifying matter and motion in powerful self-moving atoms could not admit these possibilities. Like the Cartesian position it was limited to a definite and necessary set of laws.[65]

In response to Descartes' derivation of the "conservation" of matter from the "immutability" of God, Boyle's resistance showed a further difference between their positions on law. Whereas Descartes implied that the content of laws must be mathematical, Boyle felt that Descartes' position assumed a given quantity of motion, and argued that

> the proof he offers being drawn from the immutability of God, seems very metaphysical, and not very cogent to me, who fear, that the properties and extent of the divine immutability are not so well known to us mortals, as to allow *Cartesians* to make it, in our present case, an argument *a priori*. And *a posteriori*, I see not how the rule will be demonstrated. . . .[66]

Any necessary lines between divine immutability and conserved matter (or motion) and between the same immutability and the mathematical content of explanatory laws of nature constituted an affront to the freedom of God, what He has done, and human limitations. As Boyle wrote elsewhere,

> It is one thing to contradict a catholick or metaphysical principle, or dictate of reason, and another to contradict a physical one; since the laws of nature, as they were at first arbitrarily instituted by God, so, in reference to him, they are but arbitrary still.[67]

It is difficult to overestimate the significance of Boyle's keen sense of God's "arbitrary" freedom vis-a-vis even the laws of nature. Like Newton, he felt no compulsion to construct a completely detailed natural philosophy tied to divine attributes. At the same time, both men expressed man's responsibility to observe the regularities of phenomena according to experience and experiment.

Making due allowances for his possible misreading of Descartes, Boyle gained a doctrine of matter ruled by law that was not tied to infinite extension in turn reinforced by a theologically deduced conservation of matter. Furthermore, his orientation admitted explanation according to both mathematical and non-mathematical laws. Irregardless of his proficiency in mathematics, Boyle's critical concern was the content rather than a final systematic statement of the laws of nature, especially in the presupposed framework of a divine establishment. In short, he was open to a greater range of observed regularities, and his thought was less hampered by fidelity to a complete and detailed metaphysical system.[68]

Furthermore, it is striking that for all his emphasis on God's authorship of law, Boyle did not advance examples directly embodying such law in his chemistry or pneumatics. That is, he did not seek to justify his own particular results or even specific laws by claiming that they were of God. It is likely that here again Boyle's critical respect for the distinct freedom of scientific inquiry was shaped by his deep resistance to easy Spiritualist confusions of the ways of God and man. In any case, Boyle like Newton was content to exemplify budding natural science as man's quest for and statement of the positive laws of nature. Accordingly, he described the twofold task of the new natural philosopher as one who discovers and formulates laws of nature. In *Reason and Religion*, for example, he gave clear expression to God's properly arbitrary will:

> If we consider God as the author of the universe, and the free establisher of the laws of motion . . . we cannot but acknowledge, that, by with-holding his concourse, or changing these laws of motion, which depend perfectly upon his will, he may invalidate most, if not all the axioms and theorems of natural philosophy: these supposing the course of nature, and especially the established laws of motion among the parts of the universal matter, as those upon which all the phaenomena depend.

Moreover, in precisely this context, he went on to articulate the natural philosopher's proper goal, the laws of nature. For human

> framers of these rules [laws of nature] having generally built them upon the observations they had made of natural and moral things . . . must not think it impossible, that there may

be rules, which will hold in all inferior beings for which they were made; and yet not reach to that infinite and most singular Being, called God.[69]

Boyle not only distinguished positive (or specifically framed) laws of nature from God's law, but also expressed the very task of the natural (and moral) philosopher as one of formulating laws (from observations) while yet convinced of the reality of law to be discovered.

Although the scientific task for Boyle was not as ultimate as God's own will and law, it did presuppose the Creator's own relation to creation. The discovery and formulation of laws manifested the dialectical unity of God's will and law, His freedom and power as expressed in the *potentia absoluta* and *ordinata* rubric. Thus Boyle's presupposition of the voluntarist theology of creation pervaded his understanding of the laws of nature in such a way that the form (although not specific theories or results) of scientific inquiry oriented to God's law was a religious task. The vocation of the new natural philosopher was rooted in creation and transposed into his own activity. A divine dialectic of will and law toward creation was manifest in laws of nature both ultimately given and arbitrary, and this double dialectic was in turn worked out in a disciplined scientific quest for laws of nature so deeply presupposed that the search had no finite terminus. This was vocation of a high order. It expressed Boyle's image of the natural philosopher as a reformed priest, an inquiring minister of natural creation.

One major point remains to be discussed. The epochal issue of the character of scientific law may be seen in a high point of the *Notion of Nature*, Boyle's critique of Helmont. At issue here was the structure of nature. Helmont's doctrines of elements, seeds, and matter as water were epitomized in a view of law virtually alive in spiritual creation. Although Boyle began with praise for Helmont's "rejecting the *Aristotelian* tenet of the contrariety or hostility of the elements" and even held that with proper modification Helmont's doctrine was "capable of a fair construction," he faulted the view which "will have the nature of everything to be only the law, that it receives from the Creator." To hold that

the *nature* of this or that body is but the law of *God prescribed to it* is but an improper and figurative expression. . . . I must freely observe, that, to speak properly, a law being but *a notional rule of acting according to the declared will of a superior*, it is plain, that nothing but an intellectual Being can be properly capable of receiving and acting by a law.[70]

For Boyle, Helmont not only reified linguistic entities but also confused both animate and inanimate realms and God and the world. Whereas atomic matter was subject to laws of nature without respect to any kind of internal tendency or "obedience" on its part, Helmont mistook both that which was according to divine law and that which was linguistically figurative for a single realm in which entities tended to realize the unity of law and nature.

Such confusion showed a fundamental divergence on the character of law. The Helmontian view presupposed that law was immanent in and intrinsic to physical entities. Indeed, such law, identical with the inner nature of creation, was coincident with the order integral to generative seeds and aqueous matter, and, at the same time, it literally represented the Spirit of the Creator in creation.[71] On the other hand, for Boyle, who presupposed the distinct Lawgiver of creation, the divinely imparted and regulated laws of nature were *imposed* upon a creation of totally subject atoms. Whereas this presupposition issued in a search for physical laws which fostered differentiated modern sciences, Helmont's presupposition of divine law immanent in (and intrinsic to) nature precluded a finite establishment of such laws. In the intrinsically legal and divine *nature* of all things, there was little possibility for differentiated inquiry into the content of particular laws of nature.

Boyle also argued that Helmont's doctrine

gives us but a very defective idea of nature since it omits the general fabric of the world, and the contrivances of particular bodies, which yet are as well necessary as local motion itself, to the production of particular effects and phenomena.[72]

In this critique, Boyle was uncomfortable with Helmont's omission, if not his account, of particulars. It is likely that Boyle's own view of irreducible atomic particulars (not Helmont's seeds), which fostered the imposed character of laws of nature because it implied external relations between the smallest units in creation, was presupposed.[73] But more clearly, he was attacking the Spiritualist view of the entire structure of nature on the basis of his more general presupposition that nature was characterized chiefly by legal-mechanical structures.[74] Helmont omitted the "general fabric" and "contrivances" of things.

Indeed, the shift from immanent to imposed laws of nature was part of the general transition in seventeenth-century thought from an organic to a later, strictly mechanical outlook. According to the classical natural law tradition, law was immanent in the ways of nature. Similarly, in the seventeenth-century revival of Spiritualism, law was obviously immanent in, if not outrightly identical with the divine Spirit of nature. Presupposing a sharply transcendental and voluntarist theology of creation, the seventeenth-century development of imposed laws of nature clearly broke new ground. Yet it would be claiming too much for the representative thought of Boyle to equate it with that of solely and strictly positive laws of nature in later mechanistic orientations, in turn moved by presuppositions of both human autonomy (as well as creativity) and a largely impotent deism.[75] The imposed laws of nature, which were congruent in the early modern period with the achievement of differentiation and the legal-mechanical images of nature as divine creation, also presupposed the Creator as Author, a richer theological presupposition than later views of a removed Maker.

Newton's natural philosophy, like Boyle's, was marked by a profound employment of the laws of nature which presupposed a voluntarist orientation to divine creation.[76] Indeed, his views on the laws of nature were prominent in some of his most venturesome efforts to answer the problem of the general structure of nature. This is evident in a number of texts, some of which have only recently been brought to light. Yet, notwithstanding the support of his voluntarist theology, such presuppositions alone could not settle the complex issue of the structure of nature for Newton.

Writing in the broadest terms of the natural universe, Newton affirmed the dialectical freedom of God in establishing the laws of nature, which in turn could be changed if God so willed. Thus in Query 31 of his *Opticks*, he wrote that because

> matter is not necessarily in all places, it may be also allow'd that God is able to create Particles of Matter of Several Sizes and Figures, and in several Proportions to Space, and perhaps

of different Densities and Forces, and thereby to vary the Laws of Nature, and make Worlds of several sorts in several Parts of the Universe. At least, I see nothing of Contradiction in all this.[77]

Moreover, he saw the laws of nature as imposed upon things. Thus in his first letter to Richard Bentley, he wrote that ". . . the motions which the planets now have, could not spring from any natural cause alone, but were impressed by an intelligent agent."[78] In his early *De Gravitatione*, he affirmed a similar divine regulation of bodies, much as a human will regulates its body. Also, it is clear from Cotes' Preface to the second edition of the *Principia* that the recommendation that the natural philosopher study the laws of nature was opposed to the divination of "occult qualities."[79]

Of equal if not greater significance were the variety of explanations Newton entertained in wrestling with the issue of the structure of nature by seeking to comprehend the "invisible realm," the micro-level of the universe. Newton's presupposition of law appears throughout the course of these efforts. From 1687 to 1705, Newton held that the cause of the universal force of gravity was simply God's will, rejecting both secondary causes and a mechanical or fluid aether. Refining his earlier explanatory references to chemical phenomena and seeking with a general "analogy of nature" to understand this realm, he suggested "active principles."[80]

In a series of early (1705) drafts to the Queries of the *Opticks*, Newton searched further to understand the invisible realm.[81] These interesting drafts led to the following proposal published in the *Opticks* of 1717-18. He wrote that

particles have not only *Vis inertiae*, accompanied with such passive Laws of Motion as naturally result from that Force, but also that they are moved by certain active Principles, such as that of Gravity, and that which causes Fermentation, and the Cohesion of Bodies. These Principles, I consider not as occult Qualities, supposed to result from the specific Form of things, but as general Laws of Nature, by which the things themselves are form'd: Their truth appearing to us from Phaenomena, though their Causes be not yet discover'd.[82]

Turning to the earlier drafts, Newton wrote that

we meet with very little motion on the world besides what is

> owing to these active principles & therefore we ought to inquire diligently into the general Rules or Laws observed by nature in the preservation & production of motion by these principles as the Laws of motion on which the frame of Nature depends & the genuine Principles of the Mechanical Philosophy & the inward parts of the earth are constantly warmed.

Distinct from the intriguing matter of the content (and implications) of these "active principles,"[83] this passage clearly relates them to laws of motion in a most intimate way. In any case,

> without some other principle than the *Vis inertiae* there could be no motion in the world. (And what that Principle is & by (means of) laws it acts on matter is a mystery or how it stands related to matter is difficult to explain). And if there be another Principle of motion there must be other laws of motion depending on that Principle. And the first thing to be done in philosophy is to find out all the general laws of motion (so far as they can be discovered) on w[hi]ch the frame of nature depends. (For the powers of nature are not in vain [two words are illegible]. . . .[84]

On God as the source of gravity, he stated:

> Whence it seems to have been an ancient opinion that matter depends upon a Deity for its (laws of) motion as well as for its existence. The Cartesians make God the author of all motion & its as reasonable to make him the author of the laws of motion. Matter is a passive principle & cannot move itself. It continues in its state of moving or resting unless disturbed. It receives motion proportional to the force impressing it, and resists as much as it is resisted. These are passive laws & to affirm that there are no other is to speak against experience. For we find in ourselves a power of moving our bodies by our thought. Life & Will (thinking) are active Principles by which we move our bodies, & thence arise other laws of motion unknown to us.[85]

From this striking series of passages, it is clear that Newton presupposed law in seeking to render the invisible realm of active principles as intelligible as the visible realm of principles in the cosmos at large. Furthermore, he presupposed law not only in seeking to grasp this other realm but also in understanding its relationship with the visible world. Thus, he spoke of "general Rules or Laws" and not simply the laws appropriate to passive and active principles, respectively. Finally, Newton affirmed "Laws of Nature" in the invisible realm against "occult Qualities" and "Forms," just as he affirmed law against the occult in the visible world.

Moreover, the source of these physical laws was God, the Author of all laws of motion and of that universal law which is in turn presupposed throughout the structure of nature. Newton did not assume that the physical laws of nature were divinely originated simply to make a place for God in the world. Rather, he was absolutely convinced of God's law in natural creation and employed it to render intelligible the grand vision of a "Principia" even of the invisible world.[86] In short, he shared with Boyle a voluntarist presupposition of the lawful structure of creation grounded in its Author.

Theology, Atoms, and Qualities

.Turning to a third component in Boyle's idea of nature — particular units, which may be relatively distinguished from the components of totality and structure — the critical bearing of his theology will be more apparent than its positive significance. Nevertheless, the general spread of individuation (as well as differentiation) in early modern thought tended to set the conditions for "atomism" in natural philosophy; it also set conditions for "simple ideas" in epistemology, for "individuals" in literature, and for strong personal "conscience" in religious practice. Once again, it is important to understand that Boyle's theology was not the *cause* of his atomism. Indeed, the term "atomism" is a methodological construct which must be used with great care, for it is not adequate to the complexity of his thought on particulars. Furthermore, with respect to particulars in nature as compared to its totality and structure, he related God indirectly to atoms, corpuscles, and the like. The latter were part of larger structures of action and order in nature more directly related to God.

Critical Atomism

In one of his typical emphatic statements on the way particular bodies should not be conceived, Boyle wrote that ". . . inanimate bodies acting without knowledge or design of their own, cannot stop or moderate their own action, but must necessarily move as they are determined by the Catholic laws of motion."[87] Clearly, he opposed any attribution of life, spirit, or intelligence to things. Indeed, he rejected the idea that the basic relations between things were referred to their inner natures, a central notion in organic or spiritual views of nature. His presupposition of divinely imposed laws of nature did not allow such views. Its implication of basically external relations between things is explicit in his claim that

> since motion does not essentially belong to matter, as divisibility and impenetrableness are believed to do; the motion of all bodies, at least at the beginnings of things, and the motions of most bodies, the cause of whose motions we can discern, were impressed upon them, either by an external immaterial agent, God; or by other portions of matter (which are also *extrinsical impellers*) acting on them.[88]

Boyle affirmed both options; the external action of both God and particles was in agreement with his view of imposed laws of nature.

With respect to the large design of creation, Boyle developed a conception of particulars which represented the modern idea of nature. In regard to corpuscles, which were more complex than simple impenetrable atoms, he proposed a concept of texture for the designed creation within which larger particular bodies function. Resisting any framework for particulars as being an "aggregate of powers," Boyle relied upon the texture of regularized or designed groupings of atoms and corpuscles rather than the more animistic "conventions" and "agreements" of many distinct natures. This was reinforced in his recommendation that one should speak of the "system of the universe" or a "cosmical mechanism."[89]

Boyle's development of early modern atomism warrants closer examination. The idea of particular atoms with "primary affections" of size, shape, and motion constituted a major building-block for Boyle. In a careful statement in the *Usefulness of Natural Philosophy*, he wrote that

> there are divers effects in nature, of which though the immediate cause may be plausibly assigned, yet if we further inquire into the causes of those causes, and desist not from ascending in the scale of causes, till we are arrived at the top of it, we shall perhaps find the more catholick and primary causes of things to be either certain, primitive, general, and fixed laws of nature (or rules of action and passion among the parcels of the univer-

sal matter,) or else the shape, size, motion, and other primary affections of the smallest parts of matter, and of their first coalitions or clusters.[90]

In this passage even the reality of causality tends to recede in face of the more basic realities of primitive atoms and laws of nature. Accordingly, in the *Notion of Nature* Boyle deliberately replaced the idea of "internal principles of motion" alleged in falling stones and rising flames (by Helmont as well as by the Schoolmen), with "local motion," which in turn was subject to law.[91] Thus the main direction of Boyle's early modern atomism diverged from both the Helmontian view of particulars as "seeds," and the persistent scholastic (as well as Epicurean) doctrine of powerful (literally "power-filled") essences and atoms. In all these cases, the crucial systematic point was the congruence of (impenetrable) atomic particulars with external law and design throughout creation.

One can now see remarkable coherence in the presupposition of both external relations which bind together particulars, especially atoms, and of divinely imposed laws of nature. Whereas both the medieval and Spiritualist views of immanent natural law and power-filled particulars presupposed internal relations, not only among things in the physical world but also in relation to God, Boyle's thought was especially marked by a differentiation of nature into particulars. The laws of nature limited, set boundaries, and regulated atoms externally.[92] This was a major step beyond any divine realization within the tendencies and conventions of seeds and essences.

The epochal and critical scope of Boyle's atomism may be indicated if it is seen as the middle one of three stages in the roughly parallel development of both atomism and laws of nature.[93] It has been noted that the progression from the Stoic and medieval view of immanent natural law to the widespread early modern view of imposed laws of nature was followed by a positivistic conception of law chiefly as a comprehensive heuristic device. Similarly, the ancient Epicurean atoms, the medieval essences, and the Spiritualist's seeds presupposed that motion and power were inherent to particles, a view congruent with the doctrine of immanent natural law, whereas late Enlightenment thought held that atoms were hypothetical constructs in accord with its doctrine of heuristic natural law. However, in the seventeenth-century thought represented by Boyle, Gassendi, and Newton, the conception of particular impenetrable atoms ruled by imposed laws of nature was dominant.

A telling manifestation of Boyle's critical atomism was evident in the limited inferences one might draw from the external laws of nature to particulars, and vice versa.[94] (The effects of presupposing external relations contrasted sharply with the direct inferences which obtained given internal relations constitutive of particulars.) For example, Boyle criticized Helmont's proposal that the "nature of things" be understood as "the law of things." On this view, the natural philosopher divined the seeds of things through knowledge of the divine law or Spirit which constituted those things. As a correlative to such direct inferences, the Helmontian natural philosopher came to know the intrinsic laws of nature through knowledge of the directions and tendencies, if not decisions and intentions, of particular seeds. Boyle's critical alternative prohibited any inference of the essence of particular atoms from external and imposed laws. One could conclude that hard impenetrable atoms manifested diverse legal-mechanical behavior or exhibited a certain texture, but this was not to know the inner essence of things. This empirical point could be put the other way around: one could not deduce the content of (divinely grounded) laws of nature simply from particular atoms. In general, Boyle's natural philosophy was neither wholistic nor hierarchical, but legal-mechanical, atomic, and corpuscular. As such, it represented an epochally new departure in the growth of Western science.

Boyle's "Choice" of Atomism

Boyle oscillated a great deal, especially in his initial leanings toward Helmont's theory of matter, before he settled for "atomic" legal-mechanical philosophy. The immediate source of his final views was Gassendi, whose works were promoted by Charleton. Without settling the moot issue of Boyle's originality, it is significant that just as Gassendi had to do battle with the Spiritualist Fludd in establishing his position, so too Boyle was locked in a tussle with the attractions of Helmontian Spiritualism.

Although Boyle read Gassendi as early as 1645, and may

have studied his major *Syntagma Philosophicum*, he remained impressed with the Helmontian theory of matter based upon elemental water. For example, his *Reflexions*, an early version of the *Sceptical Chemist*, accorded the place of honor to Helmont's theory.[95] Even though Boyle had performed the "water culture" experiment which in turn neutralized the powerful support of Helmont's "willow tree" experiment for the theory of aqueous matter, he nevertheless honored Helmont's theory as a formidable theory of matter.[96]

In the *Sceptical Chemist* of 1661 the picture is much different. The discussion of Helmont is given secondary place and attention. Moreover, Boyle increased his criticism of "Scholastics" and "Spagyrists" (Spiritualists) and advanced an atomic theory of matter. The omission of such a theory in the *Reflexions* was not because Boyle was unfamiliar with atomism, as may be seen by his very early *Of Ye Atomical Philosophy*, written no latter than 1653.[97] Nor can the water culture experiment as such account for this shift. Not only was it the principal feature of the earlier *Reflexions*, but it had probably been performed earlier by Robert Sharrock.[98] Yet, Boyle did employ that experiment in a way markedly different from Sharrock and in this may lie the clue to an answer. He sought to gain distinct leverage from the experiment in order to criticize a universal theory of matter, although he did not fully settle that question until the time of the *Sceptical Chemist*.

Of equal significance, and in line with Boyle's genuine theoretical interests in contrast to Sharrock, is the fact that when Boyle set aside Helmont's theory in the *Sceptical Chemist*, he prefaced his treatment with the crucial *proviso* that he was speaking as a "naturalist," not as a theological "philologer." He had achieved a liberating differentiation in his theoretical orientation. This freedom to "naturalize," in contrast to the way Helmont confused natural philosophy and theology, fostered his own settlement for atomism.[99]

A Critical Account of Qualities

Boyle's views on the qualities of bodies also showed formal congruity with his theology of creation. Indeed, at one point in his critique of the persistent scholastic error of "real qualities," he held that they were no more and no less than "substantial forms" and should be dismissed for the same reasons.[100] His objections to the Spiritualist doctrine of "occult qualities" and the Cartesian view of "porous quality" were equally extensive and detailed. However, one general criticism of all three positions manifested the modernity of his corpuscular philosophy. He vigorously opposed a direct grounding of the quality of physical things in theological or metaphysical realities which necessarily determined their form and content. Noting the theological basis of the scholastic forms and qualities, Boyle said that he would carry on as a naturalist, not as a theologian — or as one who mixed the two.[101]

The real conflict here was not between theological and atheological natural philosophy. Rather, an economical theology which eschewed speculation in favor of a free yet externally regulated natural philosophy was opposed to theology and metaphysics run together and determinative of natural philosophy. Thus, Boyle's most general critique was not just against scholastic theology but also against the hegemony of the metaphysical (Aristotelian) distinction between act and potency in scholastic natural philosophy.[102] Having perceived that the persistent strength of the scholastic doctrine of real qualities was in its metaphysical support, he deliberately engaged in a comprehensive attack upon the scholastic view of qualities. It must be emphasized that his thoroughness was not simply of empirical extent but also had critical theoretical integrity.

Boyle's objection to scholastic thought also appeared in his criticism of Descartes' deduction of the conservation of matter from the immutability of God, which he extended in the *Origin of Forms and Qualities*. He refused to deduce the (porous) physical quality of bodies from the *materia subtilitas*, holding that when one accepts one metaphysical doctrine of this sort one soon has an entire system on one's hands. The less sophisticated but equally confusing synthesis of theology and metaphysics in the Spiritualist espousal of "occult qualities" was subjected to similar criticism.[103]

Boyle's position was representative of the line of English natural philosophy which sought to eschew metaphysical entanglement. The theoretical part of the *Origin of Forms and Qualities* began by criticizing hypostatized "real qualities."[104]

Accordingly, the chief concern of the "excursion on the relative nature of physical qualities" was that the various powers of physical things not be made into separate qualitative entities. Thus, the negative function of distinguishing between primary mechanical affections (qualities) and other qualities was the prohibition of the proliferation of separate "real qualities." Boyle saw no defensible way to control the proliferation of real qualities once one allows distinct being to the various powers of physical things.

Moreover, Boyle argued that, in addition to its metaphysical bondage, the Cartesian view considered quality only in relation to us at the expense of the mutual relations of particular qualities. He claimed that Descartes

> speaks but very briefly and generally, rather considering what they [qualities] do upon the organs of sense, than what changes happen in the objects themselves, to make them cause in us a perception sometimes of one quality, and sometimes of another.[105]

Descartes failed to acknowledge the impenetrability of physical things, their definite physical particularity. This was the other side of Boyle's critique of the inutility of the doctrine of *materia subtilitas* in dealing with hard physical bodies.

Boyle's positive understanding of particular physical qualities represented an epochal modern distinction between primary and secondary qualities. Moreover, his two-fold distinction between primary and secondary qualities also bore witness to the weight of his basic presuppositions. In one sense, Boyle advanced the key distinction as follows: What was primarily and simply qualitative in physical bodies was distinguished from their powers or capacities to affect each other or our senses.[106] This distinction not between two kinds of qualities but between the quality of physical bodies per se and the powers relative to such qualitative entities was the exact opposite of the false hypostatization of "real qualities."[107] Accordingly, Boyle also affirmed cosmical physical qualities and appreciated the different qualities in differently contextured bodies. Moreover, he anticipated the discovery of "new qualities."[108] When Boyle wrote of simple quality in this sense, he presupposed openness to creaturely variety or quality in the designed creation. Thus, he could assume the corpuscularian philosophy without embracing either the atomic or Cartesian doctrines of matter as final.[109]

Extending the Baconian exhortation and program to attend to the full particularity of immediate and efficient causes, Boyle insisted upon the primacy of simple qualities in distinction from attendant powers. Just as Bacon resisted appeal to a hidden teleology in particulars, so Boyle ruled out misleading "real" qualities in favor of primary qualities, which were minimal requirements for a truly comprehensive yet nonrestrictive explanatory base in natural philosophy.

> It is chiefly by the knowledge, such as it is, that experience (not art) hath taught us, of these differing qualities of bodies, that we are enabled, by a due application of agents to patients, to exercise the little empire, that we have either acquired or regained over the creatures.[110]

Boyle also advanced the distinction between primary and secondary qualities in a second and different sense. He regarded primary qualities as the more or less mechanical affections of size, shape, and local motion. Such qualities were more primitive than the secondary qualities which were derived from them and also conditional upon the senses.[111] This crucial distinction was intended to counter not only the hypostatization of separate real qualities, but also the power of occult qualities which Boyle regarded as fictitious. He felt that this second distinction helped prevent the fallacious occult qualities or the spurious three elements of "spagyrist" traditions. Once again the basic level of his thought moved against both traditional and Spiritualist natural philosophy. His distinction of mechanical primary qualities from more complex secondary qualities presupposed his framework of divine law, and especially the mechanical affectivity central to insensible atoms subject to law. Boyle further held that it was speculative to go "behind" atoms in discussions of their infinite divisibility.[112] He granted that this was possible for the mind but insisted that the natural philosopher should deal with more given realities.

In brief, Boyle's two-fold distinction between primary and secondary qualities, as a distinction of simple quality and its powers, as well as a sharp distinction between mechanical and non-mechanical qualities, was congruent with the critical and guiding power of a voluntarist theology of creation.

* * * * *

In conclusion, this chapter has shown quite simply that Boyle presupposed the natural world to be God's creation. In his highly representative thought the idea of nature by itself was a mere notion. In truth, however, this idea stood for the physical world as divine creation. Apart from creation, nature was nothing. Boyle did not merely assume that this was or might be the case, say, from the point of view of some relative or even absolute thinker. On the contrary, this was a basic theological presupposition; he took it for granted.

This central thesis has been developed in some detail in relation to the images, categories, and distinctive positions that marked Boyle's early modern view of nature — all of which is briefly summarized in the concluding chapter. Meanwhile, it should be noted that the contextual method employed here — a search for basic presuppositions — has disclosed a definite efficacy range of deeply held theological convictions.[113] These convictions amounted to a lively context for wide-ranging and discriminating criticism. They also shaped and characterized a number of root metaphors and some potent legal answers to the problem of the structure of nature. Moreover, it is likely that Boyle's theology was at work most specifically in his settlement for a particulate theory of matter. Simultaneously, in a formal but not empty way, the same theology was at work in his critical views of atoms and qualities. This broad and rich efficacy range of basic presuppositions shows that they were far from idle. In a time of deep conflict, they were fruitful for the problems of forming an epochally new understanding of the totality, structure, and particular units of nature.

CHAPTER SEVEN:

Conclusion

The foregoing detailed textual explications of the thought of Helmont and Boyle have shown that the central texts in their natural philosophy and science manifested diverse theological/religious orientations which were less determinative than direct causes but more determinative than simple conditions. Helmont was a powerful thinker who not only represented the profundity and attractiveness of Spiritualist orientations but also generated an impressive wholistic unification of thought, practice, and piety. Indeed, in his coherent and thoroughly knit position science and piety were not simply fused; they were expressed and synthesized in a remarkable unity of natural philosophy and Spiritualist theology. This unity, in turn, was manifest in the concrete practice of a chemistry and medicine simultaneously cosmic, humane, and divine in scope and purpose. Boyle's contrasting forays into historical inquiry and literary soundings, taken together with his diverse and well-known contributions in chemistry, natural philosophy, and religion, reveal a pattern that clearly bespoke the modern mind. His way was oriented to an exclusive One rather than inclusive Spirit. Presupposing divine transcendence, law, and design, he advanced the critical as well as soberly systematic edge of modern thought against both traditionalists and Spiritualists. The many aspects of his thought were marked by a unity of differentiation and critical reconstruction of particulars that stands forth historically as modern in contrast to the hierarchical and wholistic unities, respectively, of traditional and Spiritualist orientations.[1]

The arguments and contrasts between Boyle and Helmont, Boyle and the traditionalists, Bacon and his antagonists, Newton and his opponents, and, not least, Boyle and Descartes have highlighted the drama of the epochal rise of modern thought. In this drama, the rise of modern natural science was more than a simple change of scene from medieval to modern outlooks, anticipated in late medieval criticism and initially established in early modern developments. The inner drama of this development was richly contested and concentrated, particularly in mid-seventeenth-century English thought. Traditional natural philosophy did not simply expire. It persisted, and was met by the virtually total opposition of renascent Spiritualism. In the midst of this encounter, the achievement of the mainline early modern figures was by no means assured. Boyle's determined early modern effort was partly moved by Helmontian attractions, which he came to criticize so thoroughly. Thus, mechanical images did not merely replace organic ones. Law-like basic images of nature overcame those that featured nature as a Spiritual process. Such lively and critical mediation was integral to the outcome of a more mechanical outlook. Similarly, a new critical empiricism struggled with both Spiritualist enthusiasm for the concrete and traditional modes of inquiry.

In this dramatic force-field of the rise of modern science, different questions were raised, diverse answers assumed, and different positions presupposed. Nevertheless, my contextual inquiry, a search for basic presuppositions, has shown a powerful fundamental which was often neglected in the economy of Christian thought itself. Through early modern times, Christian thought took God the Creator largely for granted. It was held in a powerful trust. Of course most of the principals were far from fully aware of this, for it had not been otherwise for centuries.[2]

While it is a truism that the rise of modern natural science occurred within Christendom, I have sought to show in the broadest sense that belief in creation constituted a definitive context within which the basic questions of major figures in the advent of the new science were raised, pursued, and developed. Systematically, the principals who gave shape to the new science (traditionalists, Spiritualists, and moderns) took for granted an orientation to God as Creator, His relation to creation, structure in creation at large, and the human creature's special place in creation. The efficacy of these basic presuppositions was manifest historically in the dramatic conflict of competing orientations to the Creator, created order, etc. In short, belief in creation was the rich yet common intellectual arena for profound conflict and debate within which long-established ontological orientations, renascent Spiritualist orientations, and highly visible voluntarist orientations to reality engaged each other.

The new science emerged in a milieu that in the deepest sense was theologically secure and lively by virtue of moving religious interests in creation and culture. Since much was taken for granted, there was something worth fighting about that went beyond the Spiritualist's highest vision of a wholly new science, the traditionalist's determined retention of perennial natural philosophy, and the modern's remarkably successful advancement of "mechanical" philosophies and sciences.

Besides this universal sense in which belief in divine creation was a nurturing presupposition of the new science, there was a second way in which creation was presupposed. Helmont's natural philosophy was more than nurtured by Spiritualist religion and theology. His thought virtually exuded the Creator Spirit. The whole as well as each part of his undifferentiated vision was totally oriented to the Creator as inclusive and pervasive Spirit, divine omneity. Nature as a vital process (from "water" and "seeds" to aerial ferments), the spirituality of man, and knowledge as Spiritual understanding were immediate manifestations of the Father of Lights and Life. Even Helmont's stress on the immediacy of attention and the necessity of certainty were fused with the Spiritual virtues of charity and humility.

The full historical role of undifferentiated Spiritualism in the rise of modern science has not yet been determined. Yet, distinct from estimating particular contributions, it is clear that this orientation was massively opposed to traditional natural philosophy and its metaphysical supports. The philosophy of Aristotle, Galen, and the medieval thinkers was pronounced to be ignorant of both Creator and creation, and utterly lost in the pride of reason at the expense of understanding. Nevertheless, without underestimating the role of this condemnation, it is clear that the dominant early modern thinkers chartered a very different course. In this respect the role of Spiritualism was that of a foil and catalyst.

In the face of the wholistic Spiritualist position and negation, there was a third and most pointed way that belief in divine creation was movingly presupposed in the advent of early modern science. The largely voluntarist theological orientation to creation of Boyle, Bacon, and Newton was as thoroughly differentiated as that of Helmont was undifferentiated.[3] No less genuinely theological, they represented both the cutting and the building edges of modern science. Their careful constructions were epochally different from those of traditional natural philosophy, but no less formative for subsequent centuries. And their criticism, severe as it was, was not locked into the sheer opposition to tradition which marked so much of the Spiritualist renaissance; it was discriminating. Their way has been at the heart of this study.

These early modern thinkers were determined reformers. Their belief in creation had all the force of a new and highly focused sense of the supreme will of God. The Creator was much more than the power of being; He was the single source of the chief order in creation. Some of the moderns were converted natural philosophers, but all were moved and disciplined by praise of the Creator. Belief in the transcendent otherness of God, who was the Author of all law and design in creation, was at the moving center of their thought. Venerable unities of the hierarchy of being (and therefore of everything else) and renewed unities of wholistic reality gave way before belief in a willful and lawful Creator whose field was the entire natural creation and all sorts of creatures within it. This kind of pointed belief was highly determinative in epochally new ideas of nature, of knowledge, and of modernity itself.

Nothing was more basic to Boyle's representative new view of nature than his broadside against the many ways of deifying nature. Closely associated with such egregious errors, the reign of traditional organic and renewed vitalist images of nature was critically overcome by new images of nature as law-like and mechanical. The very economy of these modern images bespoke the transcendent Creator and His law. Perennial images of design, now ordered to the divine Author, were reappropriated in legal-mechanical images. Moreover, the venerable categories of matter and form were reevaluated. The formerly intractable stuff of matter was raised to a new level of equity and economy while, at the same time, the favored status traditionally accorded to form(s) was ruled out. The new "Catholic" principles of divinely originated laws of motion sharply distinguished from particulate matter constituted a new categorial rubric. (Ironically, the end result of denying any semi-divine "plastick power" was a new grasp of nature more radically plastic, i.e., malleable and disposable, for divine will and human projects.)

Once nature was presupposed as an entire legal-mechanical creation subject to divine law, imposed physical laws of nature were taken for granted. Boyle, Bacon, and Newton were largely responsible for this shift from the older immanent natural law and the vital inner law of Spiritualism. Moreover, the new establishment of imposed laws was an economical structure of creation which further called for a new view of particulars — atoms, corpuscles, and the like. Atoms were externally linked to other atoms with universal mechanical affections, and a critical economy of primary qualities formed a new center of scientific imagination and construction. Helmontian seeds and forms as well as the qualities and essences of traditionalists had no place in such a newly conceived universe subject to imposed law. A rigorous egalitarianism of the individual units of nature overcame the dense entities of more elaborate hierarchical and wholistic structures of natural being and Spiritual life. (The older conventions and inner affinities of diverse particles, which presupposed complex internal relations and many fundamentally different qualitative bodies, now gave way to external relations of impenetrable atomic particulars.)

Partly due to convictions of divinely imposed laws of nature, knowledge in the new science was marked by a disciplined search for and positive statement of laws. Furthermore, the modern relation to nature, similar to the relation to God, was expressed in a relatively simple epistemic economy, which involved more than "simple ideas." Simultaneously moved by many constructions, the sharp edge of modern knowledge was its rule over nature, a utilitarian expression of knowledge as power. The necessarily involved (and elaborate) discernment of types and archetypes was overcome. Likewise, the Spiritualist practice of understanding, a more passive yet concrete involving of all powers of the self with those of Spirit in nature, was set aside.

In perhaps broader yet equally critical terms, the modern view of knowledge presupposed an epochally new distance between knower and known, much as God and man in their own ways transcended creation; neither was subject to nature. Accordingly, the classic (and medieval) order of knowledge following being was reversed, and the process of knowing was no longer centered in participation or identification with the known. Quite otherwise, there was a widespread differentiation of knowledge — of natural philosophy from elaborate theological/metaphysical entanglements, of incipient natural sciences from natural philosophy, and of empirical attention as careful observation distinct from framing and testing hypotheses. Even the reflective reconstruction (and justification) of the knowledge process itself (including tolerance to balance its many elements) now became part of the differentiation of knowledge. The critical presupposition of transcendence in knowledge was both profound and far reaching.

Empirical knowledge was now linked to will, and there was no longer any long or short cut to knowledge of the world through divine Mind or Spirit. That world, a creation radically dependent upon divine will and ruled by God's law, both required and called for direct inquiry with distinct modes of observation and hypothesis, among others. Indeed, the very search to fashion laws while taking law for granted manifested the same voluntary yet rational bent at the center of critical-dialectical voluntarist theologies of creation. For this orientation, revelation in creation at large was neither a sealed answer nor the hidden truth; it was an invitation to a highly disciplined scientific research.

Finally, the rise of modern natural science involved more than new views of nature and knowledge; it was *modern*. This arrival of modernity showed the force of a pointed voluntarist theology. One of the principal axes in the structure of modernity was that God's work of creation was sharply differentiated from that of redemption. This was supported by an emergent religion of creation — featuring the Creator's mandate to Adam — with an integrity distinct from that of redemption. Impatient with the immediacy of visions, Bacon, Boyle, and Newton presupposed that history itself was a regular but progressive divine creation. Scientific (and other) discoveries were signs anticipating a new age; they were not symbolic deliverances from the past or into the future. Returns to Paradise and ascents to Heaven were ruled out. The sobriety of signs rather than symbols or hieroglyphics bespoke a linear sense of history in which the distinct realities of past, present, and future were not reduced but tensed. Such historical stretching out of creation meant that science itself was no longer the Spiritualist's gift nor a venerable tradition.

The new science was a task which called for the productions and reformations of that faith which issued in works. This was at the root of Bacon's call for a concrete faith. The early modern sense of reform was more optimistic than Reformation Christianity, more progressive than classic Roman Catholic Christianity, and more sober than Spiritualism. Joining the sharp differentiation of God's work to a heightened sense of His transcendence as the supreme individual, it gave shape and direction to a differentiation of human works as literary, historical, religious, and scientific. The early modern course of differentiation in both divinity and natural philosophy (as well as other spheres) fostered newly distinguished disciplines of religious and scientific practice. Relatively new genres of communication — ranging from pious meditations on creation to laboratory reports, from historical inquiry to the beginnings of the novel — appeared, just as atoms of matter, conscience in religious consciousness, simple ideas in knowledge, and the events of history stood forth for both practice and inquiry. But the law of the Creator as Author was consistently taken for granted in spheres as diverse as nature, morals, and religion. For the highly disciplined sense of modernity this was no idle presupposition.[4]

Notes

Notes to Chapter One

[1]See the works of Joseph Needham, particularly *Science and Civilization in China* (London: Cambridge University Press, 1954), and the discussions in *Changing Perspectives in the History of Science: Essays in Honour of Joseph Needham* (Dordrecht: D. Reidel, 1973), ed. by Mikulas Teich and Robert Young.

[2]"The Early Modern Revolution in Science and Philosophy," *Boston Studies in the Philosophy of Science*, ed. by Robert S. Cohen and Marx W. Wartofsky (New York: Humanities Press, 1968), III, 1.

[3]New York: Scribner's, 1948.

[4]From a vast literature, see the quite different works of Lynn White, Jacques Ellul, and Jerome R. Ravetz, *Scientific Knowledge and its Social Problems* (New York: Oxford, 1973).

[5]Notwithstanding the differences between Walzer and Little, taken together their works amount to a significant demonstration of the influence of religion in seventeenth-century political-ethical life. See Michael Walzer, *The Revolution of the Saints* (Cambridge: Harvard, 1965), and David Little, *Religion, Order, and Law* (New York: Harper, 1969).

[6]For example, see E. J. Dijksterhuis, *The Mechanization of the World Picture* (New York: Oxford, 1961).

[7]Precisely this perspective is lacking in the "internal-external" dichotomy that plagues history (and historiography) of science, especially efforts to understand those broad meanings of nature which antedate the eighteenth-century conception of special "natural sciences." Moreover, the dubious dichotomy multiplies problems when one deals with diffuse rather than compact scientific traditions and disciplines, particularly in times of great change. Toulmin's attempt to fashion an "ecological" epistemology is, in part, a philosophical response to such problems. See Stephen Toulmin, *Human Understanding* (Princeton: Princeton University Press, 1972), I, 300-318, and his earlier "Conceptual Revolutions in Science," *Boston Studies in the Philosophy of Science*, III, 347.

[8]In addition to the works of Merton, Collingwood, and Whitehead discussed below, see Raven, *Natural Religion and Christian Theology: Volume I, Science and Religion* (London: Cambridge University Press, 1953), and Hooykaas, *Religion and the Rise of Modern Science* (Grand Rapids: Eerdmans, 1972).

[9]2 vols.; New York: Appleton, 1896. The apologetic literatures on behalf of both science and religion are immense. They deserve a separate discussion mainly because of their effects upon subsequent historiography.

[10]But see Thomas F. Torrance, "The Influence of Reformed Theology on the Development of Scientific Method," *Theology in Reconstruction* (London: SCM Press, 1965), pp. 62-75, for a fascinating combination of history, the independence of theology, and Christian apologetics. Torrance's argument is far more sophisticated than ordinary apologetics, even though his historical case is less than solid.

[11]A conception of the "history of Christian thought" is programmatic for Heiko A. Oberman's influential *The Harvest of Medieval Theology* (Cambridge: Harvard, 1963); see below, chap. 2. On the Spiritualists or radicals, see George H. Williams, *The Radical Reformation* (Philadelphia: Westminster, 1962), and others considered in chap. 3 below.

[12]For a wise estimate of the mere beginnings of historical-critical study of the vastness of religion in the context of its heavy history, see Richard R. Niebuhr, *Experiential Religion* (New York: Harper, 1972), p. 33.

[13]Thomas S. Kuhn, *The Structure of Scientific Revolutions*, 2nd ed. (Chicago: University of Chicago Press, 1970), and Toulmin, *Human Understanding*. Methodologically, I have chosen to follow one of Kuhn's major sources, i.e., the work of Collingwood, which is also a subject of debate between Kuhn and Toulmin. However, since Kuhn, Collingwood, and Toulmin share a loosely "contextualist" historiographical standpoint in sharp contrast to positivist standpoints in history and philosophy of science, their work warrants a separate methodological discussion.

[14]Edwin A. Burtt, *The Metaphysical Foundations of Modern Science*, rev. ed. (New York: Doubleday, 1954), and Alexandre Koyré, *From the Closed World to the Infinite Universe* (New York: Harper, 1958).

[15]See below, chaps. 4 and 6, for discussions of these studies. Although the distinction between elucidation and explanation is not rigid, it does reflect a difference in the goals of writing history. For example, Westfall's careful study of *Science and Religion in Seventeenth-Century England* (New Haven: Yale, 1958) is mainly an elucidation of their connections, althouth it also argues that the new science did bring adjustments that weakened religion.

[16]See Douglas S. Kemsley's "Religious Influences in the Rise of Modern Science: A Review and Criticism, Particularly of the 'Protestant-Puritan Ethic' Theory," *Annals of Science*, 24 (1968), 199-226, and Westfall, *Science and Religion*, p. 7.

[17]Other good accounts are those of A. N. Whitehead and M. B. Foster. Whitehead's historical and metaphysical argument for the importance of religion and theology for the new science assumes acquaintance with an original synthesis of experience and thought, which in turn is expressed in a complex technical vocabulary. See Whitehead's *Science in the Modern World*. The philospher of religion, M. B. Foster, has also developed a significant argument, but compared to the work of Collingwood it is deficient in one important respect. Foster's claim that new (and old) methods "presuppose" views of creation or nature which, in turn, "presuppose" theology is correct, but he does not unfold what is involved in the crucial relation of presupposing. See M. B. Foster, "The Christian Doctrine of Creation and the Rise of Modern Natural Science," *Mind*, 43 (1934), 446ff., recently reissued in D. O'Connor and Francis Oakley, eds., *Creation: The Impact of an Idea* (New York: Scribner's, 1969), pp. 29-53. See also Foster, "Christian Theology and the Modern Science of Nature," *Mind*, 44 (1935), 439ff., and 45 (1936), 1ff.

18Zilsel, "The Sociological Roots of Science," republished in Hugh F. Kearney, ed., *Origins of the Scientific Revolution* (New York: Barnes and Noble, 1964), pp. 86-99. Hill, *Intellectual Origins of the English Revolution* (London: Oxford, 1965). Merton, *Science, Technology, and Society in Seventeenth-Century England*, republished with a new Preface (New York: Harper, 1970), and *Social Theory and Social Structure*, rev. ed. (Glencoe, Ill.: Free Press, 1957).

19Merton, *Science and Society*, pp. 56-60, 112-115. Hooykaas' survey of subsequent statistical research corroborates Merton's estimates. See Hooykaas, pp. 98f.

20*Science and Society*, pp. 60ff., 73-76.

21*Ibid.*, pp. 60-64.

22*Ibid.*, p. 93.

23*Ibid.*, p. 157. Some of Merton critics on "Puritanism" have overlooked this parallel line of argument; see further *ibid.*, pp. 137-207.

24For Zilsel's general thesis, see his "Sociological Roots of Science," and his "The Origins of William Gilbert's Scientific Method," *Journal of the History of Ideas*, 2 (1941), 1-32. Although Hooykaas' account of the significance of Protestant teaching, i.e., the priesthood of all believers, the duty of free inquiry, and the sanctification of work, speaks directly to a crucial problem in general economic arguments for modern science, it falls short of a comparative sociology of Protestant and Roman Catholic figures. See Hooykaas, pp. 83-97.

25King shows that Merton's lack of historical penetration is rooted in a dichotomous general theory, i.e., society is the realm of work and science is the realm of thought. M. D. King, "Reason, Tradition, and the Progressiveness of Science," *History and Theory*, 10, no. 1 (1971), 9-21. Sorely needed is a sociology that does not labor under either Merton's tendency to *separate* science and society, or Zilsel's tendency to *collapse* them at the expense of the distinct integrity of science. Specifically a more adequate and historical (non-dualistic) sociology of knowledge of Puritanism, Anglicanism, and Spiritualist groups — no small task — would be helpful. Such a sociology could draw richly from the fierce church polity conflicts in seventeenth-century England, and might employ Weber's three-fold categorization of traditional, rational, and charismatic forces in society. Moreover, such a sociology could be of particular value in judging the immensely suggestive but as yet inconclusive claims for millenarianism and latitudinarianism, as well as Puritanism, that have sparked a series of *Past and Present* debates among early modern historians. See the articles, and particularly Webster's careful Introduction, in Charles Webster, ed., *The Intellectual Revolution of the Seventeenth Century* (London: Routledge and Kegan Paul, 1974).

26Among many critics of Merton's understanding of Puritanism, see A. Rupert Hall, "Merton Revisited or Science and Society in the Seventeenth Century," *History of Science*, 2 (1963), 1-16. For a good survey, see Kemsley, pp. 199-226. For a partial correction to Merton's line of argument, see the employment of Anglican figures in Raven's *Science and Religion*.

27*Science and Society*, pp. 97-107, 109; see also pp. 62f. Merton stresses the doctrine of predestination at the expense of belief in Providence.

28I have chosen Collingwood for primary discussion because his argument is highly suggestive, and his methodology enhances that argument, even though they must be carefully distinguished. Whitehead's argument may be better metaphysically, and that of Hooykaas is more empirically solid, but neither is advanced with the historiographical sensitivity of Collingwood. Collingwood's argument explaining the rise of modern science is found chiefly in his *Idea of Nature* (London: Oxford, 1945), and his relevant methodological proposals are mainly in his *An Essay on Metaphysics* (London: Oxford, 1940). Henceforth abbreviated *IN* and *EM* respectively.

[29]The term "modern," here used loosely, covers post-Reformation and post-Renaissance thought in general. Collingwood uses the term for eighteenth- and nineteenth-century thought. Generally, we shall follow this lead, and also discriminate sixteenth- and seventeenth-century thought as "early modern." For such periodization, see Collingwood, *IN*, pp. 4ff., and Robert Bellah, *Beyond Belief* (New York: Harper, 1970), pp. 36ff.

[30]For example, Burtt tends to overestimate the efficacy of highly reflective epistemological positions, particularly that of Descartes, in his *Metaphysical Foundations*, chap. 1, although he is far from reducing theological presuppositions. In general, the close ties to what is common and efficacious in communities binds theologians more than philosophers.

[31]*EM*, pp. 253-256. Collingwood adds that if positivists ". . . knew a little more about the history of science, they would know that the belief in the possibility of applied mathematics is only one part of the belief in God." *EM*, p. 257.

[32] Collingwood, *The New Leviathan* (London: Oxford, 1942), pp. 253, 254.

[33]*IN*, p. 5.

[34]*Ibid.*, pp. 94-105.

[35]*Ibid.*, p. 103.

[36]*Ibid.*, p. 99. See also pp. 94-96.

[37]*Ibid.*, p. 95.

[38]*Ibid.*, pp. 99, 100.

[39]*Ibid.*, p. 103.

[40]*Ibid.*, pp. 103ff.

[41]Collingwood, EM, pp. 213-227. In turn, Collingwood's background argument from Augustine was built upon an interpretation of earlier Greek "polytheistic" and "monotheistic" science, EM, pp. 185ff.

[42]Collingwood, EM, pp. 222-226.

[43]Collingwood's supporting argument is too cryptic, yet highly concentrated, to admit discriminating judgment without much further inquiry. Yet one can see that the Greek failure to promote *experimental* science turns upon its high estimation of eternally given rather than contingent nature. Similarly, Greek thought takes motion for granted, so much so that nature was held to be lively and purposive. This is very different from the anti-common-sensical overcoming of such natural motion in the principle of inertia. See Foster, "Theology and Science," pp. 439ff.

[44]Gilbert's study of the concept of "method" shows that a new power of method as discovery rather than merely organization emerged in the seventeenth century. Neal W. Gilbert, *Renaissance Concepts of Method* (New York: Columbia, 1960), chap. 1.

[45]My consideration and partial adoption of Collingwood's methodology focuses on his view of presuppositions, particularly in *EM*, which I have interpreted as

a proposal for systematic historical inquiry. See also his *Idea of History* (London: Oxford, 1946), and Louis O. Mink, *Mind, History and Dialectic: The Philosophy of R. G. Collingwood* (Bloomington: Indiana University Press, 1969), and "Collingwood's Historicism: A Dialectic of Process," *Critical Essays on the Philosophy of R. G. Collingwood*, ed. by Michael Krausz (Oxford: Clarendon, 1972), pp. 154-178. See also J. F. Post, "A Defense of Collingwood's Theory of Presuppositions," *Inquiry*, 8 (1965), 332-354. Collingwood's approach is more sophisticated than the term "method" suggests. In general his historiographical work has not been sufficiently related to his philosophical labors (but see Mink's basic corrective), and neither of these has been sufficiently related to his actual practice of intellectual history, particularly his efforts to show the presuppositions of modern science.

46Although Bacon does not belong here chronologically, his thought in natural philosophy and religion was of considerable significance for the Royal Society, at which time it was revived after a lapse in the 1630's. See Purver on Bacon's influence upon the Royal Society. Margery Purver, *The Royal Society: Concept and Creation* (Cambridge: M.I.T. Press, 1967).

47This period is typical of early modern thought. However, this assumption does not necessarily imply that the beginnings of modern science were in decline on the continent during a remarkably creative phase of English thought. That is another issue. Moreover, it may well be the case that *different* religious sources than those so effective in our period, were more operative in the passion for truth of the great astronomical pioneers before the mid-seventeenth-century. See further Benjamin Nelson, "The Early Modern Revolution in Science and Philosophy," and " 'Probabilists', 'Anti-Probabilists', and the Quest for Certitude in the 16th and 17th Centuries," *Actes du Xme Congrès international d'histoire des sciences*, I (1965), 269-273.

48*Metaphysical Foundations*, p. 167. See also R. Westfall's judgment in his introduction to three "Unpublished Boyle Papers Relating to Scientific Method," *Annals of Science*, 12 (1956), 64. Furthermore, to justify the assumption I am making, namely, that Boyle was a particularly representative early modern thinker, would require additional investigation. Newton, of course, would also make an excellent choice for primary concentration. Although Boyle's wide range of interests (and accomplishments) may have exceeded those of Wilkins, Hooke, Charleton, and Ray, he was not beyond the ranks of these peers.

49I am resisting the scholarly tradition of treating Boyle as a specialist, as either the "father" or obstacle to the emergence of modern chemistry. Among other things, Boyle was (in J. E. McGuire's phrase) the great "father figure of English natural philosophy." In and through his thought a major issue is that of the emergence of what were later called natural sciences from various early modern natural philosophies. Here the crucial point is not the general validity of Boyle's chemical theory — a moot point. For example, the debate between Marie Boas Hall and Thomas Kuhn on whether Boyle's chemical theory advanced or impeded chemical advance turns largely upon their general estimates of such conceptions as atoms, elements, laws, etc. Hence it is crucial to see Boyle's natural philosophy on its own terms and in the light of basic presuppositions manifest in his thought. See Marie Boas Hall, "Boyle as a Theoretical Scientist," *Isis*, 41 (1950), 261-268; and Thomas S. Kuhn, "Robert Boyle and Structural Chemistry in the Seventeenth Century," *Isis*, 43 (1952), 12-36.

[50]Collingwood, *EM*, pp. 213-227. See also Toulmin on "ideals of natural order" in his *Foresight and Understanding* (New York: Harper, 1963), pp. 44ff.; Burtt's understanding of "metaphysical foundations" in his *Metaphysical Foundations*; and Koyré's way of attending to correlative concepts of space and divinity in his *From World to Universe*. It may be argued that these works embody approaches roughly similar to the boldness and comprehension of Collingwood's. However, Collingwood's effort to understand anthropological and theological presuppositions, as well as cosmological presuppositions, distinguishes his approach from the more school-oriented (and less epochal) rubric of "paradigm" in Kuhn's usage. See Kuhn, *Structure of Scientific Revolutions*, chap. 5.

[51]*EM*, p. 48; *Autobiography* (London: Oxford, 1939), p. 2; and *IN*, pp. 3-13.

[52]This interpretation is drawn mainly from *EM*, pp. 21-33, but see also Collingwood's *Autobiography*, pp. 29ff.

[53]See Mink, *Mind, History and Dialectic*, for an excellent account of the many levels of consciousness for Collingwood.

[54]As such their order falls between that of stictly logical and loosely ordinary language. For a different account of informal logic see G. Ryle, *Dilemmas* (Cambridge, Eng.: Cambridge, 1956), pp. 111ff. Against a strictly logical reading of "logical efficacy," note that in his principal discussion of absolute presuppositions Collingwood does not treat implication. *EM*, pp. 23, 52.

[55]*EM*, p. 27; *IN*, p. 1.

[56]*EM*, p. 76.

[57]See Bellah, *Beyond Belief*, pp. 1-50, and below, chap. 4.

[58]*EM*, pp. 41-47. This also distinguishes presuppositions from assumptions; *ibid.*, p. 27.

[59]My use of the term "basic presuppositions" is to acknowledge the specific forms which I shall henceforth employ, and particularly the notion of context, as well as my general interpretation of Collingwood on absolute presuppositions. One of the difficulties with Collingwood's term "absolute presuppositions" is that in relation to "relative presuppositions" this terminology accentuates the logical difficulties of relations between presuppositions without mapping the internal structure of diverse presuppositions. Although the distinction Collingwood makes is important to prevent the sheer dependence of one presupposition "deduced" from another (Collingwood speaks of the "consupponibility" of absolute presuppositions, and "constellations" of presuppositions to safeguard his position. *EM*, p. 66), it does precious little to clarify the family relationships among basic presuppositions. In using the notion of basic presuppositions I am following more closely Collingwood's actual methodical practice of intellectual history as the search for presuppositions. For in this search the complex relationships of family and fellow presuppositions, e.g. of self, God and world, take on a significance lost in strictly logical types of relations such as deduction and implication. Yet, the actual structure of presupposing, questioning, and answering is not reducible to a mere pattern. All of this is not to deny the logical problematic involved, much less to "solve" it. That would require an extensive inquiry into relations *and* relationships in both formal and informal logic.

[60]For a suggestive account of the function of "limiting questions," see Toulmin, *An Examination of the Place of Reason in Ethics* (Cambridge, Eng.: Cambridge, 1950), pp. 204ff.

[61]"Images" of nature here should be understood in a comprehensive sense much like Pepper's "root metaphors." See Stephen Pepper, *World Hypotheses* (Berkeley: California, 1961), Part One.

Notes to Chapter Two

[1]For a classic statement, see F. D. E. Schleiermacher's Introduction to *The Christian Faith* (New York: Harper Torchbook, 1963). The twentieth-century emphasis on the dominant eschatological character of primitive Christianity, by A. Schweitzer and R. Bultmann, has strongly reinforced the view that Christianity is a religion of redemption.

[2]There are, however, numerous historical studies of selected topics, figures, and problems of this doctrine; the broad historical soundings of Langdon Gilkey's *Maker of Heaven and Earth* (New York: Doubleday, 1959) are useful.

[3]The question remains unresolved as to how much Thomas' thought on causality and Anselm's on intellect and will were harbingers of developments subsequent to the classic medieval synthesis. That question, however, remains one of "to what extent" these fathers of the scholastic achievement went beyond their intellectual and spiritual father, Augustine.

[4]Although Collingwood claims more for Christian presuppositions of creation established by Augustine, at least this much is surely solid.

[5]The chronological and religious dependence of belief in creation upon belief in historical salvation is a staple of twentiety-century historical-critical Old Testament scholarship. As such, belief in the Creator is held to be a part of the chiefly historical character of Israel's faith, and opposed to Canaanite nature religions. For a representative statement of this scholarly consensus see B. W. Anderson on "creation" in the *Interpreter's Dictionary of the Bible*. It can be further argued, however, that the truth of this consensus should be recast in a larger literary, theological, and historical perspective.

[6]This is powerfully argued in Barth's historical (and theological) critique of eighteenth- and nineteenth-century liberal Protestant thought for selling out to an optimistic estimate of human power that proved disastrous to Christians and non-Christians alike. See Karl Barth, *Protestant Thought: From Rousseau to Ritschl* (New York: Simon and Schuster, 1959).

[7]*The Christian Faith*, p. 131. However, the dominant and purely critical force of Schleiermacher's rigorously systematic (and undramatic) doctrine of creation is apparent throughout Propositions 36-41 of *The Christian Faith*, pp. 142-156. He even finds its Old Testament basis to be a concession to curiosity, p. 149. Endangered for Schleiermacher is the purity of absolute dependence, in turn ordered solely to absolute causality (God), see pp. 200ff.

[8]My account of late medieval voluntarist or nominalist theology of creation is largely drawn from the work of these scholars, particularly that of Oberman. See H. A. Oberman, *The Harvest of Medieval Theology* (Cambridge: Harvard, 1963), and "Some Notes on the Theology of Nominalism, with Attention to its Relation to the Renaissance," *Harvard Theological Review*, 52 (1960). For a recent indication of the wide range of religious and non-religious subjects illumined by the rediscovery of late medieval theology, see the publications from the 1972 University of Michigan Conference on Late Medieval and Renaissance Religion edited by C. Trinkaus and H. Oberman, *The Pursuit of*

Holiness in Late Medieval and Renaissance Religion (Leiden: Brill, 1974). See also Paul Vignaux, *Philosophy in the Middle Ages: An Introduction* (New York: Meridian Books, 1959); E. Gilson, *History of Christian Philosophy in the Middle Ages* (New York: Random House, 1955); and F. C. Copleston, *A History of Philosophy: Vol. III: Ockham to Suarez* (Westminster: Newman Press, 1953).

[9]On March 7, 1277, Etienne Tempier, Bishop of Paris, condemned 219 propositions of Averroistic-Aristotelian philosophy at the request of Pope John XXI. Eleven days later, the Archbishop of Canterbury, Robert Kilwardby, condemned another 30 propositions. On the targets of the Condemnations, and their significance as a turning point from high scholasticism to late medieval "nominalist" or "voluntarist" theology (I have chosen the latter term because it is more comprehensive), see Vignaux, p. 86; Gilson, pp. 385-427; and F. C. Copleston, *Medieval Philosophy* (New York: Harper Torchbook, 1961), pp. 100-106. See also Francis Oakley's *The Political Thought of Pierre d'Ailly: The Voluntarist Tradition* (New Haven: Yale, 1964), and "Medieval Theories of Natural Law: William of Ockham and the Significance of the Voluntarist Tradition," *Natural Law Forum*, 6 (1961), 65-83.

[10]The majority of the condemned propositions are philosophical and theological. On the text and classification of the propositions, see Gilson, *History of Christian Philosophy*, NS. 50-54, pp. 727-729. On their significance, see also R. Hooykaas, "Science and Theology in the Middle Ages," *Free University Quarterly*, 3 (1954).

[11]On this view more than one natural motion for an earthly body is impossible, and their circular and projectile motion was seen to be unnatural or violent. See R. Hooykaas, "Science and Theology," pp. 86-88. The analogous distinction in chemistry denied the integrity of artificial in favor of natural compounds.

[12]Gilson notes that the listing and numbering of the condemned propositions, as well as their targets (Siger, Thomas, *et al.*), are disputed by Franciscan and Dominican editors. Gilson, *History*, n. 52, p. 728. Selecting and translating from the list of Pierre Mandonnet, OP., *Siger de Brabant* (Paris, 1930), II, 175-181, Gilson finds Avicenna to be the target of the following proposition on God and motion: "64, That God is the necessary cause of the motion of superior bodies and of conjunctions and divisions in stars. . . ." Gilson, *History*, n. 54, p. 729. Hooykaas translates a similar proposition from the complete listing of H. Denifle, S. J. *Chartularium Universitatis Parisiensis* (Paris, 1889), I: "186, That the heaven never stands still, because the generation of things below, which is the aim of the motion of the heaven, may not cease, or, because the heaven has its being and its virtue from its mover and this preserves the heaven through its motion. Consequently, if it would cease to move, it would cease to be." Hooykaas, "Science and Theology," p. 91.

[13]Gilson translates the condemned proposition (#34 in Denifle's list) as follows: "That the Prime Cause cannot make several worlds (Mandonnet's list, 27)." Gilson, *History*, n. 52, p. 728. As Hooykaas has shown, although Thomas does not simply deny the possibility of other worlds, his more rationally conceived universe is evident in his treatment of the question. He argues that such worlds would be either similar or dissimilar to this world. If similar, then another like world would be superfluous and this casts aspersion on the divine wisdom. On the other hand, if another world is dissimilar, all such worlds would be required for a perfect universe. Thus, chiefly in the interests of the divine wisdom Thomas demurs. Thomas Aquinas, *De Coelo*, lib. I, lect. XIX, cited from Hooykaas, "Science and Theology," p. 95.

[14]Gilson, *History*, n. 54, p. 729.

[15]See Oberman, *Harvest*, pp. 30-56. See also Oberman, "Notes on Nominalism," pp. 47ff. This transcendence meant that even the ordinary course of events could be seen as miraculous.

[16]Oberman, "Notes on Nominalism," pp. 56, 57. The distinction was formulated at the beginning of scholasticism when Hugh of St. Victor (1096-1141) argued that God's omnipotence is limited only by the law of noncontradiction. Thomas defined the *potentia absoluta* as God's power in isolation and the *potentia ordinata* as including His intention and action. See also Ernst Borchert, *Der Einfluss des Nominalismus auf die Christologie der Spätscholastik* (Munster, 1940), pp. 46-74, and especially W. J. Courtenay, "Nominalism and Late Medieval Religion," in Trinkhaus and Oberman, *Pursuit of Holiness*, pp. 26ff.

[17]Ockham did not celebrate divine caprice. The *potentia absoluta* is held in dialectical tension with His *potentia ordinata*. And by His *potentia ordinata* God freely and graciously commits himself to a framework of creation and a framework of redemption according to which he accepts sinful man into the final company of the beatified. Oberman defines this framework as a protective dome within which man freely does the best which is in him. See Oberman, "Notes on Nominalism," p. 63. See also Oberman, *Harvest*, pp. 132-134. This dome may also be considered as an arc in which from man's point of view the points are connected, yet from God's perspective there is a series of points which are never closed to His *potentia absoluta*.

[18]Oberman, *Harvest*, pp. 37. 38.

[19]Francis Oakley, *The Political Thought of Pierre d'Ailly: The Voluntarist Tradition* (New Haven: Yale, 1964), p. 22. Oakley does not pursue d'Ailly's stress on the unity of God, but it is clear that it should not be read as uniformity. See Francis Oakley, "Pierre d'Ailly and the Absolute Power of God: Another Note on the Theology of Nominalism," *Harvard Theological Review*, 56 (1963), 59-73. See also Oberman, "Notes on Nominalism," pp. 61, 62, and Frederick C. Copleston, *A History of Philosophy, Vol. III: Ockham to Suarez* pp. 71-76.

[20]In this respect late medieval thought echoes the Old Testament view of law in contrast to classical Stoic views so prominent in medieval thought. As Oakley summarizes,

> . . . the pantheistic Stoic view . . . conceived of natural law as the expression of the divine reason immanent in the universe. It was regarded as embracing the universal practice of men, in all times and in every country, and as analogous to the principle of harmony or cohesion which governed the movements of the heavenly bodies and the habits of animals. . . . In such a view, then, the natural law and the laws of nature are conceived as being at least in essence one, a body of rational principles inherent in the fabric of nature and possessing divine or cosmic sanction.
>
> *The Political Thought of Pierre d'Ailly*, p. 166.

On the crucial point that law in voluntarism did not exclude reason, see Oakley, "Medieval Theories of Natural Law," pp. 66-72.

[21]Biel and d'Ailly follow Ockham in relating the legal order of creation to God's will, for it is the presupposition of God's imposed law that marks their notion of "right" reason as a "sign," but not a guarantee of the dialectics of God's

power. See Oberman, *Harvest*, pp. 116, 90-117. See also Oakley, *The Political Thought of Pierre d'Ailly*, pp. 191-196. "Right" reason, which must conform to an external norm, is very far removed from Kant's doctrine of pure (or substantial) reason and its self-legislating power.

[22]Gilson, *History*, n. 52, p. 728. The significance of this new voluntarism appears in late medieval models of Church (the rise of conciliarism) and State. See Oakley, "Medieval Theories of Natural Law," and Oakley, *The Political Thought of Pierre d'Ailly*, chaps. 3, 6.

[23]*Harvest*, pp. 330, 323ff. See also S. Ozment's "Mysticism, Nominalism and Dissent," in Trinkhaus and Oberman, *Pursuit of Holiness*, pp. 67ff.

[24]*Harvest*, pp. 339, 323-360. On the nature of piety Biel sounds the same note as Gerson, but he develops the logic of voluntary piety in stressing its availability to all rather than a spiritual elite.

[25]These suggestions have been partially developed in many quarters. See Hooykaas, *Religion and the Rise of Modern Science*, pp. 32-35. Crombie has noted the parallelism of the logic of explanation in Grosseteste and the seventeenth century, but refrains from claiming much historical influence. A. C. Crombie, *Robert Grosseteste and the Origins of Experimental Science: 1100-1700* (London: Oxford, 1953), pp. 290-319, and "The Significance of Medieval Discussions of Scientific Method for the Scientific Revolution," in *Critical Problems in the History of Science*, ed. by Marshall Clagett (Madison: Wisconsin, 1959), pp. 79-101.

[26]Oberman, *Harvest*, p. 41.

[27]This was a major issue in the late medieval debate on the status of universals. The pressing historical question here is how much the denial of ontological/theological universals affected nominalist philosophy of universals, and vice versa. Historical scholarship has not yet sufficiently related these questions. See Oberman's suggestive discussion of Biel and Ockham on universals in the context of their general views on man and faith. *Harvest*, p. 61.

[28]John T. McNeill, *The History and Character of Calvinism* (New York: Oxford, 1954), pp. 290-330.

[29]The bulk of Calvin scholarship per se, a circle that seldom intersects the interests of those who examine his work in extra-ecclesiastical contexts, remains oriented to the great divide of Roman Catholic and Protestant thought — the issue of redemption. Moreover, among those historians, sociologists, philosophers, and a few theologians, who argue for his influence upon the rise of modern science there is little agreement on what is most important or relevant in his thought. My account considers Calvin's theology of creation in terms of four structural components: the view of the Creator, the act of creation, created order, and man as a special creature, all of which are apparent in historically developed Christian orientations to creation.

[30]John Calvin, *Institutes of the Christian Religion*, trans. by Ford Lewis Battles and ed. by John T. McNeill (Philadelphia: Westminster Press, 1960), Book I, Chaps. 16 and 17, pp. 197ff. Henceforth, references to the *Institutes* will be cited with the abbreviation *ICR*, followed by book, chapter, section, and page number.

[31]On the origin of the soul, Calvin's preference for creationism underlines his affirmation of the contingency of creation (*ICR*, II:1:7, p. 249), as does his sense of active Providence (not just *pro-videre*), and his presentation of the

doctrine of creation by tracing the history of God's increasingly more particular acts.

32For Calvin there was no hierarchy or graded order of essential beings. The crucial essence-existence distinction of Thomas did not function for Calvin. Accordingly, the interplay of the Thomistic distinction between primary and secondary causation and a scale of higher and lower causes was also absent.

33*ICR*, I:16:3, p. 200; I:5:2, p. 53; I:14:4-12, pp. 163-172. In general, the modesty of Calvin's teaching on angels is striking; they are not intermediaries between God and man. See *ICR*, II:12:1, p. 464.

34This contributed to a major theological shift in early modern thought, evident in its differentiation. Properly theological "work" meant both God's acts and his productions. Calvin was far from collapsing creation into God. Although Luther opposed works in the name of faith, Calvin insisted on the same conclusion for more explicitly theological reasons. It is not clear that Merton and the Weberian tradition see this.

35*ICR*, I:5:2, p. 53.

36*ICR*, I:13:1ff., pp. 121ff. The other epithet that Calvin claimed theologically sufficient, were it not for human weakness, was God's "infinite" essence, which stressed both power and will. The result of these auspicious beginnings was a trinitarian map of Christian life in the world which stressed the rule of the Spirit. However, Calvin was far from realizing the map he drew, as the radical Spiritualist "third wing" of the Reformation rightly insisted. Perhaps the basic theological problem was subjection of the Spirit to the Word. In any case, it is crucial to see that he did not subordinate his theology of the Holy Spirit to a doctrine of the Church (compare the order of topics in Thomas' *Summa Contra Gentiles*). Hence, Calvin was vulnerable to the charge of the "third wing" Radical Reformers.

37*ICR*, I:16:4, pp. 202-203; I:15:2, p. 184.

38*ICR*, I:13:14, p. 138. For Calvin this inspiration is universal motion, not vital breath.

39*ICR*, I:5:1, pp. 51, 52. Brackets by the translators.

40*ICR*, I:5:10, p. 63.

41*ICR*, I:5:5, pp. 56ff.

42*ICR*, I:18:1, p. 229; I:16:1-3, pp. 197-201.

43*ICR*, I:5:6, 7, pp. 59, 60.

44*ICR*, I:18:3, pp. 233-235; I:17:2, p. 212.

45This distinguishes Calvin's thought from that of Augustine and Luther, for whom the Genesis account of creation in six days served as the standard scriptural basis for hierarchy (and teleology) in creation.

46*ICR*, I:5:5, p. 58; I:5:5, p. 59.

47*ICR*, I:14:20, 21, pp. 179-181. See Calvin's total celebrations of creation as a spectacular theatre of God's glory, a magnificent edifice of His artifice, and an open book of the divine Author.

48*ICR*, I:5, pp. 51ff. Calvin's "argument" may be interpreted as a primitive version of the seventeenth-century staple in arguing for God's existence, i.e. the argument from design. Congruent with his latent theory of the divine attributes of power, wisdom, and goodness, Calvin represents a shift away from the classic cosmological argument to the teleological argument. The cosmological demonstration of Thomas turns upon cause and proportionality, but Calvin's argumentation attends to the liveliness of God's own Spirit in the concrete design of things. For Calvin concrete things invite sense to perceive God. This contrasts with their function as occasions for intellectual abstraction for Thomas. Typical for Calvin is his citation of David's celebration of the common marvel of breastfeeding. (*ICR*, I:5:3, p. 55.) It is difficult to overestimate the importance of this new way of showing forth God, which bloomed in the seventeenth century.

[49]*ICR*, I:16:7, 8, pp. 206, 207. The presupposition of legal order in creation is partly responsible for Calvin's effort to discipline the "nature enthusiasm" of Renaissance thought. All creation is subject to God's law and ordered to *His* glory. Yet, on balance, it is remarkable how much aesthetic notions of order, undergirded by a disciplined theology of Spirit, kept Calvin's thought from systematic or arbitrary legalism. This is frequently overlooked in interpretations of Calvin.

[50]*ICR*, I:14:20, p. 180; II:2:15, p. 273. See Calvin on the extensive work of the Holy Spirit in art and science, *ICR*, II:2:16, pp. 275ff.

[51]John Calvin, *Commentary on Psalm 8:6*, cited in T. F. Torrance, *Calvin's Doctrine of Man* (Grand Rapids: Eerdmans, 1957), p. 24.

[52]*ICR*, I:3:3, p. 46; I:2:2, p. 42; I:5:3, p. 54.

[53]Richard Hooker, *Treatise on the Laws of Ecclesiastical Polity* (London, 1594), Book I: chaps. 8 and 16.

[54]Ames, *The Marrow of Theology*, trans., ed. from the 3rd Latin ed. (1629), and introduced by John D. Eusden (Boston: Pilgrim Press, 1968), I, vi, pp. 91-100. Henceforth abbreviated *Marrow*.

[55]More precisely, any ontology that included the Being of God within its frame was excluded. The voluntarists were far from denying the uniqueness of *creatio ex nihilo*. Furthermore, like Calvin, for this tradition Providence was very closely tied to the presupposition of God as Creator. Hence disorder would ensue if Providence were withdrawn, much as chaos would obtain if there was no Creator. However, this was not equivalent to collapsing the distinction between divine creation and Providence. The latter presupposed the former, irreversibly. There were many providences, and many kinds of Providential work, but only one creation. In part this resistance to collapsing creation and Providence was to guard against a speculative ontology. Not only intellectual speculation, but thought that strayed from the religious order of passage from creation through the fall to redemption. This interpretation goes against many dismissals of seventeenth-century theology as (Protestant) "scholasticism."

[56]John Flavel, *The Mystery of Providence* (1678) (London: Banner of Truth, 1963), pp. 113ff. Compared to Calvin's doctrine of Providence, notwithstanding his stress on "benefits," the highly person-forming teachings of the English writers generated a strong sense of personal history in the believer.

[57]See Michael Walzer, *The Revolution of the Saints*, and David Little, *Religion, Order, and Law*. On grounding the institution and duties of marriage in creation and Providence, rather than the sacraments, see James T. Johnson, *A Society Ordained by God* (Nashville: Abingdon, 1970). On the institution of the Sabbath rooted in creation, see Eusden's Introduction to Ames' *Marrow*, p.

19. In general these works show that belief in Providence did much to generate a sense that man under God lives in history.

⁵⁸For suggestive accounts of belief in Providence and God's *potentia absoluta* and *ordinata* on the part of these figures among others, see J. E. McGuire, "Force, Active Principles, and Newton's Invisible Realm," *Ambix*, 15 (1968), 187-194; and F. Oakley, "Christian Theology and the Newtonian Science," *Church History*, 30 (1961), 439-441, 454. See also Oakley, "The Absolute and Ordinary Powers of the King," *Journal of the History of Ideas*, 29 (1968), 332ff.

⁵⁹For example, Ames reached back to Thomas to affirm the distinct reality of second causes. However, he also precluded any positive theology of God's "sufficiency," the Being of God. Instead he stressed both the mystery of God's transcendence and His universal "efficiency" by appropriating the late medieval dialectic of *potentia ordinata* and *absoluta*. Ames, *Marrow*, I, vi, p. 93.

⁶⁰Nathaniel Culverwell, *Of the Light of Nature: A Discourse* (1652), ed. by John Brown (Edinburgh, 1857).

⁶¹Oakley shows that Suarez, a traditional natural law thinker, identified the voluntarist tradition, and particularly its view of imposed law, in such late medieval figures as d'Ailly, Gerson, Holcot, Biel, Almain, Major and deCastro, as well as such diverse seventeenth-century figures as Grotius, Pufendorf, Richer, and Hobbes. See F. Oakley, "Theology and Newtonian Science," p. 440. For Oakley's main effort to trace voluntarism in political philosophers, see his "Medieval Theories of Natural Law: William of Ockham and the Significance of the Voluntarist Tradition," and *The Political Thought of Pierre d'Ailly*, and with E. W. Urdang, "Locke, Natural Law, and God," *Natural Law Forum*, 11 (1966), 92-109.

⁶²This basic religious dynamic of law and gospel stood in a peculiar tension with the doctrine of the two kingdoms, the Kingdom of Christ and that of the world. In the separation of these kingdoms, law was accorded another function — to maintain order. Thus, at best, pious life may become thoroughly paradoxical, caught within a religiously foreign state. But whether purely pious or paradoxical, disciplined reform of properly created social-political orders is not a normal religious task.

⁶³From the Anglican side, Sanderson, whose work was patronized by Boyle, and from the Puritan side, Ames, were definitive figures in ethics of the "cases" of conscience. See Ames' second major work, *Conscience with the Power and Cases Thereof: Divided into Five Books* (1643), trans. from first Latin ed., 1630, and reproduced with *Marrow* in a limited facsimile edition (Cambridge: Harvard Divinity School Library, 1964). See also Perry Miller's suggestive account of New England law related to the conscience tradition in ethics. Miller, *The New England Mind: The Seventeenth Century* (Boston: Beacon, 1961), pp. 192ff. See also H. R. McAdoo, *The Spirit of Anglicanism* (New York: Scribner's, 1965), pp. 1-80.

⁶⁴For a classic example, see John Bunyan, *Pilgrim's Progress*, and *Grace Abounding to the Chief of Sinners*. See also Gerald R. Cragg, *From Puritanism to the Age of Reason* (Cambridge, Eng.: Cambridge, 1950), pp. 37-60.

⁶⁵R. F. Jones, *Ancients and Moderns*, 2nd ed. (Berkeley, California, 1961), pp. 87-118. See below, chap. 4, on Bacon's *New Atlantis*, and Newton's work on Daniel.

[66]This is apparent in Toland's *Christianity not Mysterious* (1696) and Tindal's *Christianity as old as the Creation, or the Gospel a Republication of the Religion of Reason* (1702).

Notes to Chapter Three

[1]See George H. Williams and Angel Mergal, *Spiritual and Anabaptist Writers* (Philadelphia: Westminster, 1957); George H. Williams, *The Radical Reformation* (Philadelphia: Westminster, 1962); Rufus M. Jones, *Spiritual Reformers in the 16th and 17th Centuries* (Boston: Beacon Paperback, 1959); Norman Cohn, *The Pursuit of the Millennium*, rev. ed. (New York: Oxford, 1970). For path-breaking inquiry into Spiritualism, see Francis A. Yates, *Giordano Bruno and the Hermetic Tradition* (Chicago: University of Chicago Press, 1964), and "The Hermetic Tradition in Renaissance Science," *Art, Science, and History in the Renaissance*, ed. by C. S. Singleton (Baltimore: Johns Hopkins, 1968). For an introduction to some of the scientific figures in Spiritualism, interpreted as a "magical" tradition, see H. Kearney's *Science and Change, 1500-1700* (New York: McGraw-Hill, 1971).

[2]John Ferguson has noted that ". . . between the years 1650 and 1675 or 1680 more alchemical books appeared in English than in all the time before and after those dates." Cited in Ronald S. Wilkinson, "The Hartlib Papers and Seventeenth-Century Chemistry," *Ambix*, 15 (1968), 56. On Hartlib, see Charles Webster, *Samuel Hartlib and the Advancement of Learning* (Cambridge, Eng.: Cambridge, 1970). On Cambridge (and other) Platonists see *The Cambridge Platonists*, ed. by G. R. Cragg (New York: Oxford, 1968); E. Cassirer's *Individual and Cosmos* (New York: Barnes & Noble, 1964); and D. P. Walker's *The Ancient Theology* (Ithaca: Cornell, 1972).

[3]The theme of Ames' *Marrow* is sounded in its first sentence: "Theology is the doctrine or teaching [*doctrina*] of living to God." Ames, *Marrow*, I,1,1, p. 77.

[4]On Fludd, see Allen G. Debus, "Renaissance Chemistry and the Work of Robert Fludd," *Ambix*, 14 (1967), 42-59. Among English Paracelsians, Debus has noted various *images* of creation, which were drawn from fields as diverse as alchemy and mathematics. Debus cites John Dee's view that the Creator's "numbryng . . . was his Creatyng of all things, and his Continuall Numbryng, of all thinges, is the Conservation of them in being." Allen G. Debus, "Mathematics and Nature in the Chemical Texts of the Renaissance," *Ambix*, 15 (1968), 10f. See also Thomas Browne, *Religio Medici* (1643), ed. by Denonain (Cambridge, Eng.: Cambridge, 1955), part I, section 39, p. 52.

[5]See Allen G. Debus, *The English Paracelsians* (London: Oldbourne, 1965), and Alexandre Koyré, *Mystiques, spirituels, alchimistes: Schwenckfeld, Sebastian Franck, Weigel, Paracelse* (Paris, 1955). On Charleton's temporary promotion of Helmont, see Nina R. Gelbart, "The Intellectual Development of Walter Charleton," *Ambix*, 18 (1971), 149-177.

[6]In spite of the long scholarly habit to dismiss Spiritualists in natural philosophy as "mystics" and "sectarians," special note should be taken of the following studies. Debus has argued that early seventeenth-century English Paracelsians omitted the mysticism of much continental Paracelsian thought. *The English Paracelsians*, chap. 2. Others have underlined the importance of religious traditions and mystical thought. See J. E. McGuire and P. M. Rat-

tansi, "Newton and the 'Pipes of Pan'," *Notes and Records of the Royal Society*, 21 (1966), 108-143; J. E. McGuire, "Force, Active Principles, and Newton's Invisible Realm," *Ambix*, 15 (1968), 154-208; and Charles Webster, "Henry Power's Experimental Philosophy," *Ambix*, 14 (1967), 150-178. See also Walter Pagel, "The debt of science and medicine to a devout belief in God. Illustrated by the work of Van Helmont," *Transactions of the Victoria Institute*, 74 (1942), 99-115; Pagel, *Paracelsus: An Introduction to Philosophical Medicine in the Era of the Renaissance* (Basel: S. Karger, 1958); and Pagel, "Paracelsus and the Neoplatonic and Gnostic Tradition," *Ambix*, 8 (1960), 125-166.

[7]On Boyle's early indebtedness to Helmont, and his subsequent decisive differences, see Wilkinson, "The Hartlib Papers," pp. 57-63; and the judgment of Marie Boas Hall, *Robert Boyle on Natural Philosophy* (Bloomington: Indiana, 1965), pp. 83ff. Many of the decisive theological and natural philosophical issues between Boyle and Helmont were also evident in Gassendi's opposition to Fludd's mystical views of nature and the Bible. See Debus, "Renaissance Chemistry and the Work of Robert Fludd," pp. 49ff. The earlier critical relationship of Bacon to the pantheistic Paracelsians and Platonists was of a similar order. On a more sophisticated level there was the debate between Cartesian mechanism and More's espousal of the "Spirit of nature." See Burtt, *Metaphysical Foundations*, pp. 135-142. Newton's relationship to both alchemy and the rational and ecumenical enthusiasm of Leibnitz is not dissimilar.

[8]Besides the work of Pagel, Partington gives Helmont special attention in pre-Boylean chemistry for isolating and classifying various gases, and his promising work on ferments. J. R. Partington, *A Short History of Chemistry* (New York: Harper Torchbook, 1960), pp. vii, 49, 53. Note also Debus' general estimate of Helmont:

> "It is thus becoming increasingly evident that van Helmont is a key figure in seventeenth-century science and medicine (a) because of his own contribution to chemical and medical thought, (b) because of the decisive influence his work played in the development of the Chemical Philosophy, and (c) because of the impact of the Helmontian corpus on major figures and major trends in the mid- and late seventeenth century." Debus, "Some Comments on the Contemporary Helmontian Renaissance," *Ambix*, 19 (1972), 149.

[9]Johan Baptist van Helmont, *A Ternary of Paradoxes*, trans. by Walter Charleton (London, 1650); and Johan Baptist van Helmont, *Oriatrike, or, Physick Refined, the common Errors therein Refuted, and the whole Art Reformed and Rectified, being a new Rise and Progress of Phylosophy and Medicine, for the Destruction of Diseases and Prolongation of Life*, trans. by John Chandler from the first Latin ed., *Ortus Medicinae*, 1648 (London, 1662). Henceforth abbreviated *Oriatrike*. References cite chapter and section numbers, e.g., I:1. On recent editions of Helmont's works in Flemish, German, and Latin, see Debus, "Comments on the Contemporary Helmontian Renaissance," pp. 145-150.

[10]*Oriàtrike*, pp. i-iv.

[11]*Ibid.*, p. i.

[12]*Ibid.*, pp. i-iii. In general the English resisted the alleged Egyptian origin of gnosis. See Yates, *Giordano Bruno and the Hermetic Tradition*, pp. 21ff.

[13]*Oriatrike*, p. ii.

[14]The naming of God as the "Father of Lights" is frequent not only among the alchemists who rely upon the Hermetic literature, but also among the Cambridge Platonists. In the latter case, it comports with a *logos* christology, and reason understood as the "candle of the Lord." In the Hermetic literature, and throughout much Augustinian mysticism, the classic scripture reference for this central title is James 1:17. This title suggests a more adequate understanding of Spiritualist thought than Kearney on God the "Magus." Kearney, *Science and Change*, p. 118.

[15]*Oriatrike*, pp. iii, iv.

[16]The presence of the microcosm-macrocosm principle of relating man, God, and nature in continental Paracelsian thought shows how organic Spiritualist theologies of creation were. However, the Helmontian critique of the microcosm-macrocosm principle (shared by English Paracelsian thought as Debus has shown) curbed the propensity of Spiritualism to conceive the course of creation organically. Yet, Helmontian Spiritualism remained open to the belief in an *anima mundi*, by conceiving the *anima* of the world not as the mind but as the Spirit of the Creator, the processes of light and life running through man and creation.

[17]*Oriatrike*, p. iv.

[18]Scholars of early Christianity and its Jewish antecedents have found very different estimates of the future, ranging from historical promise to gradually realized and highly apocalyptic eschatologies. The latter type of vision appears in Spiritualist natural philosophy.

[19]*Oriatrike*, Preface "To the Friendly Reader," by Francis Mercurius van Helmont, "A Philosopher, by that One in whom are all things" [21 pages without pagination], henceforth abbreviated "Preface." See further, "A Prayer to the Unutterable Word, by the Author" [3 pages without pagination], henceforth abbreviated "Prayer."

[20]This category was common among the Cambridge Platonists, for whom, along with Newton and Edwards, issues in the nature and divinity of space were prominent. See also T. Browne, *Religio Medici*, part I, section 35, pp. 46, 47. Edwards' thought on omneity, Holy Spirit, space, and gravity is particularly intriguing. See Herbert W. Richardson's unpubl. 1962 Harvard dissertation, *The Glory of God in the Theology of Jonathan Edwards*, and in general, R. M. Jones, *Spiritual Reformers*.

[21]*Oriatrike*, XXI:2.

[22]*Ibid.*, XXI:3. Like other Spiritualists, Helmont also sees creation as a process of divine separation. Yet, he does not stop here, for creation is also God's way of empowering and moving things. Creation seen as separation was frequent among the alchemists, for divine and alchemical processes were similar. Debus has shown how widespread this conception was, though perhaps without sufficient sensitivity to preparation as well as separation, synthesis as well as pyrochemical analysis, and divine inspiration as well as separation. See Debus, "Renaissance Chemistry and the Work of Robert Fludd," pp. 42ff.

[23]*Oriatrike*, Promises, p. 4.

[24]*Ibid.*, Prayer.

[25]*Ibid.*, III:48. Italics mine.

[26]*Ibid.*, III:1.

27*Ibid.*, III:18, 51, 52; I:12. Reason as the "candle of the Lord," directly related to the "Father of Lights," was a staple for the Cambridge Platonists.

28*Ibid.*, II:12,19; XX:37.

29*Ibid.*, XXI:96.

30*Ibid.*, Prayer.

31See below, chap. 4. The distinction between the two books is common to voluntarist, Spiritualist, and medieval Aristotelian natural philosophy. The crucial considerations turn on how sharply the distinction between the two books is drawn, and the actual use of the two books. For example, Browne, in his *Religio Medici*, part I, section 16, pp. 21-23, expresses the Spiritualist way of running the two books together, but his usage seems less radical than Helmont. This important rubric warrants further historical study, but see Hooykaas, *Religion and the Rise of Modern Science*, pp. 105ff., and Frank Manuel, *The Religion of Isaac Newton* (Oxford: Clarendon, 1974), pp. 27ff.

32*Oriatrike*, VII:2, 3.

33*Ibid.*, VII:3, 2-4. An understanding of external or imposed command is further ruled out by Helmont's position, discussed below, that lawful subjects are vital "seeds."

34See Debus, *The English Paracelsians*, pp. 105ff. However, for Helmont this does not mean that God as Spirit is merely a divine Chemist. Thus, the early seventeenth-century English Paracelsian resistance to mystical theories should not be simply extended into mid-century English thought, at which time Helmont's Spiritualist views were attractive.

35*Oriatrike*, IV:39,31.

36Charles Webster details Boyle's careful reception and opposition to this experiment and its interpretation. See Charles Webster, "Water as the Ultimate Principle of Nature: The Background to Boyle's Skeptical Chymist," *Ambix*, 13 (1966), 97ff. For an account of the widespread influence of this experiment, see Kearney, *Science and Change*, pp. 58-63.

37*Oriatrike*, VIII:3.

38*Ibid.*, IV:23.

39*Ibid.*, VII:15.

40*Ibid.*, VIII:19; IV:1, 8. Helmont's use of Thomistic language is far from classical Thomism. "Seeds" take priority over "forms." Moreover, as Pagel has rightly argued, there is a sense in which Helmont's Deity is temporal. Walter Pagel, "J. B. van Helmont, '*De Tempore*' and the History of the Biological Concept of Time," *Osiris*, 8 (1948), 346-417.

41*Oriatrike*, IV:14, 28.

42*Ibid.*, IV:12. Helmont also argues that final causes are constructions of reason, not part of genuine understanding.

43*Ibid.*, XCII:2, 3. Italics mine. The priority of seeds is also apparent in Helmont's denial that seeds are properly elemental, or contingent upon a theory of elements. The seeds exist in the "bosom of the elements," which is ". . . as it were the storehouse of the seeds." *Ibid.*, IV:31.

44*Ibid.*, XXI:3; XXIV:1.

[45]*Ibid.*, IV:3; VIII:3. The latter text is one of many in Helmont that invites the perspective of depth psychology.

[46]*Ibid.*, VIII:7, 8.

[47]*Ibid.*, XXIII:16, 21.

[48]*Ibid.*, XXIII:21, 22, 23, 36.

[49]*Ibid.*, VIII:10. See Pagel, "The debt of science and medicine," p. 106.

[50]*Oriatrike*, VIII:3, 13, 7, 8.

[51]*Ibid.*, IV:9, 12. See Marie Boas Hall, *Robert Boyle and Seventeenth-Century Chemistry* (Cambridge, Eng.: Cambridge, 1958), pp. 88f.

[52]*Oriatrike*, V:3, 4.

[53]*Ibid.*, XIII:1. Walter Pagel, "The Position of Harvey and van Helmont in the History of European Thought," *Toward Modern Science*, ed. by Robert M. Palter (New York: Noonday paperback, 1961), II, 185ff.

[54]*Oriatrike*, XIII:2, 3, 4.

[55]Helmont, "Of the Magnetic Cure of Wounds," *A Ternary of Paradoxes*, pp. 1-93. This Spiritualist excess was influential in turning Charleton away from his early adherence to Helmont and brought about his embrace of Gassendi and the new atomism. See P. M. Rattansi, "Paracelsus and the Puritan Revolution," *Ambix*, 11 (1963), 30.

[56]In his discussion of Luther's "so-called 'Turmerlebnis'," Oberman has discovered the form and function of conversion accounts in theological tradition. Heiko A. Oberman, " 'Iustitia Christi' and 'Iustitia Dei': Luther and the Scholastic Doctrines of Justification," *Harvard Theological Review*, 59 (1966), 9ff.

[57]See Erik Erikson, *Young Man Luther: A Study in Psychoanalysis and History* (New York: Norton, 1958). Helmont's record of his vision was a dramatic testimony to his conversion from scholastic to Spiritualist natural philosophy — no matter how one might reconstruct the underlying religious experience and its psychological dimension.

[58]Martin Luther, *Preface to the Complete Edition of Luther's Latin Writings* (1545), *Martin Luther: Selections*, ed. by John Dillenberger (New York: Doubleday Paperback, 1961), pp. 11, 12. John Calvin, Dedication of the *Commentary on the Psalms* (1560), *Calvin: Commentaries*, ed. by Joseph Haroutunian (Philadelphia: Westminster, 1957), pp. 51-57. See Oberman, " 'Iustitia Christi' and 'Iustitia Dei'," p. 9, n. 5.

[59]René Descartes, *Discourse on the Method of Rightly Conducting the Reason and Seeking Truth in the Sciences* (1637), trans. by Laurence J. LaFleur (New York: Liberal Arts Press Paperback, 1950), part I, pp. 3-5. See also pp. 6f., 13, 25, 26.

[60]*Oriatrike*, Preface; I:1, 4, 13; II:7, 8, 12, 20.

[61]*Ibid.*, I:6, 7.

[62]*Ibid.*, I:6, 12.

[63]*Ibid.*, I:14; II:18, 19, 20.

[64]Francis Bacon, *Masculine Birth of Time* (1605), *The Philosophy of Francis Bacon*, trans. and ed. by Benjamin Farrington (Chicago: University of Chicago Press, 1964), pp. 59-72. See also Farrington's important introductory study of Bacon's early works. *Ibid.*, pp. 11ff. See further Ravetz' study of

"strategy" and especially "Bacon's conversion," which, he argues, may be rooted in "some current of pietistic Paracelsian philosophy"; J. R. Ravetz, "Francis Bacon and the Reform of Philosophy," *Science, Medicine and Society in the Renaissance*, ed. by A. G. Debus (New York: Science History Publications, 1972), II, 97-119, esp. p. 115. For another interpretation of Bacon's theological/religious stance *vis-à-vis* Spiritualist figures, see below, esp. chap. 4.

[65]Bacon, *Masculine Birth of Time*, p. 59. See also Farrington, *Philosophy of Francis Bacon*, p. 18.

[66]Robert Boyle, *An Account of Philaretus, i.e. Mr. R. Boyle, during his Minority*, in *The Works of Robert Boyle*, ed. by Thomas Birch (London, 1744), I, 12.

[67]The basic source here, i.e. Helmont's chapter on the *imago dei* in the *Oriatrike*, appeared separately in 1650 as *The Image of God in Man*, in Helmont's *Ternary of Paradoxes*, "translated, illustrated, and ampliated" by Walter Charleton, pp. 121-147. *Oriatrike*, XXXV:2.

[68]Henry More shared this view, which figured in his opposition to both Hobbes' "mortalism" and the dualistic basis for immortality in Descartes. See Burtt, *Metaphysical Foundations*, pp. 135ff.

[69]*Oriatrike*, XXXV:20, 21; XL:21.

[70]*Ibid.*, XXXV:10, 23, 25.

[71]*Ibid.*, III:25-29; XXXV:19. Here it seems that there is a great gulf between Helmont and the Cambridge Platonists. But this appearance is somewhat misleading, given Helmont on the divine unity of "understanding," and the Cambridge Platonists on the spiritual divinity of reason. Both positions stressed wholistic unity *vs.* multiplicity. This was central to Spiritualist epistemology. It was clearly not understood by those Puritans who opposed faith to reason. This may be seen in the Tuckney-Whichcote debate. See Cragg, *The Cambridge Platonists*, pp. 35-49, and R. F. Jones, *Spiritual Reformers*, pp. 291ff.

[72]*Oriatrike*, III:21, 25; XXXV:29.

[73]*Ibid.*, Promises, p. 4. Italics mine.

[74]*Ibid.*, III:21, 59. Accordingly, Helmont writes that ". . . man doth not measure Nature; but she him," IV:41.

[75]*Ibid.*, III:25-29. Helmont's way of securing certainty is the opposite of that of Descartes. Helmont holds body and mind, life and understanding together in the Spirit.

[76]*Ibid.*, III:31-33, 48.

[77]*Ibid.*, VI:2,13,22. Jesus' parable of the talents, interpreted as a test of faith by works, was frequently used in Spiritualist thought.

[78]*Ibid.*, Promises, p. 6.

[79]*Ibid.*, LX:66.

[80]Nicholas Le Fevre, *A Compleat Body of Chemistry*, trans. by P. D. C., Esq. (London, 1670), pp. 8,1,3. Cited in Debus, "Renaissance Chemistry and the Work of Robert Fludd," pp. 44-47.

[81]*Oriatrike*, I:14; Promises, p. 4. Johan Baptist van Helmont, *Opuscula Medica Inaudita* (Cologne, 1644). This work was later published in the *Oriatrike*, pp. 815ff.

[82]In his earliest published writing, Boyle argued on the grounds of God's bounty as well as "our Savior's prescription . . . *Freely ye have received, freely give*," that all medicinal secrets should be shared. See Robert Boyle, *An Epistolical Discourse of Philaretus to Empericus, written by a Person of singular Piety, Honour, and Learning, inviting all true lovers of Vertue and Mankind, to a free and generous Communication of their Secrets and Receipts in Physick*, p. 147. Written in 1647, this tract was published in Samuel Hartlib's *Chymical, Medicinal, and Chyrugical Addresses made to Samuel Hartlib, Esquire, etc.* (London, 1655), pp. 113-150. Republished by Margaret E. Rowbottom, "The Earliest Published Writing of Robert Boyle," *Annals of Science*, 6 (1948), 384.

[83]Francis Bacon, *Thoughts and Conclusions on the Interpretation of Nature as a Science Productive of Works* (1607), *The Philosophy of Francis Bacon*, pp. 73, 76.

[84]Bacon, *Thoughts and Conclusions*, pp. 93, 102.

Notes to Chapter Four

[1]Jones, *Ancients and Moderns*, p. viii.

[2]Collingwood has argued that eighteenth-century convictions of the autonomy of mind represent a significant departure from earlier modern thought. I have not attempted to settle this complex issue, apart from highlighting distinctive seventeenth-century thought.

[3]Thomas Aquinas, *Summa Contra Gentiles*, in *On the Truth of the Catholic Faith*, trans. by James F. Anderson (New York: Doubleday Image Books, 1956-1962), book II, chap. 6, p. 36.

[4]Contemporary views of radical transcendence, e.g. God as the "wholly other" in Barth and the "God beyond God" of Tillich, should not be confused with this. They are epochally different. Congruently, the historic modern problem of relations has been overlaid by that of alienation in our times.

[5]In Thomas' doctrine of creation the distinction of individuals is a problem rather than something original. Thomas Aquinas, *Summa Contra Gentiles*, book II, chap. 39, p. 115.

[6]The doctrine of the Trinity, powerfully shaped by Augustine, emphasized three divine *personae*, and promoted a sense of inner personality or inner space (memory, understanding, and will) in man, yet Augustine always insisted on the unity of God and His works. God's own personhood was not at issue then; belief in God as personal is a peculiarly modern problem. This is evident in the late appearance of explicitly social trinitarianism.

[7]Barth has argued that Anselm's classic statement of the ontological argument was a prayer. Teleological arguments often appear as interminably long sermons. See Karl Barth, *Anselm: Fides Quarens Intellectum* (London: SCM, 1960).

[8]Francis Bacon, *The Advancement of Learning* (1605), ed. by G. W. Kitchin (London: J. M. Dent and Sons, 1915), p. 41. Italics mine. Bacon was keenly aware of the political reality of the Reformation; he did not conceive it as a purely religious event.

[9]It was precisely in the name of reformation that many Spiritualists denied that the magisterial Reformation got beyond externals to fundamentals.

[10]This is most clear in Bacon's brief early works, and was restated in the *Novum Organum* and *The Great Instauration*. On Bacon's projects of reform, see Benjamin Farrington's Introduction to *The Philosophy of Francis Bacon*, pp. 11-55.

[11]Francis Bacon, *The Masculine Birth of Time* (1603), *The Philosophy of Francis Bacon*, trans. and ed. by B. Farrington, p. 59 (italics mine); and *The Refutation of Philosophies* (1608), *ibid.*, pp. 106, 107.

[12]See the long quotation from Bacon's *Natural and Experimental History for the Foundation of Philosophy* (1622), in Fulton H. Anderson, ed., *The New Organon and Related Writings* (New York: Bobbs-Merrill, 1960), pp. xiv, xv.

[13]Some of Boyle's earliest and most complete statements of the humble yet powerful task of a new Adamic natural philosophy are found throughout his *Usefulness of Natural Philosophy*. Robert Boyle, *Considerations touching the Usefulness of Experimental Natural Philosophy, Proposed in a familiar Discourse to a Friend, by Way of Invitation to the Study of it* (1663), *The Works of Robert Boyle*, I.

[14]Frank E. Manuel, *Isaac Newton, Historian* (Cambridge: Harvard, 1963), chap. 6. See also Newton, *The Original of Monarchies*, *ibid.*, pp. 198-221. See further J. E. McGuire, "Force, Active Principles, and Newton's Invisible Realm," *Ambix*, 15 (1968), 108ff., and with P. M. Rattansi, "Newton and 'Pipes of Pan'," *Notes and Records of the Royal Society*, 21 (1966), 112.

[15]Newton's theology is discussed further below, chaps. 5, 6.

[16]*Refutation of Philosophies*, pp. 110, 131, 132.

[17]*The New Atlantis*, in *The Works of Francis Bacon*, ed. by J. Spedding, R. L. Ellis, and D. D. Heath (London, 1857), III, 145.

[18]This interpretation differs from Ravetz' important study which also stresses religious influences; see J. R. Ravetz, "Francis Bacon and the Reform of Philosophy," in *Science, Medicine and Society in the Renaissance*, ed. by A. G. Debus (New York: Science History Publication, 1972), II, 97-119. See also Walzer, *The Revolution of the Saints*, ch. 6; and C. Webster, *The Intellectual Revolution of the Seventeenth Century*, pp. 1-13, 369-385.

[19]Preface to *The Great Instauration*, in *The New Organon and Related Writings*, pp. 28, 29.

[20]*Observations upon the Prophecies of Daniel*, and the *Apocalypse of St. John*, ed. by Benjamin Smith (London, 1733), pp. 248, 249. Last italics mine.

[21]Bacon's more explicit prophetic self-understanding is perhaps most evident in his *Refutation of Philosophies*, in which he reads navigational ventures and discoveries in the mechanical arts as the best "signs," for they meet the rule of faith shown by works. *Ibid.*, pp. 110, 126, 123.

[22]I am using the concept of differentiation in a broad sense partly suggested by Robert Bellah in his comprehensive but restrained account of the socio-cultural development of religion; see his important article, "Religious Evolution," in *Beyond Belief*, pp. 20-50. The conception of differentiation compares well with such traditional categories as monism, dualism, pantheism, etc., especially when the problem is one of understanding the course of symbolic and institutional change. Marked by structure and process, differentiation proliferates throughout the modern epoch. However, my emphasis is on the beginning of that process in early modern times. I shall give less attention to two equally significant structural components, individuation and systematization.

Schematically, early modern differentiation was apparent in the individuation of (a) religious consciousness, i.e., the centrality of "conscience" from Luther's near instant heroic example to its "cases" in Puritan and Anglican morality, (b) Scripture, i.e., versification and argument by proof texts, (c) nature, i.e., atomization, and (d) knowledge, i.e., the priority of "simple ideas" in both its activity and justification. Furthermore, modern systematization was also marked by many relatively exclusive systems. These systems exerted epochal critical force against looser modes of organization. (a) Note the mathematical models which governed reason and affectional life in Descartes and Spinoza. (b) Compare the rigorous critical principle of Scripture in Calvin's *Institutes* to the inclusive expanse of Thomas' *Summa Theologiae*. Or better, compare the many tight "bodies of divinity" in Puritanism to the common *loci* of classic medieval theology. (c) Note the systematic critical edge of both the "mechanical Philosophy" and the Westminster Confession. In general, such systematizing of individuals generated problems of how to relate atoms (hooks?), simple ideas (association?), verses (analogy of Scripture?), and consciences (cases?). This was an acutely modern problem.

[23]Boyle's work represented early modern critical responses to traditional and Spiritualist thought, English appreciation of Descartes, and the whole range of modern differentiation in religion, natural philosophy, theology, history, etc. Modern individuation, mirrored in Boyle's atomism, influenced Locke's epistemology. See Maurice Mandelbaum, *Philosophy, Science, and Sense Perception* (Baltimore: Johns Hopkins, 1964), chaps. 1, 2. In this context the unity of Boyle's quite diverse works may be further understood.

[24]*Meditationes Sacrae* (1597), *The Works of Francis Bacon*, VII, 243; and Bacon, *Confession of Faith* (1603), *Works*, VII, 219.

[25]*Of Heresies, Works*, VII, 252.

[26]*The Excellency of Theology, compared with Natural Philosophy . . . To which are annexed Some Occasional Thoughts about the Excellency and Grounds of the Mechanical Hypothesis* (1674), III, 407. *The Excellency of Theology* was written in 1665. See the Appendix for the dates of Boyle's works.

[27]*Masculine Birth of Time*, p. 66.

[28]*Some Considerations Touching the Usefulness of Experimental Natural Philosophy* (1663), *Works*, I, 488; Tome One of the *Usefulness of Natural Philosophy* was written in 1650. Boyle, *A Free Discourse against Customary Swearing* (no date), *Works*, V, 209; the *Discourse against Swearing*, published posthumously, was written in 1647.

[29]Boyle argues that Hobbes' view of impenetrable dimensions conflicts with his affirmation of the Creator. He writes that ". . . it seems difficult to conceive, how, in a world, that is already perfectly full of body, a corporeal Deity, such as he maintains in his *Append ad Leviath. cap* 3, can have access, even to the minute parts of the mundane matter, that seems requisite to the attributes and operation, that belong to the Deity, in reference to the world." Boyle, *Animadversions upon Mr. Hobbes Problemata De Vacuo* (1674), *Works*, III, 476. On Boyle's objection to Hobbes' appeal to omnipotence, see *An Examen of Mr. T. Hobbes' Dialogus Physicus de Natura Aeris* (1662), *Works*, I, 150.

[30]See Manuel, *Isaac Newton, Historian*, pp. 112ff., and below, chap. 5.

[31]Robert Boyle, *Of the High Veneration Man's Intellect Owes to God, Peculiarly for His Wisdom and Power*, no date, in *Works*, IV, 339, 340. Boyle's *Veneration Man Owes to God* was written at "diverse times."

[32]*Of the Reconcileableness of Reason and Religion* by *T. E., a layman, Works,* III, 515. (Fulton shows that the initials "T. E." were used by Boyle, and that *Reason and Religion* was probably published in 1675. See the Appendix.) See also Bacon, *Advancement of Learning,* pp. 216, 218.

[33]Boyle, *Usefulness of Natural Philosophy,* I, 432ff. Frequently, it has been argued that the (Protestant) nurture of the individual's rights and duty to interpret Scripture was part of the freedom from authority basic to the new science. This may be true; yet, apart from sharply differentiating the two books, and delimiting the direct authority of theology for natural philosophy, even such new rights and duties probably would have been much less effective. It is difficult to overestimate the significance of the sharp early modern differentiation of the works (and books) of creation and redemption.

[34]Bacon, *A Confession of Faith, Works,* VII, 221. Published in 1648, the *Confession* was written before 1603. See also Bacon, *Meditationes Sacrae, Works,* VII, 252, and Bacon, *Valerius Terminus of the Interpretations of Nature with the Annotations of Hermes Stella, Works,* III, 222. Bacon's sharp distinction of creation and redemption was instrumental in releasing the classic Christian drama of creation-fall-redemption such that preoccupation with the material content of God's work in the six days of creation was minimized. Once released, the classic drama was applied to disciplines of knowledge as well as those of religion.

[35]*Thoughts and Conclusions,* pp. 77-79.

[36]In his *New Organon,* Bacon cast his message in the form of "aphorisms" intended as "precepts" to reform natural philosophy. This style, as in his early work, showed his basic conviction that both religion and science were ultimately the work of God. Yet, hardly less important was Bacon's insistence that henceforth the study of nature be differentiated from the religious interest in redemption. (They are to be kept distinct along the lines of God's power and will.) This is the point of Aphorism LXV, which charges that traditional Greek natural philosophy superstitiously introduced final causes, an "apotheosis of error," which not only blocked the search for intermediate causes, but also damaged the heart of religion. Similarly, Bacon charges that the Spiritualist attempt to "found a system of natural philosophy on the first chapter of Genesis" is confused, and "from this unwholesome mixture of things human and divine there arises not only a fantastic philosophy but also a heretical religion." *New Organon,* p. 62. Bacon's insistence on differentiation at the levels of divine work, the book of nature, and human study also marks his *Advancement of Learning,* pp. 27, 89, 216-219.

[37]On Wallis, see Thomas Birch, *Life of Robert Boyle* (1744), in Boyle's *Works,* I, 25. See also Robert Hooke on the purpose and design of the Royal Society as quoted in J. C. Weld, ed., *The History of the Royal Society* (London, 1848), I, 146-149. Special note should be taken of a specific purpose stated by Hooke: "To attempt the recovering of such allowable arts and inventions as are lost," *ibid.,* p. 146. The attempt here is to recover original creation. See also Birch, *Life of Robert Boyle,* pp. 87, 101.

[38]*Masculine Birth of Time,* p. 65, and *New Organon,* Aphorism XXXIX, p. 47.

[39]Despite Boyle's later additions to his early *Style of Scriptures,* it is one of Boyle's most carefully written pieces. See also John Locke, *The Reasonableness of Christianity as Delivered in the Scriptures* (London, 1695). The modern historical consciousness which emerges in the seventeenth century was the

preparation for the much deeper historical consciousness of the nineteenth century, in turn dependent upon Romantic thought. The seventeenth-century effort to liberate historical events from witnesses and traditions should not be confused with the later effort to unfold the self-consciousness of historical agents.

[40]In a discussion of classical rhetoricians, Boyle writes that one should not be tied to Cicero who confounded the "system of precepts" in Scripture with the "art of rhetorick." *Some Considerations Touching the Style of the Holy Scriptures* (1661), *Works*, II, 123, 101. See also pp. 125, 103. Boyle buttresses his theological point by quoting Isaiah 55:8, "As the heavens are higher than the earth, so are his thoughts higher than our thoughts."

[41]*Style of Scriptures*, II, 98. In large measure, Boyle follows Bacon's critique of Ramus and Aristotle. See Bacon, *Thoughts and Conclusions*, p. 83. Also see Bacon's critique that just as the "schoolmen" left God's word for their theological systems, they also deserted His works for their own schemes of natural philosophy. *Advancement of Learning*, pp. 27, 219.

[42]Most Boyle scholarship passes lightly over his early life and works. An important exception is J. R. Jacob's "The Ideological Origins of Robert Boyle's Natural Philosophy," *Journal of European Studies*, 2 (1971), 1-21. Boyle's critical interest in translation is seen in his critique of the Fathers for their lack of Hebrew *(Excellency of Theology*, II, 415), and of the Christian tradition in general for its reliance upon the inaccurate Septuagint. Boyle held that most translations of the Hebrew, especially into Latin, lose its idiomatic flavor in attending to words rather than phrases. *Style of Scriptures*, II, 95, 96.

[43]*Style of Scriptures*, II, 96-98.

[44]*Ibid.*, 99, 98. Divine "accommodation" was a long-standing staple in Christian doctrines of Scripture; it is not, as such, either a witness to an intellectually threatened Church in the seventeenth century, or a positive factor in the new science.

[45]See William Haller, *The Rise of Puritanism* (New York: Harper Torchbook, 1957), pp. 298f., and Benjamin Nelson, "Casuistry," *Encyclopedia Britannica*, 1963. Robert Sanderson's *Ten Lectures on the Obligations of Human Conscience*, trans. by Robert Codrington (London, 1660), was dedicated to Boyle.

[46]See Louis T. More, *The Life and Works of the Honourable Robert Boyle* (New York: Oxford, 1944), pp. 144ff., for an interpretation which differs from ours. Boyle's *The Martyrdom of Theodora and of Didymus* (1687), *Works*, IV, 425-463, was written forty years before its publication. See also Ian Watt, *The Rise of the Novel* (Berkeley, California, 1957), and John J. Richetti, *Popular Fiction Before Richardson* (Oxford: Clarendon, 1969), pp. 4ff.

[47]On the unique emergence of narrative history in the Old Testament see G. E. Wright, *God Who Acts* (Naperville: Allenson, 1952), p. 38; on the unique yet vexing genre of gospel see William Beardslee, *Literary Criticism of the New Testament* (Philadelphia: Fortress, 1970); and on autobiography and personality see Charles N. Cochrane, *Christianity and Classical Culture* (London: Oxford, 1940), chap. 11.

[48]*Martyrdom*, IV, 433, 434, 458, 461.

[49]*Ibid.*, pp. 457, 434.

[50]*Ibid.*, pp. 426-429.

[51]See Wilfred C. Smith's excellent study of the terminology of "religion" in the

West, which is somewhat marred by reading highly developed rational assumptions of the eighteenth century into seventeenth-century thought. Smith, "'Religion' in the West," *The Meaning and End of Religion* (New York: Mentor Books, 1964), pp. 19-49, esp. pp. 40ff. On the eighteenth-century view, see Frank Manuel, *The Eighteenth Century Confronts the Gods*, chap. 2. On Calvin, see *ICR*, I:5, pp. 51ff.

⁵²This is clear in the voluminous writings of the Christian *virtuosi*, particularly Boyle's *Christian Virtuoso*.

⁵³See Smith, "'Religion' in the West," notes 111, 112.

⁵⁴For a remarkable appearance of creation piety see the works of St. Francis; and for seventeenth-century figures see Raven, *Science and Religion*, chaps. 6, 7. Far from romanticism, or even the contemplation of nature per se, seventeenth-century creation piety was ordered by the will of God and man.

⁵⁵Perry Miller's Introduction to Jonathan Edwards' meditative *Images or Shadows of Divine Things* is an insightful account of this genre. Edwards, *Images or Shadows of Divine Things*, ed. by Perry Miller (New Haven: Yale, 1948), pp. 1-41. See also Joseph Hall, *The Shaking of the Olive Tree* (London, 1660).

⁵⁶William Haller, *The Rise of Puritanism* (New York: Harper Torchbook, 1957), pp. 129ff.; and G. S. Wakefield, *Puritan Devotion: Its Place in the Development of Christian Piety* (London: Epworth Press, 1957), pp. 1-28.

⁵⁷Boyle, *Occasional Reflections upon Several Subjects. Whereto is premised A Discourse about such kind of thoughts* (1665), *Works*, II, 138-226. (Henceforth abbreviated *Reflections* and *Discourse*, respectively. On the early writing of this work, see the Appendix.) The example cited is from Boyle, *Discourse*, II, 157. Baxter's enthusiastic letter on this work was typical; Boyle, *Works*, V, 553-555.

⁵⁸*Reflections*, II, 142-146; *Discourse*, II, 147; see also p. 156.

⁵⁹*Discourse*, II, 151.

⁶⁰*Ibid.*, 155, 149.

⁶¹Moreover, in generally differentiating natural philosophy from theological and philosophical entanglement, Boyle quoted Bacon to note that both would progress as long as one did not *"unwisely mingle and confound"* them. This enabled Boyle to refute traditionalist Henry Stubbe's charges that the Royal Society was injurious to both natural philosophy and religion. See Thomas Birch, *Life of Robert Boyle*, pp. 47-50, and Boyle, *Usefulness of Natural Philosophy*, I, 458. Similarly, Newton declared "that religion and Philosophy are to be preserved distinct. We are not to introduce divine relations into Philosophy nor philosophical opinions into religion." This is the first of Newton's unpublished "Seven Statements on Religion," *Newton: Theological Manuscripts*, ed. by Herbert McLachlan (Liverpool, 1950), p. 58. Forceful as this statement is, Newton (like Boyle) did affirm a distinction, not a separation, of religion and science.

⁶²*The Sceptical Chymist* (1661), *Works*, I, pp. 315ff. Henceforth abbreviated *Sceptical Chemist*.

⁶³*Usefulness of Natural Philosophy*, I, 488. Boyle's own Christology is orthodox. Although Bacon's is less so — he affirms Christ primarily as a moral prophet and reformer — the crucial point is that their differentiation of creation from redemption removes the pressure to base their natural philosophy (or

medicine) upon Christ. On the *Sceptical Chemist* as a critique of traditional natural philosophy, see below, chap. 6, and Marie Boas Hall, "The Establishment of the Mechanical Philosophy," *Osiris*, 10 (1952); and *Robert Boyle and Seventeenth-century Chemistry* (Cambridge, 1958).

[64]*A Defense of the Doctrine touching the Spring and Weight of the Air, proposed by Mr. R. Boyle, in his new Physico-Mechanical Experiments; against the Objections of Franciscus Linus. Wherewith the Objector's Funicular Hypothesis is also examined* (1662), *Works*, I, 77, 92f., 95f., esp. p. 96. In this *Defense* Boyle gives the clearest formulation of the Law which bears his name.

[65]Compare Kearney's conception of basic differences apparent in the course of differing "scientific styles, languages, and experiments." Kearney, *Science and Change*, chap. 2.

[66]Marie Boas Hall, *Robert Boyle on Natural Philosophy*, p. 43. (Boyle had Hooke's early assistance in promoting an early form of lab reporting.) Boyle's *Defense against Linus* came shortly *after* his *New Experiments Physico-Mechanical, touching the Spring of Air, and its Effects; Made for the most part, in a New Pneumatical Engine* (1659), *Works*, I, 1-75. It was in the *Defense* of original reporting that Boyle became theoretically aware of the "weight" of air — a factor omitted from the *New Experiments* — and formulated his Law.

[67]The *Proemial Essay* appeared in the first essay of *Certain Physiological Essays, and other Tracts; written at distant Times, and on several Occasions* (1661), *Works*, I, 191-204. See esp. pp. 192, 194, 196f.

[68]Boyle, *Proemial Essay*, p. 196. See Marie Boas Hall, *Robert Boyle on Natural Philosophy*, pp. 27-29, 53f.

[69]Boyle, *A Free Inquiry into the vulgarly received Notion of Nature; Made in an Essay addressed to a Friend* (1686), *Works*, IV, 358-424. Fulton extravagantly praises this somewhat overlooked work, partly completed in 1666, as Boyle's *Principia*. Its significance is examined closely below, chap. 6.

[70]Boyle, *The Requirements of a Good and Excellent Hypothesis*, in *Robert Boyle On Natural Philosophy*, ed. by M. B. Hall, pp. 134, 135. Newton, *Mathematical Principles of Natural Philosophy*, trans. by Motte and Cajori (New York: Dover, 1966), pp. 398-400. See also Boyle, *The Requisites of a Good and Excellent Hypothesis*, and *Of Ye Atomicall Philosophy*, and *Propositions on Sense, Reason, and Authority*, in Richard Westfall, "Unpublished Boyle Papers Relating to Scientific Method — II," *Annals of Science*, 12 (1956), 111-117, especially pp. 116, 117. See further Neal W. Gilbert's thesis that from the sixteenth to the seventeenth century there was a major shift from method as a way of organization to an instrument of discovery. Gilbert, *Renaissance Concepts of Method* (New York: Columbia, 1960).

[71]*A Disquisition about the Final Causes of Natural Things* (1688), *Works*, IV, 518-520, esp. p. 519.

[72]Boyle further holds that the freedom of God in His own work is prior to that of cosmic design, which in turn is prior to its reflection in the human and animal ends of creation. Boyle's sophisticated generalization of final causes is thus undergirded by a hierarchy of wills. *Final Causes*, IV, 518, 522.

[73]*Ibid.*, p. 524. Even so, Boyle held that all creatures were "arbitrary pictures of the great creator," *Veneration Man Owes to God*, IV, 351.

[74]*Essay on the Usefulness of Mathematics in Natural Philosophy*, *Works*, III,

156-162. The reflective epistemological ventures of Descartes and Locke generated a novel modern conception of philosophy itself.

[75]Newton, *Principia*, p. xxxii.

[76]On the Clarke-Leibnitz debate, see Koyré, *From World to Universe*, pp. 238ff. On Leibnitz in relation to Newton see J. E. McGuire, "Boyle's Conception of Nature," *Journal of the History of Ideas*, 33 (1972), 527, 531ff.

[77]*Excellency of Theology*, III, 416, 417. Boyle's "very general" yet clearly theological "universal hypothesis" is a near direct statement of what we have termed a basic presupposition. Marie Boas Hall notes that Boyle sometimes meant an hypothesis was a "theological doctrine." Marie Boas Hall, *Robert Boyle on Natural Philosophy*, p. 52.

[78]The modern reversal of this basic medieval order raises the question: Why did not late medieval voluntarism get beyond the *question* of reversing the classical order of knowing following being? Early modern thought could because it was built upon a keener base of divine and human will, and the outbreak of widespread skepticism sharpened the issue; it demanded answers.

[79]See Hannah Arendt, *The Human Condition* (New York: Doubleday, 1959), chap. 6.

[80]Without belittling the questions of the great eighteenth-century epistemologists, e.g. Kant, who took empirical knowledge for granted and sought to spell out its universal and necessary conditions — a logical justification of knowledge — the more practical skeptical question of the possibility of empirical knowledge was more pressing in early modern times. Kant's philosophy presupposed considerable historic success in the natural sciences. In general, see Richard H. Popkin, *The History of Skepticism from Erasmus to Descartes*, rev. ed. (New York: Harper, 1964).

[81]This preference was neither opposed to truth per se, nor should it be identified with the stand for truth taken by some continental astronomers in another struggle crucial to modern science. See the investigations of Benjamin Nelson cited above, chap. 1, note 47.

[82]This raises the general question of the contribution of Spiritualism to modern empirical knowledge. Although I am stressing that this was manifest largely through more visible moderns such as Boyle, this is not a complete answer.

[83]Frequently, the "empirical" cast of Boylean (and English) thought is simply opposed to the "deductive" propensities of Descartes. This ignores the larger context in which, despite a large measure of agreement on the priority of divine will, Boyle remained suspicious of the closer relation of divine and human mind in Descartes. Whereas Descartes' ontological argument for God presupposed the priority of self and God, Boyle's teleological argument gave equal integrity to a third term, the world. Against Descartes, Boyle argued that God's will was distinctly manifest "as well without, upon the world, as within, upon the mind." *Final Causes*, IV, 522.

Notes to Chapter Five

[1]Boyle's claim that an amateur divine could often communicate what the professional overlooked has sufficient truth in his own case to warrant concentra-

tion on his thought. Boyle, *Seraphick Love*, I, 180. On his theological similarities to Wilkins and Glanvill (and the Christian *virtuosi*), respectively, see Hooykaas, *Religion and the Rise of Modern Science*, and Westfall, *Science and Religion*. Boyle read and wrote theology throughout his life, and was familiar with continental Reformed theology. Partington wrote that Boyle's early schooling in Geneva brought him "under Calvinist protestant influences, which remained with him all his life." J. R. Pàrtington, *A History of Chemistry* (London: Macmillan, 1961), II, 486. This is possible, given his adolescent "conversion," but such issues are not central for our inquiry. Boyle's theology differed as much from that of Calvin as did seventeenth-century English theology generally.

[2]See Westfall, *Science and Religion*. See also Jacob, who accentuates the ideological propensities of Boyle's early religious thought. J. R. Jacob, "The Ideological Origins of Robert Boyle's Natural Philosophy," *Journal of European Studies*, 2 (1971), 1-21.

[3]Thomas Birch, *The Life of Robert Boyle*, p. 87.

[4]*Usefulness of Natural Philosophy*, I, 433-434.

[5]*Style of Scriptures*, II, 118 and 137.

[6]*Some Motives and Incentives to the Love of God, Pathetically discoursed of, in a letter to a Friend* (1659), *Works*, I, 167. Henceforth abbreviated *Seraphick Love*. On the celebration of God's work among those influenced by the Cambridge Platonists, see Charles E. Raven, *Science and Religion*, pp. 110ff.

[7]On the slow rise, sudden outburst, and rapid decline of English Deism, see John Orr, *English Deism: Its Roots and Fruits* (Grand Rapids: Eerdmans, 1934), pp. 18-19, 59ff.

[8]Pp. 444ff., 449.

[9]*Excellency of Theology*, III, 407.

[10]*A Discourse of things above Reason, inquiring whether a Philosopher should admit there are any such* (1681), *Works*, IV, 47.

[11]In *Works*, III, 537. Henceforth abbreviated, *Resurrection*. See also Boyle, *Some Considerations about the Reconcileableness of Reason and Religion*, (1675), in *Works*, III, pp. 509ff. Henceforth abbreviated, *Reason and Religion*.

[12]*Resurrection*, III, 538, 539-540, 544, 545.

[13]The seventeenth-century understanding of God should not be confused with the highly domesticated Deity of much Enlightenment thought. Koyré's denomination of the God of Newton as the mighty "Jehovah" is most fortunate. In great part it captures the exalted sense of God in seventeenth-century English thought, See Koyré, *From World to Universe*, pp. 206-272.

[14]*Seraphick Love*, I, 177; *Greatness of Mind promoted by Christianity* (no date), *Works*, V, 73. This piece was appended to *The Christian Virtuoso*.

[15]*Seraphick Love*, I, 168, 169.

[16]*Veneration Man Owes to God*, IV, 356-358. This treatise opens with a keen consciousness of God's uniqueness:

> "Upon this occasion I shall take leave to declare, that it is not without some indignation, as well as wonder, that I see many men, and some of them divines too, who little considering what God is, and what themselves are, presume to talk of him and his attributes as freely, and as unpremedi-

tately as if they were talking of a geometrical figure, or a mechanical engine." *Ibid.*, p. 339.
See also *Excellency of Theology*, III, 408.

17*Veneration Man Owes to God*, IV, 339f.

18*Excellency of Theology*, III, 419, and *Veneration Man Owes to God*, IV, 355.

19For Newton's use of this title in his natural and moral philosophy, respectively, see his conception of "God the author of all motion" (below, chap. 6), and see the universal title of "true Author and Benefactor," in the final sentence of the *Opticks*, 4th ed. (New York: Dover, 1952), pp. 405, 406.

20Pp. 429 (italics mine), 430.

21*Veneration Man Owes to God*, IV, 352, 353-354.

22*Reason and Religion*, III, 516, 518, 517. See also Boyle, *Resurrection*, III, 544, and *Martyrdom*, IV, 434, on the stock voluntarist example of the rescue of Daniel.

23*Reason and Religion*, III, 517, 518. Boyle also expresses the dialectic of God's will on the issue of whether or not He will forgive sins. See *Excellency of Theology*, III, 409.

24Ames extended the covenant idea beyond divine-human relations to a conception of God's one-way covenant with the inanimate world. Ames, *Marrow*, I: 8, 9, pp. 100-110. See further the argument of Perry Miller, *The New England Mind: Vol. I, The Seventeenth Century* (Boston: Beacon Paperback, 1961), book 4, pp. 365ff.

25The task of demonstrating the content of the view of God in Newton's strictly theological writing remains to be fulfilled. One way of at least putting the central issue here is how much Newton's theology per se was indebted to voluntarist, Spiritualist, traditional, and aesthetic theologies of creation. This question is different from, although related to, that of the function of his theology in his natural philosophy. Westfall's *Science and Religion* is a valuable but historically (and theologically) limited contribution to the central issue. This is less true of Frank Manuel's *The Religion of Isaac Newton* (Oxford: Clarendon, 1974), which substantiates his earlier account of Newton's "Puritan" view of God by stressing his obsession with God as Father. Yet even here, the complex Spiritualist influence in Newton's theology is not fully credited. More to the point is McGuire's stress on Newton's voluntarist theology, but not at the expense of Spiritualism. See below, chap. 6.

26This "Scheme" was part of Newton's unpublished "Irenicum." Selections published in: *Isaac Newton: Theological Manuscripts*, p. 54.

27Newton, *Principia*, p. 544.

28Pp. 170, 171, 172. This early work is significant in showing Boyle's theological break with Helmontian Spiritualism.

29For Boyle, God is "so holy in his laws, and so concerned for them, that even the ministers of his altars shall not violate them with impunity, but find him (what the writer to the Hebrews calls him) *a consuming fire.*" *Seraphick Love*, I, 173. In this discussion Boyle makes no suggestion of any dichotomy between divine law and love.

30*Seraphick Love*, I, 175, 178. Newton also subordinated love to God's power, particularly in his stress on direct obedience to all the commandments without the service of a mediator. Newton, "Short Scheme of True Religion," *Newton: Theological Manuscripts*, pp. 48-53.

[31]*Veneration Man Owes to God*, IV, 351, 352. In this revision of the Spiritualist way of relating Creator and creation, Boyle's use of the category of occasion is reminiscent of Gassendi. However, Boyle's limited retention of teleology kept him from sheer occasionalism. Boyle went òn to articulate a legal conception of God's ". . . architectonic wisdom (if I may so call it) exerted in framing and regulating an innumerable company of differing creatures. . . ,"*ibid.*

[32]Unlike radical criticism in recent Protestant neo-orthodox theology, early modern criticism sought to reconstruct self and world according to divine law.

[33]This view, detailed in an early draft of the final Query in the *Opticks*, shows that Newton's deep soundings into the ancients discovered nothing less than the law of the Creator, no less binding in the present than at the beginning. Babson Collection of the Works of Newton, 1950, p. 129, cited by Klaus-Dietwordt Buchholtz, *Isaac Newton als Theologe* (Witten: Luther-Verlag, 1965), p. 119.

[34]*Excellency of Theology*, III, 417.

[35]*Ibid.*, p. 419.

[36]Boyle, *A Free Discourse against Customary Swearing*, V, 218. See also *Style of Scriptures*, II, 112.

[37]*Greatness of Mind*, V, 67. Italics mine.

[38]*Reason and Religion*, III, 532. Italics mine.

[39]P. 116.

[40]*Style of Scriptures*, II, 115f., 98. Elsewhere, Boyle wrote that, ". . . certainly . . . [the] . . . laws recorded in the Bible, cannot but appear more noble and worthy objects of curiosity to us Christians who know them to proceed from an omniscient deity, who being the author of mankind, as well as of the rest of the universe, cannot but have a far perfecter knowledge of the nature of man, than any other of the law-givers, or all of them put together can be conceived to have had." *Excellency of Theology*, III, 409.

[41]*Excellency of Theology*, III, 422.

[42]*Newton: Theological Manuscripts*, p. 34.

[43]Pp. 445, 446.

[44]*A Confession of Faith* (1597), *Works*, VII, 221.

[45]Boyle, *Style of Scriptures*, II, 103.

[46]Descartes should be excepted from this judgment. See Newton's General Scholium for a classic statement on God's design. In Query 28 of the *Opticks*, Newton asks the rhetorical question, "Whence is it that Nature doth nothing in vain; and whence arises all that Order and Beauty which we see in the world?" *Opticks*, p. 369.

[47]*Usefulness of Natural Philosophy*, I, 439.

[48]*Excellency of Theology*, III, 428. Boyle's presupposition of design published in creation was basic to his opposition to Spiritualist appeals to mystery rather than reason.

[49]*Style of Scriptures*, II, 131.

[50]For Boyle's further comments on wisdom see *Usefulness of Natural Philosophy*, I, 433f., 437.

Notes to Chapter Six

[1]Robert Boyle, *A Free Inquiry into the vulgarly received Notion of Nature* (1686), *Works*, IV, 358-361.

[2]I have chosen to focus on Boyle because of the thoroughness and clarity of his representative discussion of nature and its significance within wider religious, philosophical, and scientific concerns. Unfortunately, many have dismissed Boyle as a mere experimenter or imitative natural philosopher. This has obscured a sense of the whole project of Boyle's labors, and not least his lively presupposition of the natural world as creation. For important exceptions, see the works of Kargon and Westfall, and others cited below, such as M. B. Hall and McGuire. Nevertheless, even Kargon's important study is quick to see Boyle simply "purifying" atomism in the face of theology. Boyle's work, in reality, was an important reformation of atomism. Also, Westfall's valuable account of theology and cosmology in Boyle tends to regard the former more as the chief problem rather than chief presupposition of his thought. R. Kargon, *Atomism in England from Hariot to Newton* (Oxford: Clarendon, 1966); and R. Westfall, *Science and Religion*.

[3]Portions of Boyle's *Notion of Nature* were written as early as 1666, and the work was in process for a long time before its 1686 publication. Boyle's *Certain Physiological Essays, and other Tracts; written at distant Times, and on several Occasions* (1661), I, 191ff., anticipates the critical and constructive work in the *Skeptical Chemist* and the *Origin of Forms and Qualities* (1666), respectively. Henceforth abbreviated, *Certain Physiological Essays*. See especially, "The Theorical Part" of Boyle's *Origin of Forms and Qualities*, II, 460ff. See further, Robert Boyle, *Tracts written by the Honourable Robert Boyle about the Cosmicall Qualities of things, and Cosmicall Suspitions* (1671), III, 72ff., esp. pp. 82-94.

[4]*Notion of Nature*, IV, 359, 360.

[5]*Ibid.*, pp. 361, 363 *et passim.*

[6]P. 361.

[7]Usually Boyle does not name the "naturists" (in contrast to "naturalists") who mistake nature for God. However, the context usually indicates ancient pantheists (pagans) or contemporary Spiritualists.

[8]*Notion of Nature*, IV, 366.

[9]*Ibid.*, pp. 363, 369.

[10]*Ibid.*, pp. 368ff. Boyle may have had Henry More in mind, or some Spiritualists that constructed natural philosophy upon the Bible.

[11]*Ibid.*, pp. 379, 370, 374.

[12]*Ibid.*, pp. 374, 375.

[13]*Ibid.*, p. 376.

[14]*Ibid.*, pp. 376, 377.

[15]Newton, *De Gravitatione et aequipondio fluidorum* (no date), *Unpublished Scientific Papers of Isaac Newton: A Selection from the Portsmouth Collection*, trans. and ed. by A. Rupert Hall and Marie Boas Hall (Cambridge, Eng.: Cambridge, 1962), p. 142.

[16]*Principia*, p. 544.

[17]*Notion of Nature*, IV, 415, 416; see also p. 418. On Helmont's Archaeus in nature, see above, chap. 3.

[18]Boyle often preferred to speak of corpuscular natural philosophy. On the term "mechanical" see McGuire's list of its many meanings which shows that the "mechanical philosophy" of the seventeenth century should not be confused with later consolidations. See J. E. McGuire, "Boyle's Conception of Nature," p. 523.

[19]Boyle, *Notion of Nature*, IV, 380, 388. Boyle makes his critical point partly by appeal to the divine Maker of Hebrews 11:10. Moreover, he stresses that the world always depends for its design upon God. Boyle's position highlights the contingency of creation.

[20]P. 366.

[21]*Veneration Man Owes to God*, IV, 343, 344.

[22]*Veneration Man Owes to God*, IV, 348. Here it must be observed that Boyle is referring to basic images, not categories. Far too much weight has been given to Boyle's references to the Strasbourg clock for his allegedly mechanistic outlook. Franklin L. Baumer, *Religion and the Rise of Skepticism* (New York: Harcourt Brace, 1960), pp. 78-127.

[23]*Notion of Nature*, IV, 362; see also *Veneration Man Owes to God*, IV, 348.

[24]*Veneration Man Owes to God*, IV, 343.

[25]P. 373.

[26]*Usefulness of Natural Philosophy*, I, 441.

[27]See respectively Marie Boas Hall, *Robert Boyle on Natural Philosophy*, pp. 49ff.; and Harold Fisch, "The Scientist as Priest: A Note on Robert Boyle's Natural Theology," *Isis*, 44 (1953), 253.

[28]Boyle carefully quoted, but not with full approval, the *Hermetica*, and other authorities venerated in the Spiritualist tradition. In one catalogue of authorities he quoted Philo, ". . . The whole world is to be accounted the chiefest temple of God; the *Sanctum Sanctorum* of it is of the purest part of the universe, heaven; the ornaments, the stars; the priests, the ministers of his power, angels, and immaterial souls." *Usefulness of Natural Philosophy*, I, 441.

[29]*Ibid.*

[30]See above, chap. 5. A contrasting view is evident in Boyle's Spiritualist contemporary, Elias Ashmole, who wrote of the adept few initiated into alchemical mysteries and practices, "For amongst the people of the *Jews*, there was but one that might enter into the *Holy of Holies*, (and that but once a year,) so there is seldom more in a Nation, whom God lets into this *Sanctum Sanctorum of Philosophy*; but there are some." Cited by Harold Fisch from the Prolegomena to Arthur Dee's *Fasciculus Chemicus*, 1650. Harold Fisch, "The Scientist as Priest," p. 255.

[31]Cited by J. E. McGuire from an *Advertissement au Lecteur*, which Newton sent to Des Maizeaux. McGuire, "Force, Active Principles, and Newton's Invisible Realm," p. 200.

[32]Cited by J. E. McGuire from Gregory MS. 245, fols. 14, 3 in the Library of the Royal Society. McGuire, "Force, Active Principles, and Newton's Invisible Realm," p. 200.

[33]*Principia*, p. xxxii. See above, chaps. 4, 5.

[34]*Usefulness of Natural Philosophy*, I, 425, 441. Italics mine.

[35]Boyle's stress on the scientist as a reformed priest or "minister" went beyond vulgar Baconian dominion. *Usefulness of Natural Philosophy*, I, 429. This also appeared in Boyle's move beyond compiling "histories" of natural qualities to genuine experimentation.

[36]*Notion of Nature*, IV, 372, 362, 381, 421.

[37]*Ibid.*, pp. 367, 372.

[38]*Reason and Religion*, III, 530.

[39]*Notion of Nature*, IV, 381.

[40]*Origin of Forms and Qualities*, II, 476.

[41]*Origin of Forms and Qualities*, II, 479-481.

[42]*Excellency of Theology*, III, 433. Boyle affirmed the "jealousy" of God against Descartes' infinite or "indefinite" matter. See *Veneration Man Owes to God*, IV, 343. Descartes' position could be put as continual *creatio ex nihilo*.

[43]*Origin of Forms and Qualities*, II, 470. As Marie Boas Hall has argued, Boyle was distinctive here, if at all, in the thoroughgoing extent to which he carried out the critique against the scholastic tradition in natural philosophy. Hall, "The Establishment of the Mechanical Philosophy," *Osiris*, 10 (1952), 416, 492.

[44]*Origin of Forms and Qualities*, II, 476, 477, 478, 462.

[45]*Ibid.*, pp. 481, 482. For Boyle, the great divine Author had no "recourse to substantial forms" in His work, *ibid.*, p. 484. Elsewhere, he found the doctrine of substantial forms an affront to the exquisitely designed world which God in his wisdom has published. Not only the goodness, or integrity, but also the beauty and harmony of divine order is respected. Boyle's position does not rest with merely arbitrary will, and thus a world in which the seeds of destruction and chaos lie. God is the Author who published his own reliability as well as freedom. See *The Christian Virtuoso*, V, 43ff.

[46]Similarly, he rejected traditional "real and distinct qualities" marked by formal essences. Moreover, besides his broad objection to reified forms (as causes, qualities, and powers), Boyle equally resisted that mode of inquiry or explanation which put the question — What makes X different from Y? — and answered in terms of formal causes. See M. B. Hall, *Robert Boyle on Natural Philosophy*, pp. 57-59.

[47]*Usefulness of Natural Philosophy*, I, 448.

[48]*Final Causes*, IV, 527. Boyle intends this in the most strict sense, for unlike his new employment of the concept of nature, which he also criticized as a "notion," Boyle never reemployed a concept of chance. *Notion of Nature*, IV, 365, 366.

[49]*Notion of Nature*, IV, 372, 374. In maintaining this form of the basic distinction between matter and motion, Boyle's immediate target was Epicurean atomism and its confusions. Similarly, the consistent "motionalist" philosophy of Hobbes, i.e., the tendency to collapse matter into motion, as contrasted to the Epicurean tendency to collapse motion into matter, struck Boyle as erroneous if not idolatrous. *Reason and Religion*, III, 520f.

[50]*Origin of Forms and Qualities*, II, 461, 471, 475, *et passim*. Notwithstanding his use of causal language to account for local motion, Boyle accounted for

corruption as a simple form of "transposition." Moreover, the same local motion described as a second cause was also understood as God's "instrument." To sort all this out would require more than just a general theory of local motion. Equally critical are the questions of (1) the relation of laws of motion and local motion, and (2) the efficacy of divine will and motion. Generally, Boyle wrote interchangeably of laws of motion and laws of nature.

[51]On the concept of a "scale" of causes see below, p. 177. In general, Boyle subordinated the weighty traditional division of first and second causes in his voluntarist orientation. See J. E. McGuire, "Boyle's Conception of Nature," pp. 523-542, for a discussion of causality and theology in Boyle's thought.

[52]From a philosophical-historical viewpoint, Whitehead and Collingwood have suggested the novelty and epochal significance of the idea of physical *laws* of nature in modern thought, and Zilsel, Oakley, and McGuire have begun the arduous historical work of substantiating this insight. In contrast to Zilsel's assumption that the new conception of law derived from the classical natural law tradition, in relation to contemporaneous social theory, Oakley and McGuire have shown that it arose within late medieval and early modern traditions of voluntarist and nominalist thought. See Collingwood, *New Leviathan*, pp. 125-129; Zilsel, "The Genesis of the Concept of Physical Laws," *Philosophical Review*, 51 (1942), 263-276; Oakley, "Medieval Theories of Natural Law: William of Ockham and the Significance of the Voluntarist Tradition," *Natural Law Forum*, 6 (1961), and "Christian Theology and the Newtonian Science: The Rise of the Concept of the Laws of Nature," *Church History*, 30 (1961), 433-457; and others cited below.

[53]See also Bacon's strong affirmation of nature in terms of divine laws, above, chap. 5, and his conception of natural forms as laws. *New Organon*, 2, Aphorism XVII, p. 152.

[54]*Notion of Nature*, IV, 400, 380.

[55]*Veneration Man Owes to God*, IV, 341.

[56]*The Christian Virtuoso*, V, 45.

[57]P. 402.

[58]Robert Boyle, *Some Occasional Thoughts about the Excellency and Grounds of the Mechanical Hypothesis* (1665), annexed to the *Excellency of Theology*, III, 450. Italics mine.

[59]*Ibid.*, p. 452.

[60]*Notion of Nature*, IV, 372.

[61]*Ibid.*

[62]*Ibid.*, p. 400.

[63]*Ibid.*, pp. 386, 387, 423.

[64]Unlike Descartes, who held both that the world was continually dependent upon the will of the Creator, and that the world had its own "substance," but finally appealed to the *idea* (not notion) that God would not deceive human perceptions of the external world, Boyle's position was more informed by the dialectical possibilities of a voluntarist theology of creation featuring God's *potentia absoluta* and *ordinata*, as well as the contingent dependence and integrity of nature as creation. For Boyle, the creation per se had more theological variety and significance than it did for Descartes. See above, chaps. 4, 5. Although Descartes also presupposed a divine establishment, his

position was not as thoroughly informed by voluntarist (and nominalist) traditions.

⁶⁵*Veneration Man Owes to God*, IV, 345, 346ff.

⁶⁶*Ibid.*, p. 346.

⁶⁷*The Christian Virtuoso*, V, 682.

⁶⁸This openness was significant for Boyle's chemical theory. See Marie Boas Hall, *Robert Boyle and Seventeenth-Century Chemistry*, pp. 80ff.

⁶⁹*Reason and Religion*, III, 516.

⁷⁰*Notion of Nature*, IV, 367. The close relation of linguistic nominalism and voluntarist theology here is similar to late medieval thought.

⁷¹Cudworth, a sophisticated Spiritualist, stated a similar position, joined to the conception of "Plastick Nature," which Boyle and the voluntarist tradition rejected. Cudworth wrote of God and nature that ". . . the Divine Law and Command, by which the things of Nature are administered, must be conceived to be the Real Appointment of some Energetick, Effectual and Operative Cause for the Production of every Effect . . . Wherefore . . . it may well be concluded, that there is a *Plastick Nature* under him, which as an Inferior and Subordinate Instrument doth drudgingly execute that Part of his Providence which consists in the regular and Orderly Motion of Matter": Ralph Cudworth, *True Intellectual System of the Universe*, book I, chapter 3, section 28, cited by Ernst Cassirer, *The Platonic Renaissance in England* (London: Nelson, 1953), p. 141.

⁷²*Notion of Nature*, IV, 367.

⁷³See above, chap. 5, the discussion of Boyle's view of God as the Author of ethical law marked by obligation, and his stress on the Creator's right to "annihilate" Adam and Eve. Boyle was committed to the external work of God.

⁷⁴This suggests that Boyle's presupposition of creation was "larger" or more widely effective than his position on atomism. Furthermore, it is possible that Boyle was also implicitly criticizing Helmont's Spiritualist understanding of *motion*. For the distinction of motion from matter (fundamental to Boyle) was severely threatened by Helmont's doctrines of seeds and ferments, which tended to collapse the distinction between local motion and laws of motion.

⁷⁵See A. N. Whitehead's similar sketch in his *Adventure of Ideas* (New York: Mentor, 1955), pp. 107-123. Also see Oakley, "Christian Theology and Newtonian Science," p. 450.

⁷⁶See above, chap. 5, the discussion of Newton's voluntarist orientation to God's transcendence and freedom as Creator and Author. His conception of history and of nature in general presupposed a theology of God's will and agency such that He was in but not of the physical (temporal and spatial) world.

⁷⁷*Opticks*, pp. 403, 404.

⁷⁸Cited in Oakley, "Christian Theology and Newtonian Science," p. 453, n. 23.

⁷⁹*De Gravitatione*, pp. 138-140, and *Principia*, p. xxxii. Furthermore, as McGuire has argued, Newton held to the universality of law in explaining gravity partly in order to avoid Leibnitz's dilemma of a sheerly miraculous

divine cause or a mere mechanical cause thereof. Newton relied upon a free yet lawful divine cause of gravity. See McGuire, "Force, Active Principles, and Newton's Invisible Realm," pp. 182ff.

[80]McGuire's account is suggestive on the question of law, and detailed on Newton's searching appeals to chemical phenomena. See McGuire, "Force, Active Principles, and Newton's Invisible Realm," pp. 161-165.

[81]McGuire has collected some of these drafts (written in English in 1705), and arranged in parallel columns relevant passages from the Latin *Optice* (1706), and the second English edition *Opticks* (1717-18). The drafts are of Query 23 (31 in the second edition). My citations are from McGuire's "Force, Active Principles, and Newton's Invisible Realm," pp. 167ff. In these drafts one gets a revealing glimpse of Newton at work.

[82]*Ibid.*, p. 168.

[83]*Ibid.*, p. 170. See the entire text for a full statement of their content. At the least, McGuire's work has shown that they seriously bring into question interpretations of Newton as a mere mechanist.

[84]*Ibid.*, pp. 170, 171.

[85]*Ibid.*, p. 171.

[86]There are, of course, real problems in Newton's attempt to account for active principles in relation to God's will. However, Newton rested finally upon the two-fold power of God in maintaining active principles both subject to law and possessed of their own power. See McGuire, "Force, Active Principles, and Newton's Invisible Realm," pp. 201ff.

[87]*Notion of Nature*, IV, 404.

[88]*Ibid.*, p. 394. Italics mine.

[89]*Ibid.*, pp. 365, 366. Boyle underlined this point in his most systematic introduction to mechanical philosophy; see *Origin of Forms and Qualities*, II, 453, 454.

[90]*Usefulness of Natural Philosophy*, I, 444.

[91]Pp. 365ff.

[92]This also raises the chief problem of Boyle's atomism, namely, how do atoms cohere? On this typical early modern problem, see above, chap. 4.

[93]The principle of this sketch, suggested by Whitehead, is more sound than isolating either laws of nature or a history of atomism.

[94]See Oakley, "Christian Theology and Newtonian Science," pp. 435ff.

[95]Boyle, *Reflexions on the Experiments vulgarly alledged to evince the 4 Peripatetique Elements, or ye 3 Chymicall Principles of Mixt Bodies*, republished by Marie Boas Hall, "An Early Version of Boyle's *Sceptical Chymist*," *Isis*, 45 (1954), 158-168. Hall argues that it was written not later than 1657; *ibid.*, p. 154.

[96]*Reflexions*, pp. 164-168. See Charles Webster, "Water as the Ultimate Principle of Nature: The Background to Boyle's Sceptical Chymist," *Ambix*, 13 (1966), 96-107. Kearney describes (and interprets) the willow tree experiment in his *Science and Change*, pp. 58-63.

[97]Boyle, *Of ye Atomicall Philosophy*, published by Richard S. Westfall, "Unpublished Boyle Papers Relating to Scientific Method — II," *Annals of Sci-*

ence, 12 (1956), 111-113. Westfall argues that it was probably completed in 1653; *ibid.*, part I, pp. 65, 66.

98See Webster, "Water as the Ultimate Principle of Nature," pp. 103ff.

99*Sceptical Chemist*, I, 315f. One of many Helmontian "theories" thus undercut was that of the mysterious "alkahest." See further the "Historical Part" of Boyle's *Origin of Forms and Qualities*, II, 521, 522.

100*Origin of Forms and Qualities*, II, 459.

101*Ibid.*, pp. 453, 455. Hall notes that here there was a near total conflict between Boyle and his scholastic opponents. See Marie Boas Hall, "The Establishment of the Mechanical Philosophy," p. 461.

102*Origin of Forms and Qualities*, II, 456. On Boyle's thoroughness, see Hall, "The Establishment of the Mechanical Philosophy," p. 492.

103*Origin of Forms and Qualities*, II, 458, 459.

104*Ibid.*, p. 454.

105*Ibid.*, p. 458.

106*Ibid.*, p. 461. At this point Boyle is not concerned with the issue of the simplicity versus complexity of qualities.

107*Ibid.*, pp. 464, 465.

108*Cosmicall Qualities*, III, 82ff.; *Origin of Forms and Qualities*, II, 474.

109*Ibid.*, pp. 455, 457. Accordingly, I have resisted a *classification* of Boyle's natural philosophy as atomic, mechanical, or corpuscular, and instead sought to reconstruct its major ideas and presuppositions in its intellectual context.

110*Ibid.*, pp. 451f., 458.

111*Ibid.*, pp. 466f., 475.

112*Ibid.*, pp. 466, 463.

113These convictions or basic presuppositions were not as necessitating as *direct causes* nor were they simply *conditions*. Their peculiar logical or, better, structural efficacy was neither that of *pure premises* nor solely conscious *assumptions*. For a methodological articulation of these rough parameters of basic presuppositions, see above, chap. 1.

Notes to Chapter Seven

1Methodologically, this inquiry into many texts of both Boyle and Helmont shows that a (generally Collingwoodian) contextualist inquiry need not be merely suggestive, and that it is well fitted to understand basic change. Moreover, Helmont cannot be dismissed as a mystic or purely speculative chemical philosopher. And the unity of Boyle's thought cannot be understood apart from his many diverse works. There is no sufficient historical reason for championing Boyle's chemistry at the expense of his natural philosophy, or either of these at the price of his theology.

2This may serve to qualify the long standard interpretation of historic Christianity as a religion of redemption. At least it would if (1) the systematic significance of ontological, Spiritualist, and voluntarist theologies of creation for Christian views of sin and redemption was shown, and (2) the historic break between seventeenth-century Christendom and late Enlightenment culture was shown from the side of the latter as well as the former. These are tasks for another day.

[3]At least through the seventeenth century, important historic indices of this orientation were to be found in the rubric of *potentia absoluta* and *ordinata*, and allied articulations of Providence.

[4]At least two major questions remain: What about other basic presuppositions besides those discussed? Could the argument here advanced be sustained in a detailed analysis of mathematics, physics, etc. in mid-seventeenth-century thought?

To reply to the second question first: since the basic presuppositions shown in the rise of modern science were neither so direct as causes nor so indirect as conditions, there is no reason in principle to doubt that they were also at work in other sciences besides Boylean chemistry as distinct from alchemy and iatrochemical pursuits. To answer the question fully, however, the inquiry would probably lead down novel historical paths which might include, for example, diverse philosophies of mathematics and mysticisms of number in the strange new world of the seventeenth century.

With respect to other presuppositions, the fact that my detailed examination of intellectual contexts, paradigmatic events, and governing moods has focused on (theologically articulate) beliefs in creation does not preclude the efficacy of socio-religious, socio-economic, and socio-political conditions. The problem is one of showing how such "material" conditions (or presuppositions?) were united with the manifest efficacy of the basic presuppositions here disclosed. This raises the stakes for an adequate historical sociology of knowledge and further critical inquiry.

Appendix: A List of Boyle's Works Cited

Many of Boyle's works which were written relatively early were not published until later in his life, and in some cases posthumously. Others were collections of tracts and experiments written "at diverse times." Boyle himself, in his *Proemial Essay*, apologizes for the disarray.

This situation hampers scholarly reconstruction of his life and the development of his thought. In particular, an exact determination of Boyle's writings before 1660 and after 1670 is difficult. Nevertheless, John F. Fulton's *Bibliography of Robert Boyle*, 2nd ed. (Oxford: Clarendon, 1961), R. E. W. Maddison's *The Life of the Honourable Robert Boyle* (London: 1969), and the extensive Boyle scholarship of Marie Boas Hall have produced results on the dates of writing and publication of his many works. Also, Margaret E. Rowbottom ("The Earliest Published Writing of Robert Boyle," *Annals of Science*, 6 [1950], 376-389), and Richard S. Westfall ("Unpublished Boyle Papers Relating to Scientific Method, I," *Annals of Science*, 12 [1956], 63-73) have inquired into the writing of Boyle's treatises.

On the basis of this scholarship, the following list of his writings is arranged chiefly in chronological order of publication with parenthetical accounts of the dates of writing in those cases in which they have been determined. Most of these works were published in five folio volumes of the *Works of Robert Boyle*, 1744, edited by Thomas Birch. A second edition of these works, in six quarto volumes, was published in 1772.

Philaretus to Empericus, 1647.
Of ye Atomicall Philosophy (completed ca. 1653).

The Requirements of a Good and Excellent Hypothesis (an early version written before 1653).

Reflexions on 4 Elements . . . 3 Chymicall Principles (written before 1657).

Seraphick Love, 1659 (written 1648).

Some Considerations Touching the Style of the Holy Scriptures, 1661 (written ca. 1652).

Certain Physiological Essays, 1661.

The Sceptical Chymist, 1661.

A Defense of the Doctrine touching the Spring and Weight of the Air, 1662.

An Examen of Mr. T. Hobbes' Dialogus Physicus de Natura Aeris, 1662.

Considerations touching the Usefulness of Experimental Natural Philosophy, Tome I, 1663 (first part written 1647-1649).

Occasional Reflections upon Several Subjects; Whereto is premised A Discourse about such kind of thoughts, 1665 (one Reflection dated 1648).

The Origin of Forms and Qualities according to the Corpuscular Philosophy, 1666.

The Usefulness of Experimental Natural Philosophy, Tome II (written ca. 1665).

Tracts about the Cosmicall Qualities of things, 1671.

Animadversions upon Mr. Hobbes Problemata De Vacuo, 1674.

The Excellency of Theology, 1674 (written 1665).

The Excellency and Grounds of the Mechanical Hypothesis, 1674.

Of the Reconcileableness of Reason and Religion, 1675.

Some Physico-Theological Considerations about the Possibility of the Resurrection, 1675.

A Discourse of things above Reason, 1681.

Of the High Veneration Man's Intellect Owes to God, 1685 (written at "diverse times").

A Free Inquiry into the vulgarly received Notion of Nature, 1686 (Preface dated 1682 and in part completed in 1666).

The Martyrdom of Theodora, and of Didymus, 1687 (written early).

Proemial Essay, . . . with Considerations Touching Experimental Essays in general, 1688 (written in 1657).

A Disquisition about the Final Causes of Natural Things, 1688 (well begun before 1677).

The Christian Virtuoso, 1690 (portions written earlier).

Greatness of Mind promoted by Christianity, 1690.

A Free Discourse against Customary Swearing, 1695 (written ca. 1647).

An Account of Philaretus, 1744.

Analytical Index of Principal Subjects

Act of Divine Creation, and/or relation of Creator and creation, 31; compared to chemical art, 63, 80, 208n22; *creatio ex nihilo*, 30, 35, 41, 59, 82, 159, 204n55, 225n42; by *fiat*, 151; free and ordered, 35-37; mathematical, 206n4; opposed to chance, 131, 154, 162, 166; opposed to self-creativity, 29; as Spiritual process, 57, 59; by the Word, 39, 59, 141. *See also* Relation of Creator and Creation

Air, and gas, 70f.; and Spirit, 70f.; efficient Archaeus of, 70f.; elemental, 69; elasticity and weight of, 117, 218n66; presuppositions of conflicting theories of, 100, 117

Alchemy, 53f., 80, 157f., 162, 206n2, 207n7, 208n14, 224n30

Assumptions, v, 18f., 198n58

Atomism, Boyle's development of critical, 176-180, 223n2, 228n92; concept and conditions of, 176; Epicurean, 163, 169, 178; in relation to various concepts of laws of nature and of relations, 167, 172, 178f., 189; presuppositions of early modern, 163, 167, 176, 178f., 189

Atoms, and corpuscles, 177; impenetrable, 177-179; mechanical, 167, 179; powerful self-moving, 163, 169, 178. *See also* Particulars

Belief in Divine Creation, classic meaning and cultural significance of, 29-32; equivalent to presupposing creation in Christendom, 29-32; eighteenth-century reduction of, 32, 87, 199n7; four structural components of, 31, 46, 86; three historically developed types of, vf., 32, 46, 53f., 85f., 90f., 185ff.; formative periods of: early modern, 12-15, 45-52, 85f., 89-104, 108, 113-115, 120-124, 127-146, 149-184, 188ff.; Enlightenment, 13, 32, 87, 115, 173, 199ns6f.; late medieval, 32-39, 88; medieval, 15f., 30f., 34, 90f., 140, 160-162, 178, 181; Reformation, 39-45, 50f., 115, 202n29; Renaissance, 13f., 41, 45, 112. For structural analyses, *see* Act of Divine Creation, Creator, Man as Creature, Order of Creation, Relation of Creator and Creation. For historical types, *see* Theological Orientations to Creation. *See also* Creation, Nature

Boyle, as a representative early modern figure, 19, 97, 108, 130, 197ns48f., 207n7, 214n23; as chemist, 197n49; as natural philosopher, 147ff., 197n49, 223n2; as theologian, 129ff., 140, 219n1

Causality, efficient Archaeus of, 70; efficient seeds of, 65; efficient and final, 119-121, 163; final, 47, 66, 70, 119f.; and gravity, 100, 174; and local motion, 163; material, 63-65; particular, 150; relation of causes and effects, 36; second causes, 42, 59, 174, 203n32; subordinate to laws of motion and matter, 163, 177, 226n51; theological presuppositions of, 119f.; Helmont's "totall cause," 59

Particulars, as a category for analyzing basic units of nature, knowledge, and differentiation in different traditions, 147, 149, 176, 213n22; as atoms, 163, 167, 169, 177-179; as concrete and/or discrete objects and phenomena of knowledge, 77, 121-123, 125, 150; of conscience in modern ethics and religion, 108, 176, 213n22; as corpuscles, 177; as historical events, 106f.; as individuals in modern literature and religion, 47, 109f., 112f., 176; as qualities, 180-183; as seeds, 64-66, 125, 171f., 178f; as simple ideas, 121, 176, 214n22; critical modern view of, 125, 171f., 176-183

Platonism, 12, 15f., 41, 53; Cambridge, vii, 51, 53, 88f., 92, 94, 99, 137-139, 148, 152, 208n14, 208n20, 211n71

Predestination, 8, 10, 46, 133, 195n27

Presuppositions, basic unifying capacities of, 16, 25f., 30f., 49ff., 62, 87-91, 135, 198n58; three basic forms of, 25-27, 129, 198n59; content of Boyle's theological, 127ff.; as contexts, 11, 26, 30, 91f., 184, 186; critical and constructive, 66, 127, 147ff., 176ff., 183; efficacy of, 24-26, 54, 67, 70f., 122, 147, 165, 167, 184, 186ff., 191, 227n74, 229n113, 230n4; epochal historical change in, 3, 20-22, 87, 90; logic of, 24f., 165, 198n54, 198n59; as paradigms, 26, 91f.; perennial persistence of, 15, 21, 31, 91; and questions, 12, 23, 149, 153; social, 24f., 49-52; Spiritualist, 54f., 58, 60, 62f., 67ff.; taken for granted, 25, 92, 149, 184, 186f., 189, 191; theological, 11-13, 15-17, 31f., 34, 39-41, 48, 54f., 58, 60f., 69f., 85, 86ff., 147, 176, 184; voluntarist, 29, 34, 39-41, 49, 85, 90, 97, 112, 117, 123, 127, 135-140, 146, 171, 173, 176, 188-191

Protestantism, vii, 3, 5, 7, 9, 11, 39, 45-52, 53, 88, 91f., 112, 128. *See also* Puritanism

Providence, 40-44, 46-48, 52, 56, 87f., 92, 94, 96, 116, 155, 166, 195n27; ordinary and extraordinary, 43, 48

Puritanism, and modern science, 4f., 7-11, 194n16, 195ns25f.; common interests in creation of Anglicanism and, 46-50, 129

Qualities, Boyle's critical view of, 180-183; distinctions of primary and secondary, 182f.; elements and, 68; occult, 174, 181; real and distinct, 180f., 183, 225n46

Reason, autonomous, 29, 130; ontological views of, 30f., 39, 46, 73f., 121f.; presuppositions of experimental, 121f., 124f.; in seventeenth-century religion, 8, 50f., 132, 135; significance of voluntarist views of, 37-39, 121f., 124f., 201n21; Spiritual understanding vs., 60, 74, 76-78. *See also* Knowledge

Redemption, variously related to and distinguished from creation, v, 29, 49-52, 59, 96, 102-104, 111, 190, 215ns34-36, 229n2

Reformation, vii, 16, 29, 32, 39, 46, 53, 73, 88, 91f., 108, 112, 115, 133, 191, 212n9; early modern, 86-91, 91-97, 188

Relation of Creator and Creation, being and *logos* in the, 30f., 90, 123f., 140; contingent, 33, 35, 39-41, 48, 120f., 149, 153, 159, 168, 202n31, 221n31; dependence in the, 29, 40, 153, 159, 168; dialectical, 35-37, 171; and the distinction between Creator and creation, 97-102, 124, 139f., 149, 152, 190; opposed to confusion, 42f., 98-100, 103, 150f.; participation in the, 33, 139f.; as soul of the world, 94, 152, 158, 208n16; Spirit as the unity and principle of the, 59-61; work in the, 40f. *See also* Act of Divine Creation, Order of Creation

Religion, concepts of, 110-112; congruent with theology, 10f., 49; modern differentiation of, 110-115; of creation and/or redemption, 29, 49-52, 199n1, 229n2; of creation in seventeenth-century England, 49-52, 111-115, 129ff., 217n54. *See also* Science

Religious, conversion and its significance, 60, 72-76; genres, 31, 109, 112-115,

Index of Names

242